Rockefeller Foundation

Innovation for the Next 100 Years

SHARED JOURNEY

THE ROCKEFELLER FOUNDATION, HUMAN CAPITAL, AND DEVELOPMENT IN AFRICA

By Kathryn Mathers, Ph.D.

Innovation for the Next 100 Years
Rockefeller Foundation Centennial Series

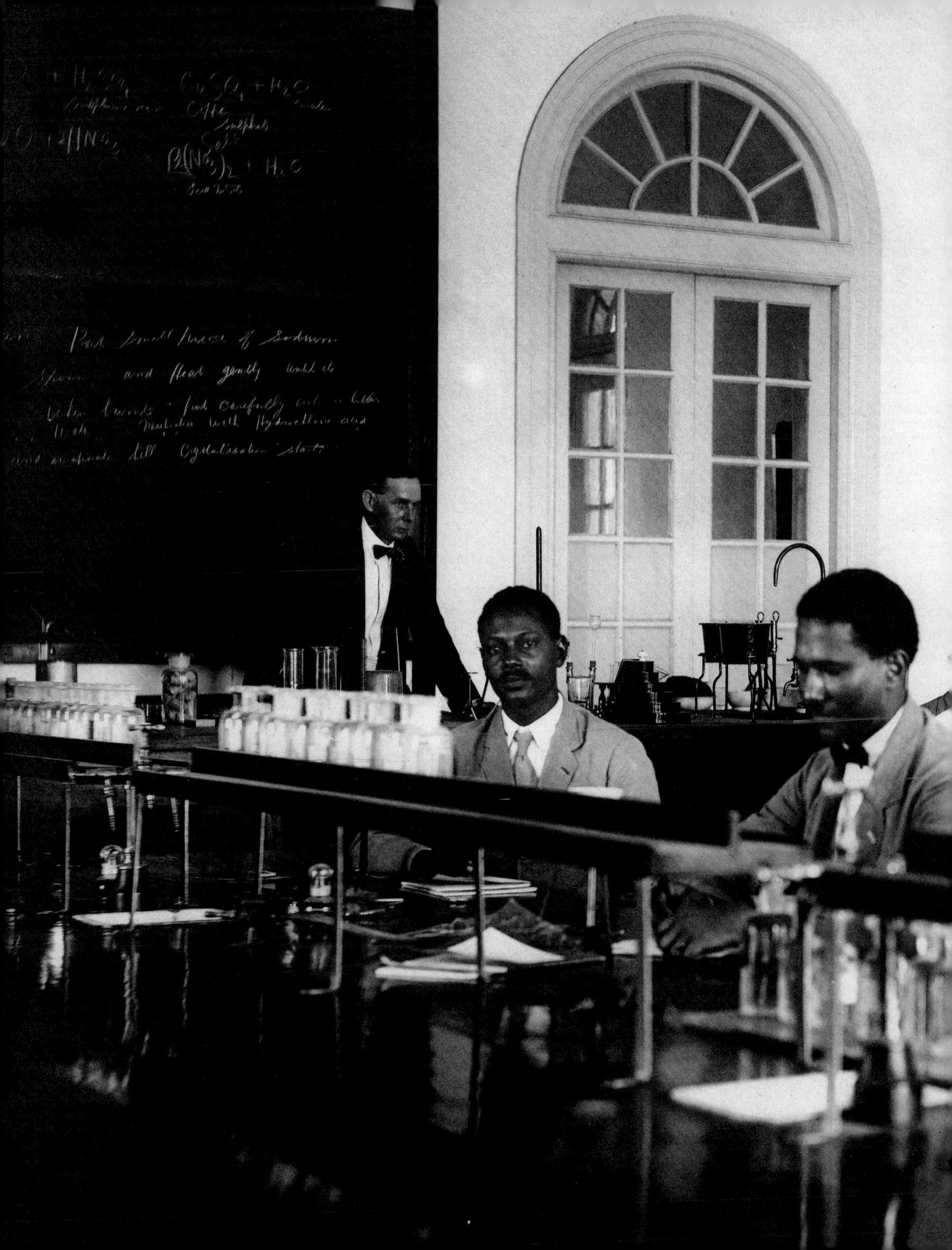

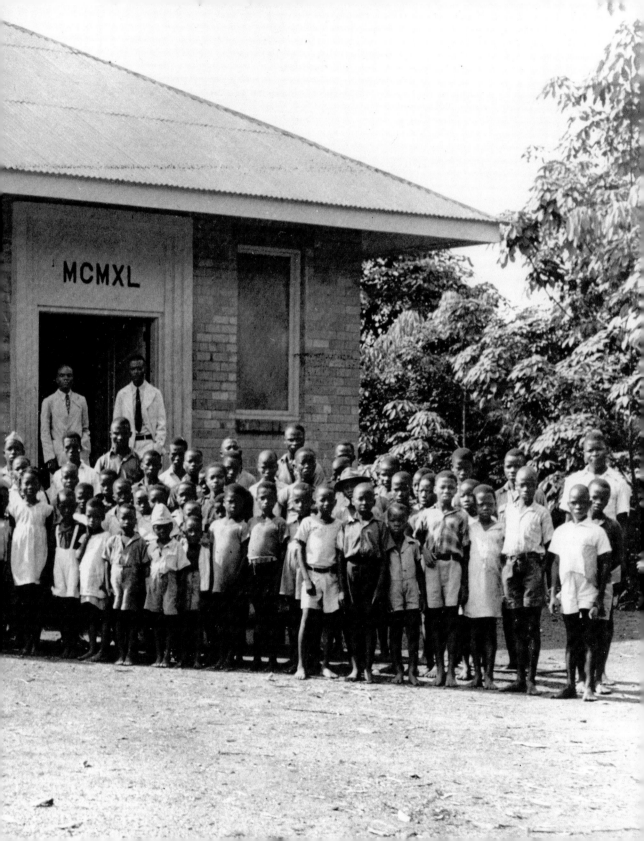

Cover:
Top: Photo by Anthony Pappone.
Getty Images.
Bottom: Photo by Image Source.
Getty Images.

Book design by Pentagram.

Shared Journey:
The Rockefeller Foundation, Human
Capital, and Development in Africa

Printed in Canada.

Published by
The Rockefeller Foundation
New York
United States of America

In association with Vantage Point
Historical Services, Inc.
South Dakota
United States of America

ISBN-13: 978-0-9796389-7-8
ISBN-10: 0-9796389-7-6

Rockefeller Foundation Centennial Series

Books published in the Rockefeller Foundation Centennial Series provide case studies for people around the world who are working "to promote the well-being of humankind." Three books highlight lessons learned in the fields of agriculture, health, and philanthropy. Three others explore the Foundation's work in Africa, Thailand, and the United States. For more information about the Rockefeller Foundation Centennial initiatives, visit www.centennial. rockefellerfoundation.org.

Notes & Permissions

The Foundation has taken all reasonable steps to ensure the accuracy of the information provided in the book; any errors or omissions are inadvertent. This book is published without footnotes or endnotes. A manuscript version with citations and references for all sources used is available at www.centennial. rockefellerfoundation.org.

Captions in this book provide information on the creator and the repository from which the images in this book were obtained. The Foundation has made its best efforts to determine the creator and copyright holder of all images used in this publication. Images held by the Rockefeller Archive Center have been deemed to be owned by the Rockefeller Foundation unless we were able to determine otherwise. Specific permission has been granted by the copyright holder to use the following works:

Jonas Bendiksen: 2-3, 22, 62-63, 98-101, 190-191, 207, 208, 212, 213, 225, 244-245, 250
Antony Njuguna: 6-7, 17, 132-133, 214-215
Steve McCurry: 10-11, 232-233, 252, 260
Zerihun Sewunet: 46-47
London School of Economics: 67, 73
Jeff Attaway: 76-77
Los Angeles Public Library Photo Collection: 87
New York Public Library: 91, 106
Stevie Mann/ILRI: 102-103
Fabian Bachrach: 107
United Nations: 111, 119, 178, 182, 185, 188, 235
Courtesy Paul Jackson: 116-117
Courtesy Jeremy D. Kark: 130, 131
Getty Images: 138
Associated Press: 157
University of Arizona Herbarium: 194
Marion Kaplan: 201
Wendy Stone: 221
Vince Smith: 262-263
Rodger Bosch: 264

By Dr. Judith Rodin
President of the Rockefeller Foundation

John D. Rockefeller gave hundreds of millions of dollars to philanthropy, but he believed that Standard Oil, the company he created to manufacture oil to light cook stoves and streetlamps around the world, also had a profound effect on the well-being of humanity. If Rockefeller could visit Africa today, his faith in the ability of entrepreneurs and innovators to improve the quality of life in their communities and nations would be reconfirmed.

I hope Rockefeller would also be delighted to know that the Foundation he created is working closely with other donors, non-governmental organizations, international agencies, governments, and the private sector to promote systemic changes in Africa. He was a big believer in coordination, collaboration, and integrated systems that lower the cost of delivering products and services—in business and in philanthropy.

When the Rockefeller Foundation was established in 1913, people in Africa, like those in many parts of the world, lived close to the land. Today, a growing majority live in cities. The Foundation's first projects on the continent aimed to help rural people battle endemic diseases like hookworm and to promote institutions that would train health care workers in mining towns and agricultural or pastoral communities. For many years, however, the Foundation's efforts were hindered by the oppressive institutions of colonialism and racism. It was hard to find partners, but the Foundation did achieve some important successes that impacted the people of Africa and the world, including the development of treatments for various tropical diseases and a vaccine against yellow fever.

Insights gained from these early years, however, provided some guidance for the Foundation and a host of newly emerging nations and multinational organizations in Africa after World War Two. We partnered with Africa's new leaders, other American foundations—like the Ford Foundation and the Carnegie Corporation—as well as development agencies to help train a new generation of African professionals and intellectuals in health care, education, and agriculture. These were challenging times for many people in Africa, characterized by political instability, economic distress, and, all too often, shortages of basic foods and medicines. Philanthropy made a difference, but the legacies of colonialism were all too pervasive.

Still, the people of Africa faced the future with extraordinary resilience, and the Rockefeller Foundation kept looking for ways to be more innovative and effective. Through the years of the Green Revolution and then the AIDS crisis we discovered ways of convening, collaborating, networking, and institution-building that would have impressed even John D. Rockefeller. In agriculture and food security, we played a key role in building an international network of scientists and researchers bent on improving agricultural technology to increase the food supply. Over time we came to understand the importance of localizing these research facilities in the countries that would benefit most from improvements in agricultural production methods. Moving in this direction went hand in hand with investments in human capital, particularly through our Rockefeller Foundation fellowship program and our investments in women's education, to enhance the capacity of local communities and individual nations to prioritize and address their own needs.

Lessons learned in agriculture provided the framework for responding to the AIDS crisis as it emerged in the 1980s. We invested in scientific research to fund an ongoing effort to find a vaccine for HIV. We invested in building clinical epidemiology and health data collection capacity. At the same time, we helped to develop health care systems that could respond to local needs and recognized AIDS as an issue for the whole family and the community, as well as the individuals afflicted by the virus.

With agriculture and health care, inspired by John D. Rockefeller, we built bridges between the philanthropic and private sectors to tap the innovative capacity of corporate research facilities and the vast potential of private sector capital.

Today, the insights gained from a hundred years of learning-by-doing in Africa are driving the way we work and partner with others on efforts to make health care more accessible and effective, increase the availability and affordability of local food supplies, address environmental sustainability, and foster communities resilient enough to withstand the effects of climate change and other shocks and stresses of our time. In agriculture, we launched the Alliance for a Green Revolution in Africa in partnership with the Bill and Melinda Gates Foundation.

And as we enter our second century, we have launched Digital Jobs Africa. This $100 million initiative will improve the lives of more than one million people in six African countries through skills training and jobs for youth, harnessing the dynamism of the continent's booming digital and technology sectors.

All of these efforts build on our history in Africa, but they also look to an exciting future. As the economic potential of Africa is unlocked in the coming decades, we see an extraordinary opportunity for philanthropy, government, and the private sector to work together to promote the well-being of the entire continent, including those who are marginalized today by poverty. Indeed, in Africa, more than any other region in the world, we are today inventing the future of philanthropy.

FOREWORD

By Archbishop Desmond Tutu

T he world has tended to laud us South Africans to the skies for achieving the notable goal of defeating the vicious system of racist oppression called apartheid. Now I do not for one moment want to diminish the contribution that our people made to accomplish this remarkable - yes indeed epoch making success. Their resilience, their courage, their determination to persist against considerable odds. But I want to put in an important caveat - we would not have scored this resounding victory without the support and the dedication of the international community.

This volume describes the exploits, the determination, the reverses, and eventually the successes scored by one U.S. institution, admittedly not an insignificant player in the global setting. We would have been in a massive predicament had the Rockefeller Foundation been working against us and the evolution of our continent. Mercifully for us, the opposite has been the case.

It is a good place to pay a very warm tribute to the Foundation for all the enthusiasm and dedication that were its hallmark on behalf of our continent, which has been the beneficiary of this institutional dedication and commitment. Organizations such as the Rockefeller Foundation contributed to our spectacular victory.

When one surveys the African continent one is struck by the presence of some quite outstanding educational tertiary institutions which owe their excellence to the initiatives and support of the Foundation - places such as Makerere University in Uganda, Ibadan University in Nigeria, tertiary institutions in Ghana and Sudan, Congo. These and others may later have had somewhat checkered histories because of political vicissitudes.

Some of the most significant investments by the Foundation have been in its scheme of fellowships. Almost without exception those who have benefited from this strategic investment made by the Foundation have been some of the brightest stars in our firmament - political stalwarts, scholars, workers and thinkers such as Ali Mazrui, Chinua Achebe, Dr. Josephine Namboze, Ngugi wa Thiong'o, Milton Obote, etc. But I have restrained myself.

Surveying the enormous impact that the Foundation has had in Africa it is almost difficult to believe that the beginnings of its work in Africa were really so insignificant in size. The Foundation was interested only in education, health, and possibly agriculture. It followed up an initiative of women students who had just graduated from Spelman College in Atlanta and who set off to improve the lot of former American slaves in Liberia with a campaign to eradicate hookworm in parts of Egypt.

"You cannot be neutral in the presence of injustice and oppression. When you claim to be impartial, then you are really supporting the current status quo and you have chosen to side with the oppressor."

One has to be restrained in things like forewords from sounding too vociferous but without shouting from the top of our voices, we must commend the support the Foundation gave so enthusiastically to establish the London School of Hygiene and Tropical Medicine which has covered itself in academic glory and become a distinguished and highly regarded place. Another initiative helped white people to understand Africans a little better— certainly a great deal better than former colonial overlords—and that was the International Institute of African Languages and Cultures headed by the distinguished anthropologist Bronislaw Malinowski.

The Rockefeller Foundation gave a significant push to the antiapartheid struggle. It abandoned its former nonpolitical stance of impartiality. Fantastic. You cannot be neutral in the presence of injustice and oppression. When you claim to be impartial, then you are really supporting the current status quo and you have chosen to side with the oppressor. Franklin Thomas, president of the Ford Foundation, chaired the Rockefeller Foundation's commission which produced its report three years later entitled, tellingly, "South Africa: Time Running Out." We the former oppressed say "Thank you."

The Foundation has invested significantly to improve the health, education, and agriculture of Africa. It has been at the forefront of the struggle against the AIDS pandemic and invested in human capital with its fellowship program as we have seen and now it is joining arms with women who are the new face for positive change. This book brings us back where the Foundation's African story began - Liberia and to salute Liberia's recent women Nobel Peace Laureates - one Ellen Johnson Sirleaf the president of the country, the other Leymah Gbowee a leading peace activist.

But also there are other women activists. The African Union has just last year elected its first woman Commission chair, Nkosazana Dhlamini-Zuma of South Africa. The women are on the march. In South Africa they say, "You touch the women - you touch a rock".

Forewords are not usually meant to be an encomium. I will deviate from the tradition. I am not uncritical, but I want to end by paying a very warm tribute to the Rockefeller Foundation. We in South Africa are free in part because of your support. Thank you on behalf of my compatriots - yes, and thank you for everything you have done for our Mother Continent, Africa.

To promote the well-being of people
in Africa, the Rockefeller Foundation
has invested in talented individuals who
have the potential to transform society.
Educating girls and women has played a
key role in promoting Africa's prosperity.
(Jonas Bendiksen. Rockefeller Foundation.)

Vida Yeboah, Paulette Missambo, Alice Tien-drébéogo, Simone de Comarmond, and Fay Chung are five remarkable women from different African countries. But what they have in common brought them together to fight a battle for women across the continent. All had grown up with a mother or another mentor who helped and encouraged them to take advantage of every possible opportunity for a good education. All had come of age in places where few women went to high school, let alone college, and where women were under-represented in all spheres of public and professional life. These five women, however, used their education for much more than success in their own careers. They committed themselves to making sure that more African women had opportunities for education, professional development, and respect in their societies. In the process, they hoped to improve the livelihoods and well-being of all Africans.

In October 1991 all five women began their conversation in Manchester, England. Manchester had played an important part in the Pan-African movement in October 1945, months after the end of World War Two, when Kwame Nkrumah from the Gold Coast, Jomo Kenyatta from Kenya, Hastings Banda from Malawi, and other nationalist leaders gathered there to discuss Africa's postcolonial future. As Nnamdi Azikiwe later wrote, these meetings marked "the turning point in Pan-Africanism from a passive to an active stage." In 1991 the city would become the launching pad for a new Pan-African movement, focused on increasing educational opportunities for women.

As their conversation developed in Manchester, the five women from different parts of Africa articulated a shared belief that more women should be in decision-making positions in Africa and that educating girls was key to long-term development goals. Each came to this conclusion from personal experience, and each was or would be in a position to influence policy to achieve their shared goal.

Vida Yeboah would serve in Ghana's legislature for eight years and be minister of tourism and a deputy minister of education. She would lead the implementation of Ghanaian educational reforms, increasing access to an education system that was more effective for individual and national development. "Working for social and political justice and equity has been a central focus in my life," she would later say, "whether fighting for national sovereignty and human rights in Africa or raising awareness of gender or health inequities that plague women and children throughout the world. In working for change it is crucial to ensure that we see and hear the voices and stories of the people and communities with whom we work."

Paulette Missambo of Gabon would go on to a long history of public service, including positions such as Minister of State in charge of Education and the Status of Women; Minister of Education and Sports; and Minister of State in charge of Labour, Employment and Professional Training. Missambo believed that the most important intervention policymakers could make in the lives of women in Africa was at the elementary school level.

Alice Tiendrébéogo, a Burkinabe historian and teacher, had worked steadily to improve education for girls and women in Burkina Faso and would later serve as Minister of Women's Affairs. She believed that girls needed technical training opportunities to enable them to contribute to national economies in

Africa. Tiendrébéogo had also spoken out on the important role women needed to play in the legislature. As she would note in 2002, "The participation of women in decision-making processes in Burkina Faso does not depend solely on implementing laws, but on women's capacity to define themselves as citizens who are endowed with capabilities and autonomy, to mobilize, and to negotiate with men."

Simone de Comarmond, the first woman Minister of Education in the Seychelles, had been in public service her entire adult life. Taking advantage of the Seychelles' commitment to girls' education and spurred by her mother's insistence on hard work, she had earned a scholarship to attend Regina Mundi Convent for girls, where she achieved the Cambridge University Ordinary Level then in use throughout the British Commonwealth countries. During her participation in community clinics she learned that there was a "need to empower those very women that we had assumed were already empowered!"

The last of these five women, Dr. Fay Chung, had grown up in colonial Rhodesia in the 1950s, a third-generation member of a Chinese immigrant family. Educated in segregated schools, she went on to earn a doctorate in education from the University of Zimbabwe and an M.Phil. in English literature from the University of Leeds as well as a B.A. in Economics from the University of London's School of Oriental and African Studies. She had been appointed Deputy Secretary of Education in Zimbabwe in 1980 and became Minister and a member of Robert Mugabe's cabinet in 1988. During her tenure, Zimbabwe had achieved an unprecedented 95 percent primary education rate, had vastly improved secondary education, and had developed a progressive curriculum for teacher-training institutions. Chung believed women could play a pivotal role in African development. "Unless we develop a strong and progressive leadership of women," she would say in 2002, "we will not be able to go forward. Women in Africa have not been able to play their full role in development, as a result of feudal traditions that place women in a supportive role, with little economic and political power. Women are not well represented at [the] tertiary level, particularly at [the] university level, and this has serious repercussions for the type of leadership that women enjoy."

In Manchester, the five women were attending a World Bank meeting of Donors to African

In September 1992 the Rockefeller Foundation organized a conference on women and education in Africa. Leading policymakers and educators who attended outlined the framework for a new organization—the Forum for African Women Educationalists (FAWE) to advocate on behalf of school-age girls in sub-Saharan Africa. (Rockefeller Archive Center.)

Education as representatives of their respective governments. Between lectures and seminars, they met behind the scenes to discuss the challenges facing girls and women across the continent. They recognized that collectively they were in an exceptional position to address the uphill battles faced by African girls and women in their quest for education. By collaborating they would be able to support one another and encourage women in other African nations to fight for education as well. They resolved to create a network of prominent women to propose measures and advocate for the transformation of African education to achieve greater gender equality. But to put their plan into effect, they would need partners.

The Rockefeller Foundation had long recognized the importance of education for women in Africa. Indeed, the Foundation's first contributions toward the well-being of people in Africa had been given nearly a hundred years earlier to support, in part, the education of African women at Spelman College in Atlanta, Georgia, in the United States as well as the training of African-American women for missionary work in Liberia, South Africa, and other countries. These missionaries had helped to bring Africans to the United States, who then returned to become religious and political leaders in the early fight against colonialism.

By 1991 the Foundation had been deeply engaged for nearly eight decades in a host of development projects in Africa—including public health and agricultural development as well as education—and the Foundation's staff had already convened a subcommittee of Donors to African Education to foster girls' and women's participation in education. As a result the Foundation's trustees were primed to support a new initiative with similar goals.

To forge a partnership with leading African educators, the Foundation organized a meeting in September 1992 of the five women at the Foundation's Bellagio Center on Lake Como, Italy. They were joined by 19 senior women policymakers in education, including the Rockefeller Foundation's associate vice president Joyce Moock, an anthropologist who had been a Peace Corps volunteer in Malawi in the 1960s. Her research on urban-rural ties in Kenya in the 1970s represented an early example of research in the new field of applied anthropology.

Moock had joined the Rockefeller Foundation in 1979 as a program officer, working closely with the Foundation's long-time Africa representative David Court. A political scientist, Court had taught school in Tanzania before earning his Ph.D. at Stanford University and then returning to East Africa to teach at the University of Nairobi. In Nairobi he worked closely with Katherine Namuddu, an educator who had established the innovative Minds Across Africa school project in Uganda before joining the Foundation. Namuddu had received her B.Sc. in Biological Sciences from Makerere University College before earning her Ph.D. in Science Education from Columbia University. All three of these individuals would work to help push forward the vision for the education of African girls and women.

At Bellagio the conferees outlined the framework for a new organization, the Forum for African Women Educationalists (FAWE), which intended to advocate on behalf of the estimated 24 million school-age girls who were not attending school in sub-Saharan Africa. Outlining their plans, FAWE's leaders identified key insights that would drive their strategy. Gender equity would require a strong political base able to initiate and sustain policy reform. It would also demand a conceptual framework and vision that would support sound policymaking. The project would have to win supporters by demonstrating success. As FAWE's leaders noted, seeing is believing. The value of educating girls and women would have to be demonstrated by the accomplishments of the students. Finally, FAWE's goals could be achieved only with the full participation of local communities, national governments, and international donors.

FAWE's goals were big and bold. The social revolution it envisioned was as far-reaching as the political agenda articulated by the Pan-African leaders who had assembled in Manchester 36 years earlier. Given the shortage of resources for education in many African countries and the deep cultural and institutional biases against women's education in many communities, philanthropy had a role to play in supporting FAWE's leaders as they launched their campaign.

A Philanthropic Vision

FAWE provides an outstanding example of the investment in human capital that is opening the door to new opportunities for many people who have historically been marginalized by colonialism, racism, sexism, and economic inequalities. It also raises important questions about the role of American and European philanthropy in Africa today. These questions will be answered by innovators in communities all across the continent, but they must be informed by a deep and honest understanding of the past. The story of the Rockefeller Foundation's work in Africa over the past century offers one path toward that deeper understanding.

This book explores the history of the Rockefeller Foundation's work in Africa from the beginning of the twentieth century to the early decades of the twenty-first. Based on materials collected in the Foundation's archives, the book traces the Foundation's efforts to engage with African communities in places as different as Egypt, South Africa, Nigeria, and Kenya. For many years prior to the end of World War Two, as colonial powers maintained their grip on the continent, the Foundation's initiatives to improve public health and enhance medical education were stymied by a lack of institutional support and outright resistance to its efforts to provide opportunities for Africans. Nevertheless, those years provided forward momentum.

Even during the colonial era, the Foundation helped to develop new knowledge about tropical diseases, including hookworm and yellow fever, and made initial efforts to promote public health systems to address these pathogens. It also supported efforts to understand African cultures and institutions that would eventually help the Foundation and other NGOs work with African communities on development projects. And along the way it contributed to the development of various individuals who would become leaders in the movement for African independence.

With the end of World War Two and the collapse of colonial empires, Africans asserted their rights and autonomy. As new governments and emerging nations charted the future, the Rockefeller Foundation's work transitioned from the library and laboratory to the fields and streets of Africa to help train a new generation of leaders and thinkers, and to forge networks of experts and community builders across borders and between countries in health, agriculture, and education.

This intensive, operational approach to philanthropy lasted through the 1970s, but changes in the institutional environment, the economy, and the Foundation's financial situation demanded that it reinvent itself and its way of working in the last part of the twentieth century. Multinational agencies like the World Bank and the United Nations commanded resources in the postwar era that far exceeded those of private philanthropists like the Rockefeller Foundation. At the same time, rampant inflation and a decline in the stock market diminished the Foundation's ability to maintain a large operating staff based in the field.

In the last decades of the twentieth century, the Foundation transitioned to being a convener and partner, a catalytic agent in arenas suffering from a lack of insight and imagination. In this era, the Foundation focused more intensively on the needs of the poor and marginalized throughout the world. Many of the Foundation's primary partners and grantees were in sub-Saharan Africa, working to promote agricultural production and improve public health in close partnership with a new generation of African leaders.

Even in its earliest years, working on five continents, the Foundation had to be sensitive to differences in culture and politics as it tried to advance science-based solutions to problems mostly related to public health and medicine. In seeking to hold to these principles, the Foundation faced unique challenges on every continent, and Africa was no exception. Lessons learned from these encounters, even when political and cultural roadblocks thwarted action, informed subsequent initiatives and fueled the path of innovation as generations of program officers and grantees endeavored to understand how to connect the mission of an American foundation seeking to promote the well-being of humanity throughout the world with the unique and particular needs of the people and nations of Africa.

Over the course of this century, much has changed in the Foundation's relationship with the various peoples of Africa, but key principles articulated early in the Foundation's history still guide the organization's work. The Foundation is driven by its core belief in the promise of science and technology in addressing challenges around the world, but with the recognition that human systems and cultures play the critical role in shaping the use and impact of these technologies. As dictated by the founder, John D. Rockefeller, the Foundation focuses on the root causes of humanity's afflictions, rather than providing short-term relief or charity. It works with local leaders and governments to build institutional support for long-term solutions. Its efforts are guided by the principle of partnership; matching local funding paves the path for self-reliance. Above all, the Foundation invests in training to create the human capital to enhance local capacity.

Physician John Knowles travelled to West Africa in 1973 shortly after he became president of the Rockefeller Foundation. Knowles renewed the Foundation's interest in community health programs during his tenure. (Rockefeller Archive Center.)

Throughout this history, grantees, fellows, and program officers swam against the current of domestic and global politics. They sought to innovate in various aspects of scientific and technological development. They were not always successful. Sometimes the greatest benefits from their work were not anticipated at the start, or took decades to be fully realized. The stories of these efforts, however, offer inspiration to new generations seeking to promote the well-being of humanity in Africa.

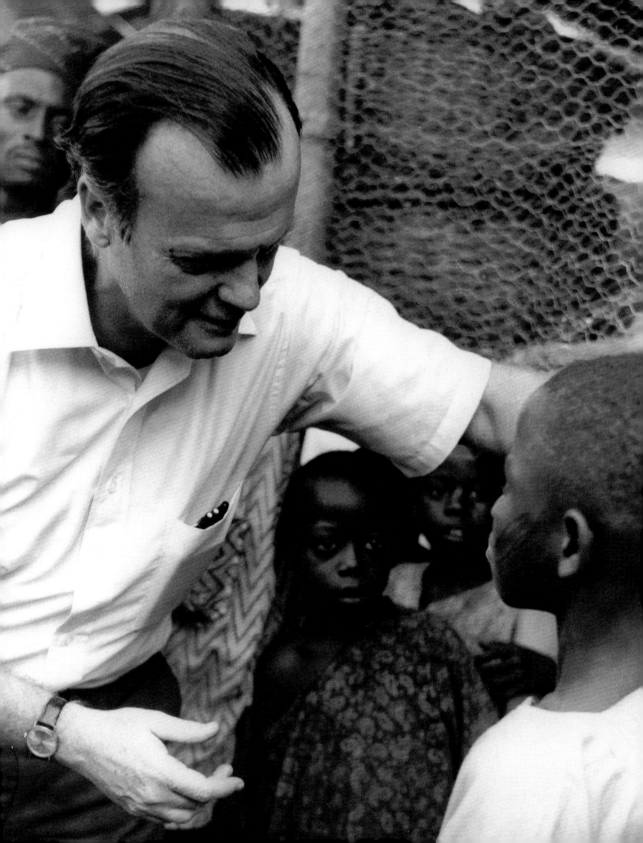

FIGHTING HOOKWORM
IN EGYPT

On March 24, 1914, Wickliffe Rose, the director of the Rockefeller Foundation's International Health Commission (later called the International Health Board), stared out the window of a train traveling from the Egyptian city of Port Said to Cairo. A former philosophy professor, Rose had a reputation as a brilliant administrator with an exacting eye for detail. He had recently guided the hookworm eradication campaign of the Rockefeller Sanitary Commission (a predecessor to the Rockefeller Foundation) through three stormy years and a thousand back-road communities of the American South. Before that, he had directed the Southern Education Board, a Rockefeller-supported organization that focused on the development of agriculture and rural communities to promote education throughout the South. Rose had a keen appreciation for what was possible; he was not inclined to either risk or haste.

In the American South, Rose had recognized that hookworm disease was grounded in the soil ecology of the region and that, quite literally, it sucked the productivity out of poor rural communities. Eradication was as much a matter of relieving poverty, providing public education, and improving community sanitation as it was of applying medical science. The integrated strategy his agents used combined medical treatment, using the potent drug thymol, with basic public health education and community development, including the development of publicly funded community health agencies. Rose's approach to disease control bridged what would later become a

yawning gulf—reflected in the evolution of professional education—between public health and medical science.

"The attack on these diseases was for him [Rose] an entering wedge, a method by which states and nations could be induced to build up permanent machinery to take care of the whole problem of public health," Raymond Fosdick, a historian and former Foundation president, wrote many years later. But the success of this method depended on the Rockefeller Foundation's ability to enlist health care providers, local political officials, business leaders, and ordinary citizens in the effort. In the American South, Wickliffe Rose understood the culture, the system of government, and the people. In Egypt, everything was new to him.

Wickliffe Rose visited the streets of Port Said in Egypt (depicted in the stereograph postcard above) before traveling to Cairo in 1914 to initiate a campaign to eradicate hookworm disease throughout the British Empire. Hookworm was a particular problem in Egypt, where parasites thrived in the soil of the Nile floodplain. (Library of Congress.)

Ldst. Batl. Aachen.
5. Komp.
27 JAN. 1915
Durchlassposten
Herbesthal.

AMERICAN CONSULATE GENERAL • ROTTERDAM •

Rotterdam, The Netherlands,
American Consulate General,
.... 28 1914

I do hereby certify as Notary Public
ex officio, that the person to whom this passport was issued, and whose signature appears
at the bottom of this document, is the person
represented on the photo hereto attached.
....He... has declared under oath, that he...........
desires it for use in visiting. Belgium...

....................American Relief Commission....
for the purpose of American Relief Commission
This passport is not valid for use in
other countries except for necessary transit
to or from the countries named.

S. Liste
Consul General.

American Consul General.

Gesehen im Kaiserlich De
Beglaubigung vorstehender
Herrn J. Liste,

Rotterdam,
Der Kaiser

Kaiserlich Deutsches Konsulat • in Rotterdam •

Kaiserlich Deutsches Konsulat • in Rotterdam •

M 6, = Fl. 3,60 frei.

UNITED STATES CONSULATE GENERAL

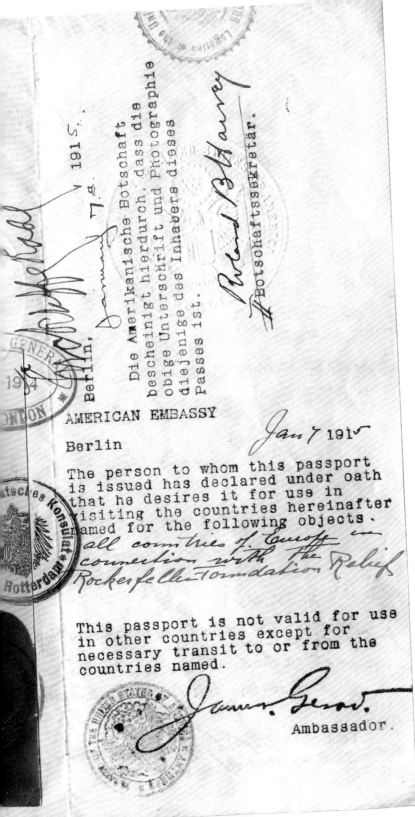

As director of the Rockefeller Foundation's International Health Commission from 1915 to 1923, Wickliffe Rose traveled extensively in support of global health campaigns against diseases such as hookworm and yellow fever. Rose hoped such eradication campaigns would encourage national governments to improve public health facilities. (Rockefeller Archive Center.)

Frederick T. Gates had asked Rose if it might be possible to transform the Southern hookworm campaign into the Rockefeller Foundation's first international initiative. Gates was John D. Rockefeller's leading philanthropic advisor. As the founder of the Standard Oil Company, Rockefeller was on his way to becoming the richest man in the world at the beginning of the twentieth century. A deeply religious man, he had been giving money to charity since he was a teenager. With his growing wealth, and with Gates's help, Rockefeller had established a series of innovative philanthropic organizations that culminated in the creation of the Rockefeller Foundation in 1913. The Foundation's mission was idealistic and ambitious: "To promote the well-being of mankind throughout the world."

Gates had asked Rose to investigate the extent of hookworm infection in other tropical regions and to consider expanding his eradication efforts. Rose painstakingly collected data and came to a stark conclusion—hookworm was endemic worldwide. A billion people were infected "in a belt of territory encircling the earth for thirty degrees each side of the equator." On the strength of this research, the Foundation's Board of Trustees on June 27, 1913, voted to "extend the work of eradicating hookworm disease to other countries and other nations, as opportunity offers."

Rose set sail for London shortly thereafter. He carried a proposal to form a joint venture between the Foundation and the British Colonial Office to eliminate hookworm throughout the British Empire. In London, Rose showed lantern slides demonstrating the work of the Southern campaign and won the blessing of Lewis Harcourt, Britain's secretary of state for the colonies.

British colonial administrator Lord Kitchener initially agreed to support the work of the Rockefeller Foundation in Egypt. The reluctance of colonial leaders to support local public health officials, however, combined with extreme poverty and a lack of basic sanitation, inhibited the Foundation's efforts. (Library of Congress.)

Eight months later Rose sailed for Egypt, at the time a protectorate of the British Empire. High Commissioner Lord Kitchener, a renowned British field marshal, served as the Empire's protectorate administrator. Rose met with him and with the leading experts of the Egyptian Public Health Service. Created early in the nineteenth century under the ruler Muhammad Ali, the Egyptian Public Health Service had included paramedical personnel who provided primary health care to rural communities, successfully reducing the number of deaths related to cholera and plague. Under British rule, however, these services had declined under administrators who favored urban, hospital-based medicine. It is unclear whether Rose was aware of the history of the Egyptian Public Health Service, but he also proposed to place emphasis on the rural population and to repeat the U.S. hookworm campaign among the poor farmers of the Nile River Delta.

Egypt was not the only country that Rose would survey, nor did it have the greatest incidence of hookworm. The sugar islands of the West Indies and the plantations of British Ceylon had higher rates of infection. But there were good reasons to look to Egypt as ground zero of the war on hookworm. Egyptian physicians in ancient times had written about hookworm, clearly part of life in the Delta even then. Year-round irrigation, made possible by the construction of the Aswan Dam on the Nile River, led to an explosion of water-borne parasites and an increase in crippling endemic diseases, including hookworm, bilharzia, malaria, and pellagra—just as engineers had warned.

An American Campaign in Egypt

There were many reasons to expect that a campaign against hookworm in Egypt might not progress as it had in the American South. The species of hookworm native to Egypt (*Ancylostoma duodenale*) was particularly aggressive, and sanitary conditions in the poor villages were among the worst in the world. Initial surveys indicated that well over half of the fellahin (agricultural laborers) who worked in the irrigated fields along the Nile were infected. The parasite left whole villages disabled by lethargy, anemia, stunted growth, and vulnerability to myriad diseases.

But Egypt had an important asset essential to Rose's integrated strategy that he would not find in other colonies. Cairo was home to an influential group of British scientists and physicians who had long experience with hookworm, several of whom were already working on a small eradication project when Rose arrived. Cairo's Kasr El Ainy Hospital and Medical School—one of only two medical schools in Africa at the time—was a center

for both clinical treatment of hookworm and scientific research. Some of the earliest studies of the hookworm lifecycle had been done at Kasr El Ainy by Arthur Looss, a German parasitologist who established that hookworm entered the body through the skin rather than the mouth. This discovery had had a major impact on Rose's work in the American South, and Rose had corresponded with Looss when he first began to consider launching a global campaign against hookworm.

Male patients from all over Egypt were treated at this church mission hospital in Cairo, Egypt, in 1914. Due to religious and social customs, however, women were generally unable to receive care. (Rockefeller Archive Center.)

Rose toured Egypt for three weeks. In his diary he recorded details of his meetings with colonial officials, consultations with physicians on the front line of public health, and visits to hospitals, mosques, and girls' schools. After visiting a mobile tent hospital that had been staked out in the desert, he wrote: "People come from a radius of about 20 miles. Treatment is free." But he also noted that patients were expected to remain in the hospital for 28 days and receive four courses of treatment. Most patients did not stay long enough to complete the treatment.

After investigating conditions in the field, Rose offered a proposal to Lord Kitchener. The Rockefeller Foundation was prepared to guarantee six thousand pounds sterling to underwrite half the cost of a pilot hookworm

Chapter One: Fighting Hookworm in Egypt

eradication program in the Egyptian province of Al-Sharqiyah, with a population of nearly a million people. An advisory board of scientists, including Arthur Looss, agreed to oversee the fieldwork and monitor results. The campaign would be based on in-patient treatment at mobile tent hospitals already in use by the Egyptian Department of Public Health. "All are in agreement that treatment, at least in the beginning, must be administered under hospital conditions," Rose explained to Dr. John A. Ferrell, the associate director of the International Health Board. Lord Kitchener was deeply interested in the work, according to Rose, and would "back it to the limit."

When the hookworm project was launched, the differences between the American South and North Africa quickly became apparent. As poor as American Southerners were, they were comparatively middle-class in the context of global poverty. In Egypt, land ownership was extremely concentrated. There was no middle or professional class in the countryside. Public expenditures to improve education or community sanitation were meager. In rural Egypt, basic sanitation was beyond the reach of all but a few. Fellahin were too poor to purchase or build outhouses. Pit latrines, which had been highly effective in the American South, were

Mobile tent hospitals were set up to treat Egyptian hookworm patients. Farmers often walked long distances to reach these hospitals for treatments that could take up to one month. Poor farmers, unable to leave their fields and families for so long, often left the hospital before their treatment was complete. (Rockefeller Archive Center.)

21375 a

impractical in Egypt because the water table was only a foot or two below the surface in many areas. Reinfection rates were high, and hookworm was only one of many diseases the peasants battled, often several at once. In the American South, patients had been treated in mobile hospitals or outpatient settings and gone back home the same day, returning for follow-up treatments over the course of a few days. In Egypt, poor farmers had to walk long distances to the mobile hospitals and admit themselves for nearly a month. No sharecropper could afford to be away from his fields this long.

Egypt's damp, sandy soil created ideal conditions for hookworm infestations. As in other areas of the developing world, the lack of proper sanitation and the tendency of people to go barefoot also contributed to the spread of hookworm. (Rockefeller Archive Center.)

British doctors told Rose that it was virtually impossible to keep patients for the entire course of treatment. To improve cure rates and encourage farmers to participate, the British tried to reduce the time patients had to stay in the hospitals. Arthur MacCallan, the head of the British eradication effort, eventually reduced the stay to three or four days, but the treatment's efficacy dropped off.

The success rate of the Egyptian hookworm campaign fell below that of the Rockefeller Sanitary Commission's work in the United States. In one hospital, Rose noted, "of 373 cases of ankylostomiasis received in hospital during the year 1913, only 53 were recorded as cured, and 261 as relieved."

The implications were daunting. In a land of 12 million people, where 60 percent of the farmers were infected and the worms were endemic, it was a pipe dream to believe that hookworm could be eradicated with cure rates of 15 percent.

In the American South, the hookworm campaign had succeeded because disease control had been tied to education and to increasing public awareness of the science of disease. Local physicians had been critical to the campaign's success. Although initially suspicious, they had been convinced by the science. They could look through a microscope and see hookworms in their patients' stool samples. They could show their patients what hookworms looked like. Won over by the Rockefeller Sanitary Commission, these local doctors had served as intermediaries with a doubting public.

But there were no doctors among the fellahin in Egypt. During the previous quarter century of colonization, the British had invested less than one percent of total state expenditures in education and sanitation. Kasr El Ainy was the only medical school for Egypt and Sudan. British and European medical staff dominated the school. In his diary Rose recorded a personal appeal from Henry Keatinge, the director of Kasr El Ainy: "If Egypt is ever to have an adequate supply of doctors they must be trained in Egypt. Neither the English doctor nor the native trained in England will ever devote himself to practice out in the villages among the Fellahin. These people, who are the great sufferers in Egypt, are very largely without medical aid."

Without village doctors, Rose was hampered in his ability to reach out to fellahin where they lived. Decades of imperial neglect of the rural public health system meant that full participation in the hookworm campaign was difficult to achieve. The Foundation's options for administering thymol were limited to field hospitals.

Cultural differences also affected the hookworm campaign. In the American South, women had participated in the hookworm campaign just as men did. In Egypt, cultural and religious restrictions kept women away from the hospitals, limiting the campaign's ability to reach half the population.

Many years later, MacCallan described the dilemma. The hookworm teams had found a high level of interest among the fellahin. Villagers came to learn about the disease. They listened to lectures by the field workers and watched flickering educational films. But without a sufficient system of latrines that could permanently be managed locally, and without the provision of realistic courses of treatment for those who already were infected, the effort offered "no permanent value."

Rose's "wedge" strategy of using disease eradication as a means to empower local communities and develop a class of health professionals also faced major obstacles in Egypt. The strategy required the leadership of well-trained local doctors and public health organizers; a cohesive infrastructure of civic institutions; and a desire by government to continue the campaign after the initial Rockefeller investment. None of these prerequisites existed in Egypt at the time. The motive of British colonial authorities and wealthy property owners for participating in a hookworm campaign had been to improve the fellahin's productivity. The last thing they wanted was to train a professional class and run the risk of mobilizing local communities to challenge British rule.

Patients at an Egyptian field hospital received thymol, a relatively inexpensive and effective cure for hookworm disease. The treatment program developed by the Rockefeller Sanitary Commission, an organization that preceded the Rockefeller Foundation, was adapted for use in Africa. (Rockefeller Archive Center.)

Rose's experience in Egypt exposed an increasing tension within the Foundation's leadership between those who believed the Foundation's mission required a holistic, community-based public health approach and those who favored a focus on medical scientific research and innovation. Administering thymol to Egyptian peasants under the supervision of British physicians was one thing. But for leaders such as Frederick Gates—who believed that the Foundation should focus on laboratory breakthroughs rather than community education and public works the Foundation could not sustain on its own—the specter of treating five or six million patients on a recurring basis, investing in millions of latrines (for which there was no good design and no means of distribution), bulldozing and filling the festering birkas (ponds that formed in the pits left behind after digging earth to make bricks), reengineering the dams on the Nile, and engaging thousands of local community leaders in educating the public on sanitary and preventive health measures was an expensive proposition, especially when the British were financially and politically against it.

Three months after Rose left Egypt, World War One engulfed Europe. Lord Kitchener was recalled to London to become secretary of state for war. The mobile tent hospitals were commandeered by the army. Rose tried to keep interest in the Egyptian hookworm campaign alive, even proposing that the Rockefeller Foundation foot the entire budget and go it alone. Foundation leaders suggested that they could train Egyptians to run the campaign. But the British refused.

The failed effort offered a cautionary tale. Working through local government was a first principle for the Foundation, but in colonial Africa that required working with European imperial powers whose investment in their colonies would always be secondary to investments at home. The hookworm campaign in Egypt ultimately failed because it could not sustain the combined medical and public health approach that had made Rose's Southern campaign effective.

In the United States, the hookworm campaign had helped spark an effort by Rose and other Foundation leaders to create a new academic discipline in public health and to launch the first school of hygiene and public health at Johns Hopkins University. Returning to the United States after his travels in the British Empire, Rose began to think they could do the same in Britain. Almost by accident, this effort would lead to a greater focus on Africa and the diseases that were endemic to its tropical regions.

PUBLIC HEALTH
FOR THE WORLD

A lthough Egypt was nothing like the American South, Wickliffe Rose's experiences in North Africa confirmed his belief that the world—including Africa and the United States—needed a robust public health system. This system demanded not only physicians and nurses but also sanitary engineers, administrators, and paraprofessional health care workers in villages and small towns in every nation. As Raymond Fosdick wrote, Rose "had long since come to realize that unless basic medical education could be greatly improved, there was little promise for public health in many of the countries in which he was working."

Creating such a system was beyond the capacity of the Rockefeller Foundation, but with its resources the Foundation could help others to develop the educational institutions, dispensaries, clinics, and hospitals that would make this dream a reality. The Rockefeller Foundation had only recently begun to lead this process in the United States. Its major grants to the foremost medical schools provided incentives for these schools to professionalize medical education by hiring full-time faculty, raising standards for students, expanding the curriculum to include laboratory science classes, and partnering with teaching hospitals to provide doctors and nurses in training with the opportunity to gain clinical experience. At the same time, Rose and other leaders at the Foundation pushed to establish the first

The Rockefeller Foundation used colorful posters to educate the public about communicable diseases during World War One. Created by the Commission for the Prevention of Tuberculosis in France, this image warned of the great plague of tuberculosis, which had grown to epidemic proportions during the war. (Rockefeller Archive Center.)

Un Grand Fléau

F. Galais

LA TUBERCULOSE

LE GOUVERNEMENT DE LA PROVINCE DE QUÉBEC — LE SERVICE PROVINCIAL D'HYGIÈNE

production autorisée par le Bureau International de Santé de la "Fondation Rockefeller" et par le Comité N.al de Défense contre la Tuberculose PARIS, 66.bis Rue Notre Dame des Champs

A. DELRIEU 18 Av. d'ORLÉANS, PARIS

Librairie CH. DELAGRAVE
15, Rue Soufflot, PARIS

Docteurs Edmond SERGENT
et Étienne SERGENT
de l'Institut Pasteur de PARIS

CONTRE LA FIÈVRE JAUNE

Les Moustiques qui inoculent la Fièvre Jaune sont les STEGOMYIA FASCIATA

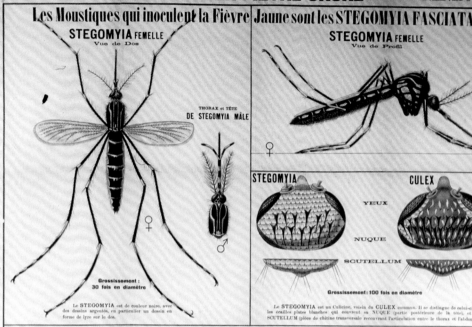

STEGOMYIA FEMELLE
Vue de Dos

THORAX et TÊTE
DE STEGOMYIA MÂLE

Grossissement :
30 fois en diamètre

Le STEGOMYIA est de couleur noire, avec
des dessins argentés, en particulier un dessin en
forme de lyre sur le dos.

STEGOMYIA FEMELLE
Vue de Profil

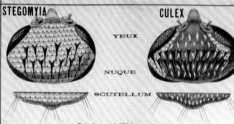

STEGOMYIA   CULEX

YEUX

NUQUE

SCUTELLUM

Grossissement : 100 fois en diamètre

Le STEGOMYIA est un Culicine, voisin du CULEX commun. Il se distingue de celui-ci par
les écailles plates blanches qui couvrent sa NUQUE (partie postérieure de la tête), et son
SCUTELLUM (pièce de chitine transversale recouvrant l'articulation entre le thorax et l'abdomen).

ŒUFS pondus, isolés,
à la surface des eaux
stagnantes. Ils éclosent
au bout de 2 à 3 jours.

LARVES d'âges différents. Elles vivent dans
l'eau. Le siphon respiratoire, à l'extrémité du corps
affleurent à la surface de l'eau, est de forme
oblaire et de couleur noire. (Après 1 à 3 semaines
de croissance, elles se transforment en nymphes).

ADULTE sortant de la
dépouille nymphale.

Les NYMPHES vivent dans l'eau.
(Après quelques jours, elles donnent
naissance aux adultes).

Comment on se protège contre la Fièvre Jaune

PÉTROLAGE OU DESTRUCTION DES GITES A STEGOMYIA

Salle d'hôpital où les lits sont mis à l'abri
des STEGOMYIA grâce à des moustiquaires de
toile métallique (avec double porte fermant)

La Fièvre Jaune est propagée par la piqûre des STEGOMYIA
FASCIATA qui ont sucé auparavant le sang de malades atteints depuis peu de jours de cette affection.

Il faut donc détruire les STEGOMYIA aux environs des habitations (dans
un rayon d'un kilomètre). Dans ce but, il faut supprimer toutes les collections
d'eau stagnante, même les plus petites; celles qui se forment dans les débris de
vaisselle, dans les tessons de bouteille, dans le creux des feuilles des arbres !

Si leur suppression est impossible (bassin d'arrosage, par exemple), verser
tous les 8 ou 15 jours, 10 centimètres cubes de pétrole ordinaire par mètre
carré de surface d'eau.

Il est prudent d'empêcher les STEGOMYIA, qui auraient échappé à ces
mesures d'extermination, de piquer les malades.

Dès qu'un cas de Fièvre Jaune est reconnu, on doit mettre le malade sous une
moustiquaire, surtout pendant les premiers jours de la maladie, et détruire tous
les STEGOMYIA adultes des maisons voisines, en brûlant du soufre :
40 grammes par mètre cube d'air.

D'une façon générale, il sera également bon de grillager toutes les ouvertures
des habitations.

school of public health in the United States, at Johns Hopkins University. The Johns Hopkins School of Hygiene and Public Health, which opened in 1918, became a template for what Rose imagined as "a series of schools of hygiene at strategic points over the world."

The flu epidemic of 1918-1919, which killed at least 20 million people, underscored the reality that disease didn't recognize flags or borders. During World War One, soldiers and refugees had died by the tens of thousands from dysentery, typhoid, and plague. Twenty-five million Russians were said to have fallen ill with typhus in the last years of the war; a million and a half died of it. Basic standards of sanitation disintegrated in battlefield trenches and refugee camps. When colonial doctors were sent to the front, rudimentary public health services collapsed in the British colonies of Africa, where epidemics of malaria and yellow fever broke out. The small gains that had been made by the Rockefeller Foundation's International Health Commission against hookworm and bilharzia vanished. As Rose and others recognized, the world was rapidly being integrated, demanding a global approach to disease that left no region behind.

To launch this global initiative in the early decades of the twentieth century, the Rockefeller Foundation had to confront the realities of empire. For centuries, European nations had projected power and influence over the continents of North and South America, Asia, and Australia. In the late nineteenth century, Britain, France, Belgium, Germany, Portugal, and Spain all claimed territories in Africa. Britain alone controlled vast regions in the eastern, central, and western portions of the continent, and continued to exert a powerful influence over South Africa and Egypt, which had recently gained a great deal of autonomy. London was the capital of this global empire and therefore the most strategic location for a new school of public health to complement the one at Johns Hopkins.

Even before the war, Wickliffe Rose had begun meeting with British officials, medical scientists, and educators and investigating possible sites for a new school. After his initial visit, the Foundation's trustees had authorized Rose to negotiate with the British on "a thoroughly matured plan and budget," but the war and its aftermath delayed decision-making.

Given his experiences in the American South, Rose had a strong interest in tropical medicine, but initially he did not see this as a critical component of this new institution. On August 18, 1914, he toured the London School of Tropical Medicine (LSTM) and had lunch with its director and faculty. LSTM, which shared space with the Albert Dock Seamen's Hospital at the Greenwich docks east of London,

Images of the development of mosquito larvae are depicted on this poster alongside methods of killing mosquitoes. Public education represented a critical component of the Rockefeller Foundation's campaign to eradicate yellow fever. (National Library of Medicine.)

was a leading center of medical research and played an influential role in the British Empire. Sailors who returned from the tropics with exotic infections were treated at the Seamen's Hospital, and colonial medical officers were routinely trained at LSTM before their postings to Africa.

Rose was impressed by LSTM. He noted approvingly in his diary that the school offered a three-month postgraduate course in tropical medicine for 84 dollars. This was the kind of initiative that would help fill the great demand for professionals in this field. But in 1914, supporting research in tropical medicine seemed peripheral to his main objective.

After the war ended, Rose had further opportunities to be impressed by the work at LSTM and learn more about its work with diseases that were endemic in Africa. In London in April 1919 to revive his talks with British authorities, he had lunch with Sir William Simpson, a lecturer at LSTM and a member of the Advisory Medical and Sanitary Committee for Tropical Africa. Simpson had been a member of the team dispatched by British authorities to the Gold Coast in 1908 to fight an outbreak of bubonic plague. Simpson was "much interested in establishing a great school of hygiene in London," Rose wrote in his diary. By this time it was becoming increasingly apparent that by involving LSTM, the Rockefeller Foundation might be able to consolidate support for a new school of public health.

Rose's negotiations with British authorities paralleled, but did not necessarily intersect with, the Foundation's interests in Africa. On January 6, 1920, for example, Rose sought approval from the Advisory Medical and Sanitary Committee for Tropical Africa, which monitored outbreaks of yellow fever and sleeping sickness, for a Rockefeller Foundation commission to study yellow fever in West Africa. On other occasions, Rose met with Africa experts and colonial officials to help Dr. Louise Pearce of the Rockefeller Institute travel to Sudan to expand her study of sleeping sickness. Through meeting after meeting, however, Rose never lost sight of the grand purpose of his visits, to work toward establishing a new school of public health in London.

During a three-day conference at the Colonial Office in 1921, the British asked Rose and Rockefeller Foundation President George Vincent to support a more diffuse project instead of a major center in London. The British believed that the bulk of the scientific investigations should be conducted in the colonies, but they complained that there were no trained staff to run laboratories in colonies such as Nigeria, the Gold Coast, Sierra Leone, Kenya, or Uganda, and no schools to train public health scientists.

The Rockefeller Foundation's leaders resisted this idea, however. They too wanted to help the people in the colonies, but they pointed out that Britain's

colonies were financially self-sustaining and thus perennially poor. Rose considered it unrealistic to suggest that the colonies, which did not yet have colleges, could host world-class medical research. As Rose suggested, "The facts of the case made it inevitable that the whole experience of the British Empire in regard to public health should be centered in London, and that in promotion of public health on an international scale London was perhaps the strategic part of greatest importance."

The London School of Hygiene and Tropical Medicine was funded by a $2 million contribution from the Rockefeller Foundation. The school was created to train public health officials while providing research and treatment of diseases endemic to Africa and other parts of the developing world. (Rockefeller Archive Center.)

   Rose and Vincent made it clear that they were focused on a pragmatic strategy. They wanted the new school to be accessible to students from all nations, not just British physicians or colonial officers. In an effort to compromise, George Vincent suggested that the Rockefeller Foundation could support a central institute of hygiene and public health that affiliated with LSTM, which might increase the focus on the public health needs of the colonies.

The group seemed to have reached an agreement by the third day of the conference, but Prime Minister David Lloyd George imposed an austerity program two months later. Minister of Health Sir Alfred Mond explained to Rose and Vincent on August 11, 1921, that he agreed with the Rockefeller Foundation's approach on every count, but Britain would be unable to finance the new school. "It is wholly out of the question for the British government or the University of London to find the necessary moneys for the expenditure involved in the establishment of such an Institute as is here recommended."

During an outbreak of yellow fever in Ogbomosho, Nigeria in 1946, Rockefeller Foundation scientist F.N. Macnamara worked with P. Ajiborisha to take blood samples for an immunity survey. Even after developing a successful vaccine, the Foundation worked to lower the cost of the vaccine to reach more people in Africa and other parts of the developing world. (Rockefeller Archive Center.)

Frustrated, Rose and Vincent were nevertheless committed to the Foundation's vision and were willing to take an enormous risk. On February 8, 1922, they made their offer: two million dollars ($26.2 million in 2013 dollars) toward the establishment of the school. The money was designated for purchase of the land and construction of the building. The Rockefeller Foundation also committed itself to funding fellowships for students to attend the school. The burden of sustaining the faculty and facilities would fall to the British. The British agreed.

At this point, the new school's relationship with LSTM was unclear. Fearing that LSTM would be made irrelevant by the new Rockefeller-funded institution, Dean Patrick Manson contacted Rose and suggested that LSTM should be incorporated into the new institution. Not wanting to embroil the Foundation in the internal politics of the British Health Ministry, Rose deftly responded that he had no authority to engineer such a move. Several months later, however, a committee organized by the British Minister of Health recommended this consolidation. In 1924 the new London School of Hygiene and Tropical Medicine (LSHTM) received its Royal Charter, and in July 1929 the school welcomed its first students.

Rose had been focused on promoting the creation of a new school to support the training of public health officials, but the project's lasting innovation had come almost by accident. The combination with LSTM created an institution with an important focus on diseases endemic to Africa and other regions that would become part of the developing world after the end of colonialism. This innovation strengthened the Foundation's link to Africa as part of its emerging vision for global health.

> "It is wholly out of the question for the British government or the University of London to find the necessary moneys."
> *Sir Alfred Mond, 1921*

In the early decades of the twentieth century, Africa's population, like others, suffered from a host of maladies, many not yet well understood. It was a continent, like others, without the institutions that could support a modern, scientific approach to medicine. But Africa was also unique, with its own history, ecology, and fabric of cultures. To work in Africa, the Rockefeller Foundation and its network of scientific experts needed to understand these differences.

"On September 21st, 1961, I joined the School of Public Health, Berkeley, University of California, where I majored in Maternal and Child Health. I learned to think in terms of the community, to identify the needs of the community, and to set priorities in programme planning. Emphasis was placed on being family centred when dealing with mothers and children, rather than treating them as individual patients."

Josephine M. Namboze
Fellowship Report, September 25, 1962

JOSEPHINE NAMBOZE: FIRST WOMAN DOCTOR IN EAST AFRICA

For many years, Dr. Josephine Namboze traversed the Uganda countryside in a lumbering Land Rover with a frighteningly wide turning radius. Home health care visits were the cornerstone of her approach to community and public health care. They were also part of her strategy to revolutionize medical training in East Africa.

Born in 1934, Namboze was the daughter of a teacher from the Nsambya Mission station. She attended a missionary primary school and earned a scholarship to Mt. St. Mary's College Namagunga for her secondary education. But there were no adequate facilities for science at this girls' school, so she made special plans to use the labs at Namilyango College, a boys' school. This lateral thinking and willingness to subject herself to criticism, and to do the unpopular thing, would characterize her life and career. In 1959 she became the first woman to graduate with a medical degree from Makerere University College and the first woman doctor in East Africa.

Namboze completed her internship in internal medicine and obstetrics and gynecology at Makerere's Mulago Hospital. Working on the children's ward, she realized that her training had prepared her to deal only with complex clinical pediatric problems, not the relentless challenge of infants and children suffering from malnutrition, diarrhea, malaria, pneumonia, worm infestations, and other preventable diseases. High infant and child mortality rates convinced her that she could be most effective in the community and in households, working on prevention and general health.

One day toward the end of her internship Namboze was summoned to the chief's office, where she met John Weir, as associate director of the Medical and Natural Sciences Division of the Rockefeller Foundation. They had a long chat about her goals. Namboze was surprised and delighted when the Foundation later awarded her a fellowship to study in London and to attend the summer course at the Institute of Child Health at the University of London.

After graduating from the University of London, in September of 1961 Namboze went on to the School of Public Health at the University of California, Berkeley, where she focused on maternal and child health and earned a Master of Public Health degree in June 1962. As she says, Berkeley taught her "to think in terms of the community, to identify the needs of the community, and to set priorities in program planning. Emphasis was placed

THE ROCKEFELLER FOUNDATION

PERSONAL HISTORY AND APPLICATION FOR

A FELLOWSHIP IN
- ☐ Agricultural Sciences
- ☐ Humanities
- ☑ Medical and Natural Sciences
- ☐ Social Sciences

APR 10 1961

(Note: Please type or print all entries in English)

FIELD OF INTEREST _Paediatrics & Child Health_

Date _17th March 1961_

Name in Full _JOSEPHINE MARY NAMBOZE_ Sex _FEMALE_

Present Address _Mulago Hospital, Box 351,_ (Street and Number) _Kampala_ (City) _UGANDA_ (State or Country)

Permanent Address _C.M. Nsambya, Box 321,_ (Street and Number) _Kampala_ (City) _UGANDA._ (State or Country)

Place of Birth _Nsambya, Kampala. UGANDA_ Year _1931_ Month _May_ Day _20th._

Citizenship _BRITISH_

Single, married, widowed, divorced _Single._ Wife's name _____

(Form of customary legal signature)

Date of marriage _—_ Number of Children _____ Age and Sex _—_

Other dependents _____

Present Position _MEDICAL OFFICER, UGANDA_ Annual Salary ████████

What part of salary and other income will be continued if a fellowship is granted?

NONE.

Have you at any previous time filed an application with The Rockefeller Foundation? _NO._

If so, give details _—_

Have you at any time held a fellowship from any other American institution or agency or are you now an applicant

for one? _NO_ If so, give details _—_

FORM 454

59

on being family centered when dealing with mothers and children rather than treating them as individual patients."

Namboze then began a whirlwind tour facilitated by the Rockefeller Foundation's global network of community health centers and clinics. She did field training at the Hospital Infantil de México and conducted research on protein-calorie malnutrition, which affects infants subjected to early cessation of breastfeeding. She went to the Institute of Nutrition of Central America and Panama (INCAP) in Guatemala and then the Candelaria Rural Health Center in Cali, Colombia, to learn about its environmental health programs.

In Kingston, she observed Jamaica's successful immunization program. In Puerto Rico, she studied methods to control tuberculosis. She finished her year-long tour with a visit to the World Health Organization in Geneva in order to gain a better understanding of public health in developing countries from an international policy perspective.

"Many diseases in the developing countries can be prevented by appropriate health education. This should be based on knowledge of the local situation, cultural beliefs and practices..."
Josephine Namboze, 1983

Namboze's Rockefeller Foundation fellowship had helped her to understand the meaning of development in the context of health. She would apply these lessons over decades in East Africa. As she says, the fellowship "laid a keystone for the development of my career." According to Namboze, her studies provided "the foundation to make a profound impact during a critical phase in the history of my country."

With support from the Rockefeller Foundation, Namboze returned to Uganda to become the first medical officer at the Kasangati Model Health Centre, which was affiliated with Makerere Medical School. Kasangati was an innovative new facility for teaching, service, and research in community health for rural settings. In 1964 Namboze became a lecturer at the Department of Preventive Medicine at Makerere Medical School, where she helped introduce antenatal outreach clinics and immunization programs backed by significant community participation. Kasangati included a nutrition rehabilitation program with a community kitchen, housing and environmental sanitation improvement, water quality protection, and home visits. The clinic's approach led to a 50-percent drop in the infant mortality rate and the elimination of whooping cough in the area. Equally important, the community learned to think of health and preventive care as an investment.

Namboze was part of the first generation of Ugandans who stepped into leadership roles after the country became independent in 1962. Their task was to foster institutional growth and promote resilience in the face of the changing political and economic environment. Her commitment to research as well as to active engagement with students fueled her rise within her profession. By 1977 she was a full professor of public health, the first woman to attain that status at Makerere University.

In 1978 Namboze was appointed head of the Institute of Public Health (formerly the Department of Preventive Medicine). In this leadership position, she came to believe in the statement by the World Health Organization (WHO) that health is a "state of complete physical, mental and social well being and not merely an absence of disease or infirmity." She also came to appreciate the importance of "indigenous beliefs and practices associated with health promotion, disease prevention and treatment as well as a variety of concepts regarding the causation of diseases." As she wrote in *Social Science and Medicine* in 1983, "Many diseases in the developing countries can be prevented by appropriate health education. This should be based on knowledge of the local situation, cultural beliefs and practices in order to effect change and establish development." In line with these insights, Namboze recommended that physicians and world health organizations should work with "traditional medical practitioners and birth attendants" who could serve as "important allies in improving health in the community."

In 1988 Namboze left Makerere University to serve as the WHO country representative in Botswana, where she established the first country HIV/ AIDS control strategy. She later served on the WHO regional expert panel for maternal and child health for Africa and its global expert panel on public health administration. From Botswana, Namboze moved to WHO's Brazzaville regional headquarters as director of Health Services Development, a position from which she retired in 1995. Even in retirement, Namboze led an active professional life, serving on the boards of several leading NGOs and dedicating herself, as a researcher, teacher, and media advocate, to the goal of integrating public health across all sectors.

PROMOTING UNDERSTANDING

The man who would become independent Kenya's first president, Kamau wa Ngengi, was born into a traditional Kikuyu family in Kenya and educated at a mission school. Here he changed his name to Johnstone Kamau and later to Jomo Kenyatta. As a young man he became the leader of the moderate anti-colonial Kikuyu Central Association. In the early 1920s, while Wickliffe Rose negotiated with the British, Kamau was in London defending Kikuyu land claims. For 18 years he navigated the arcane world of anti-imperial politics, spending a brief time in Moscow studying economics. Then, in 1935, with a scholarship from the Rockefeller Foundation, he enrolled at the London School of Economics in an anthropology seminar chaired by the renowned cultural anthropologist Bronislaw Malinowski.

In the 1920s, when Kenyatta first arrived in London, contact between European and African nations exercised a profound influence on the daily lives of many Africans. Germany, following its defeat in World War One, had lost its African colonies to Britain and France, as well as to South Africa, which had become a self-governing dominion in 1910. And as the anthropologist John Middleton has written, the academic study of Africa, except by missionary organizations, was still largely undeveloped. Despite the social dislocations of colonialism, Africans preserved historical and institutional knowledge and passed it from one generation to the next. A small number of African scholars, trained largely in missionary institutions, had received

advanced training abroad, especially in traditionally African-American colleges in the United States.

In the United States, the Phelps Stokes Fund, a philanthropy managed by Anson Phelps Stokes, a Rockefeller Foundation trustee, played a leading role in promoting educational opportunities for Africans. A study funded by Phelps Stokes led the Advisory Committee to the British Colonial Office to establish, on July 1, 1926, what later became the International Institute of African Languages and Cultures (IIALC). Operated as an independent institution, the IIALC was hosted by the London School of Economics. The institution's first chairman was Lord Frederick Lugard, who had been responsible for introducing the "indirect rule" form of administration in Britain's colonies but had also helped lead the fight to abolish the slave trade. Although the IIALC had been founded by a committee of government officials, missionaries, and others, from the beginning it was heavily influenced by academics, and particularly by the emerging social sciences, including the field of anthropology.

Mount Kenya towers above the traditional lands of the Kikuyu people. For Jomo Kenyatta and other Kikuyu leaders it was an important cultural landmark. (Library of Congress.)

In 1928 the IIALC began publishing the journal *Africa*, with monographs on "The Practical Orthography of African Languages," "Economic Changes in South African Native Life," "Division of Work According to Sex in African Hoe Culture," and "Some Conclusions Concerning the Bantu Conception of the Soul." In addition to scholarly articles, *Africa* also published "African Documents," which included texts written or dictated by Africans. Over the decades, *Africa* moved beyond a conception of itself as a service to missionaries and colonial administrators to become a leading scholarly journal.

Although the impetus for the IIALC came from missionaries and Colonial Office advisors, it was intended to be an independent entity. Initially, it focused on research by European and American scholars trying to understand the peoples of Africa, but it also began to publish work by Africans and soon recruited African scholars who provided their own view of the continent's many cultures and communities. The IIALC thus became a forum for the development of African leaders, like Kenyatta, who would challenge the colonial structure. But first, the IIALC needed funding to survive.

Laura Spelman Rockefeller Memorial and African Studies

The IIALC would not have been typical of the Rockefeller Foundation's grantees in the 1920s. For the founding generation of leaders of the Rockefeller Foundation and its affiliated boards, health and natural sciences were paramount. They believed, and had shown through programs in the United States and abroad, that science and technology held the potential to relieve human suffering and improve material well-being. But they also realized that scientific breakthroughs could be used to manufacture new instruments of war and oppression, and they were frustrated that politics, prejudice, poverty, and other social factors often made it impossible for people to benefit from new cures for disease.

The global campaign for public health launched by Wickliffe Rose and carried on by his successors at the Rockefeller Foundation depended on a better understanding of the complex social and economic problems that affected the lives of people around the world. It was impossible to eradicate hookworm or stymie the reproduction of yellow fever-carrying mosquitoes without changing the daily habits of families and communities. Increasingly, the leaders of the Rockefeller Foundation in the United States were interested in the potential for interdisciplinary, research-based social science to develop a greater understanding of people and communities in various regions of the world—including Africa.

In the 1920s, the Laura Spelman Rockefeller Memorial (LSRM), founded in 1918, was the one group within the network of John D. Rockefeller's philanthropies that focused on funding the development of the social sciences in leading universities, including the London School of Economics. Beardsley Ruml, the LSRM's director, took an early interest, for example, in women, family life, and social work. Most of the LSRM's grants were given to organizations in the United States, but its strong interest in promoting educational opportunities for African Americans led to an interest in Africa.

Bronislaw Malinowski shared Ruml's excitement about the potential of the social sciences. Malinowski had spent World War One in the Trobriand Islands of the western Pacific. His book *Argonauts of the Western Pacific*, published in 1922, became a classic of "participatory observation," the core methodology of anthropological research. The LSRM would ultimately invest well over $1.5 million in the fields of political science, economics, and anthropology at the London School of Economics to support faculty research, publication, and graduate student training. Malinowski and his students, including those from Africa, would receive a large share of this funding.

In the 1920s the Laura Spelman Rockefeller Memorial made significant financial contributions to advance the field of African Studies. This support allowed academics like anthropologist Bronislaw Malinowski of the London School of Economics to travel and to develop important ideas on race relations and African culture. (London School of Economics.)

In the spring of 1926, Ruml offered Malinowski a six-month grant to visit the United States. There is no reference in the records of Malinowski's visit suggesting that he spoke directly with anyone at the LSRM about Africa, but at his request, a trip was arranged to the American South. His observations were pertinent to the Foundation's work there, especially as it looked to those programs to guide the initiation of new projects in Africa. "It should not be forgotten," Malinowski warned, "that the present treatment of the negroes makes them very embittered, and creates a very strong prejudice among them against a friendly response to future advances from the white man." He referenced the hostility between the British and Egyptians and ended his report with a foreboding conclusion: "I believe also that in the future the problems of racial contact and the clash of cultures will become more and more urgent and important in the world's history. The white-negro configuration in the U.S., its sociological aspects, the gradual formation of a caste system under modern industrial conditions—constitute a prototype which probably will repeat everywhere."

Although he was not an Africanist, Malinowski's experiences in South Africa contributed to his evolving theory of cultural change. The methods and approaches being developed by cultural anthropologists in the 1920s were intellectually different from those used by European settlers and colonial administrators in Africa, but they had in common an interest in how and why cultures change. Malinowski's ideas would be extremely influential on both the discipline of social anthropology and the way the world understood the impact of urbanization and industrialization in Africa and elsewhere. This was in part because living and working in these spaces of contact, as

The London School of Economics, a center for African Studies, received over $1.5 million from the Laura Spelman Rockefeller Memorial. This funding supported research, publications, and graduate training across the social sciences. (Rockefeller Archive Center.)

Chapter Three: Promoting Understanding

anthropologists did, had made it obvious that there were no people without long histories of contact with other societies and cultures, in particular with colonial institutions. In southern Africa, Malinowski was first forced to consider that the focus of ethnographic inquiry could not be bounded and contained: "Roads and churches, motor cars and lorries, proclaim that we are in a world of change in which two factors are working together and producing a new type of culture, related both to Europe and Africa, yet not a mere copy of either." Malinowski, and anthropology in general, later would come under intense scrutiny and be criticized for their dependence on and contribution to colonial regimes; nonetheless, he trained students who would build a rigorous and ethical intellectual understanding of African lives in the midst of great change.

Hoping to capitalize on the Foundation's relationship with the London School of Economics and Malinowski, the IIALC requested a ten-year grant of $100,000 to support scholarships, research, and publishing. Instead, the Foundation's trustees offered $250,000 over a five-year period. They noted that "the distinctive character of the Institute is that it aims at bringing about a closer association between scientific knowledge and research and the practical interests of the administrators, educators, missionary, and colonist so that science may make an increasingly effective contribution to the solution of the immense human problems of the African continent." What the Foundation and the IIALC did not anticipate is that the grant would also provide significant support to Africans seeking to end colonial rule.

Africans and the Seminar

With a formal structure in place and its financial future secured for five years, the IIALC moved forward. Malinowski's seminar became a conduit for young anthropologists interested in Africa, and the institute, backed by the Rockefeller Foundation, supported their research fellowships. Many of them were white South Africans, including Meyer Fortes, Isaac Schapera, Lucy Mair, Audrey Richards, and a dozen others who were funded by the IIALC to conduct research in Africa.

Despite the lack of participation of black African scholars at this stage, the first generation of social anthropologists in Africa, under the influence of Malinowski's methods, had powerful real-world consequences. For the first time, scholars moved "off the veranda" and into the field. Following the example of their teacher, set in text if not in reality, they actively put themselves in the middle of village life and asked Africans to describe and explain the way they lived. As Malinowski's students began to investigate

NAME: MAIR, Miss Lucy
(M.A., Cambridge, 1927;
Cand. Ph.D., London)

PRESENT POSITION: Ass't in Internat'l Studies, London School
of Economics

PROSPECTIVE " : Lecturer in Colonial Administration, London
School of Economics

Nationality: British
AGE: 30 b. 1901
MARITAL STATUS: single
NO. OF CHILDREN
DATE APPROVED: 8/25/31
DURATION. 1 yr. 10/1/31
RENEWED:
DATE OF ARRIVAL:
FIRST STIPEND 11/16/31 **
AMOUNT:
TUITION: yes TRAVEL: yes
TERMINATION: 8/16/32**
MEETING:

STUDIES: Anthropology in East Africa (Uganda, Tanganyika and Kenya)

Subject of study: Native development in Uganda with spec. ref. to economic aspects.

Is fully prepared for field investigations she wishes to undertake; to study effects of progress on native institutions and relation between colonial admin. & maintenance & devel ment of native institutions, partic. in economic matters. Her work will be done primarily in native kingdom of Buganda in Uganda Protectorate. On way to Uganda will pass through colonies of Kenya and Tanganyika, and if possible, on her way back through the Rhodesias and South Africa.

12/3/36 TBK Interview with M: While in London, TBK had a conversation with M. concerning her present work for Lord Hailey. She was assisting in the preparation of the

**11/16/31 to 8/31/32. Suspended from 7/15/32-8/16/32.

and publish, they quickly cut through the stereotypes and racial biases of a century to reveal Africans who lived their lives within complex, sophisticated social and economic systems of culture and governance. The result was the publication of important ethnographies of life in Africa, such as C.G. Seligman and Brenda Seligman's *Pagan Tribes of the Nilotic Sudan* (1932), and the reports of government anthropologists R.S. Rattray in the Gold Coast, Charles Meek and Captain R.C. Abraham in Nigeria, and others elsewhere, followed by the most influential ethnography of all, E.E. Evans-Pritchard's *Witchcraft, Oracles, and Magic among the Azande* (1937).

The LSRM, meanwhile, was supporting Lucy Mair's work in Uganda, Audrey Richards's work with the Bemba of Zambia, Meyer Fortes's work on the Gold Coast, and Siegfried Nadel's work with the Nupe in Nigeria. The IIALC published the results of this research in texts that have become some

Lucy Mair was among the African Studies Research Fellows who received support from either the Rockefeller Foundation or the Laura Spelman Rockefeller Memorial in the 1920s and 1930s. Mair's research, as detailed on her fellowship card, focused on economic aspects of African development in Uganda. (Rockefeller Archive Center.)

Chapter Three: Promoting Understanding

of the most important contributions to understanding not only the impact of colonialism on African communities but ethnographic methods as well. These included the volume edited by Meyer Fortes and E.E. Evans-Pritchard, *African Political Systems* (1940), S.F. Nadel's *A Black Byzantium* (1942), and Audrey Richards's *Land, Labour and Diet in Northern Rhodesia* (1951).

The IIALC was becoming an increasingly important focal point for inter-racial debate and dialogue among anthropologists, other social scientists, and visitors interested in African affairs. For example, the American actor and singer Paul Robeson and his wife, Eslanda, frequently attended seminars. Most important, Malinowski's seminar began to include black Africans searching for a way to use the methods and language of the social sciences to support their fight for Africans' civil rights.

Africans and the IIALC

Jomo Kenyatta met Malinowski for the first time in December 1934. Soon afterward, Kenyatta enrolled as a graduate student in the department of social anthropology at the London School of Economics, mentored by Malinowski. Although most anthropologists at the time studied cultures other than their own, Kenyatta chose to investigate the social life of his own people, the Kikuyu. He finished his thesis in 1935, and published it three years later under the title *Facing Mount Kenya: The Tribal Life of the Gikuyu.*

Kenyatta's book marked an important bridge in the cultural conversation among Europeans, Americans, and Africans. As Malinowski noted in his introduction, the book "combines to an unusual extent the knowledge of Western ways and Western modes of thought with a training and outlook essentially African." It also helped to document "the principals underlying culture-contact and change"—principals that were important to evolving theories in anthropology and to the debate over colonialism.

Facing Mount Kenya offered a cautionary tale of the sentiment building in Kikuyu society against British colonialism. Part anti-colonial political argument, part memoir, part observation, part polemic, *Facing Mount Kenya* provided an insider's view of Kikuyu culture. One passage from Kenyatta's chapter on education illustrates the clarity of his vision of the impact of a century of British and European attitudes and behavior in Africa, even when well intended:

> In the past there has been too much of "civilising and uplifting poor savages." This policy has been based on pre-conceived ideas that the African cultures are "primitive,"

and as such, belong to the past and can only be looked upon as antiquarian relics fit only for museums. The European should realize that there is something to learn from the African and a great deal about him to understand, and that the burden could be made easier if a policy of "give and take" could be adopted. We may mention here that the African who is being civilised looks upon this "civilisation" with great fear mingled with suspicion. Above all, he finds that socially and religiously he has been torn away from his family and tribal organization. The new civilisation he is supposed to acquire neither prepares him for the proper functions of a European mode of life nor for African life; he is left floundering between the two social forces. European educationalists and others, especially those who are guided by racial prejudice and preconceived ideas of what is good for the African, usually fail to take cognizance of this vital fact. This may be due to studied indifference or to an inexcusably meager knowledge of the functions of African institutions and a lack of intimate contact with the real social life of the people they presume to teach.

> "The European should realize that there is something to learn from the African and a great deal about him to understand, and that the burden could be made easier if a policy of 'give and take' could be adopted."
> *Jomo Kenyatta, 1938*

Kenyatta's insight into the consequences of colonialism was coupled with a powerful critique of anthropology's efforts to help Westerners understand African culture. He noted, "While a European can learn something of the externals of African life, its system of kinship and classification, its peculiar arts and picturesque ceremonial, he may still have not yet reached the heart of the problem. In the mass of detail presented to him in what is called 'authoritative books,' he often loses his way as in a maze of knowledge not yet intelligible because not yet related." Kenyatta argued that the so-called objectivity of social scientists was often colored by "preconceived ideas, mingled with prejudices." As a result, the non-African anthropologist failed "to achieve a more sympathetic and imaginative knowledge, a more human and inward appreciation of the living people, the pupils he teaches, the people he meets on the roads and watches in the gardens." Without this deeper understanding of Africans' cultural consciousness, the habits of thought and expression that were intuitive to Africans were ultimately incomprehensible to Europeans.

OTHER VOICES EMERGE

K enyatta's appropriation of the theories and discourse of anthropology to resist colonial rule and assert Kikuyu rights was soon followed by similar appropriations by other black Africans involved with the IIALC. Zachariah K. Matthews, for example, had grown up in South Africa. As a young man, he received a scholarship in 1916 to the progressive Lovedale Missionary Institution, the only high school in the country open to black Africans at the time. Matthews then graduated from the newly established South African Native College (later the University College of Fort Hare). He met Anson Phelps Stokes while serving as a high school principal, and after Matthews became the first black African to earn a law degree from the

The International Institute of African Languages and Cultures, along with Bronislaw Malinowski's anthropology seminar, attracted scholars, students, and others with an interest in African affairs to the London School of Economics, where they engaged in vibrant dialogue and debate in rooms like this. (London School of Economics.)

University of South Africa, Phelps Stokes offered him a scholarship to earn an M.A. at Yale University, where he studied education, anthropology, and law.

In his Yale thesis, "Bantu Law and Western Civilization in South Africa: A Study in the Clash of Cultures," Matthews, like Kenyatta, used anthropology to create a framework for the political claims of black South Africans. From Yale, Matthews went on to the London School of Economics in 1934 to study at the IIALC and participate in Malinowski's seminar. There he interacted with Kenyatta and others. The following year, after earning a diploma in anthropology, he returned to teach in South Africa.

Like Kenyatta, Matthews appropriated the authority of social science and his association with Malinowski to critique the colonial system and assert the legitimacy of an emerging modern African identity and culture that reflected tradition and Western ideas regarding the law. In 1937, writing in the *Journal of the Royal African Society*, he challenged Frederick Lugard's undemocratic concept of "indirect rule," which left black South Africans without a voice in their own governance. He suggested that white South Africans should learn more about African institutions by encouraging and reading the work of their own anthropologists. "Africans would welcome such experts," he wrote, "provided they do not take a static view of primitive society." Matthews referred his white readers to Malinowski, who, he said, "stressed the necessity for the study of the problems of the Native with as much theoretical zeal and direct interest as the constructive study of the past."

After World War Two, Matthews would become an important leader in the African National Congress and eventually serve as Botswana's first ambassador to the United Nations. Meanwhile, 30 years after the publication of *Facing Mount Kenya* and after spending seven years in British prison during the Mau Mau rebellion, Jomo Kenyatta would become the first prime minister and the first president of independent Kenya. Sowing the seeds of African leadership in a postcolonial society had not been what the LSRM or the Rockefeller Foundation intended in the 1920s when they first began providing funding to the IIALC and Malinowski's seminar, but these results were not antithetical to the values and aspirations of many of the Foundation's early leaders. In philanthropy, some of the most important consequences are unintended. They grow out of the processes of interaction and collaboration. With the end of World War Two and the collapse of the colonial order, the Rockefeller Foundation would look for new ways to engage more directly with Africa.

After he became president of Kenya, Jomo Kenyatta's speeches echoed themes from his book *Facing Mount Kenya* (1938), in which he examined the impact of colonialism on African societies, in particular on his own Kikuyu culture. Kenyatta asserted that European colonists failed to understand African cultures and institutions, and suggested that "there is a great difference between 'living' among a people and 'knowing' them." (Marc & Evelyne Bernheim. Rockefeller Archive Center.)

" The dynamic of political change is thrusting the legal problems of Africa into the forefront. Certainly with the advance of so many territories to self-government and the prospect of full independence coming closer, there seems to be a pressing call for decisions to determine whether or not Africa is to be 'Balkanized' in the legal sense. The political institutions of the West have some vital legal and judicial presuppositions, and it is because of this that I attach considerable relevance to these legal difficulties that are now posed."

Ali Al'Amin Mazrui
Fellowship Application, May 28, 1960

ALI AL'AMIN MAZRUI: AFRICA, ISLAM,
AND THE CONFLUENCE OF CULTURES

I n 1955 Ali Al'Amin Mazrui was on his way to London to pursue his
high school education at Huddersfield Technical College. The son
of a prestigious Islamic judge from Mombasa, he would receive his
bachelor's degree in politics and philosophy with minors in English
literature and Arabic studies from Manchester University. In 1960 Mazrui
received a Rockefeller Foundation fellowship for graduate study at Columbia
University in New York and Nuffield College, Oxford, where he began his
Ph.D. on "The Idea of Self-Government and the Idiom of Nationalism in Some
Commonwealth African Countries, 1957–1963."

Mazrui is an intellectual of breathtaking range. He has written about the
history and cultural impact of European colonization, the relationship of the
Islamic north to Central Africa and the politics of North/South relations. He
became an ardent supporter of an authentic non-socialist path for African
development, and criticized efforts to impose European (or Soviet-style)
socialism on the developing nations of Africa. When civil war broke out in
the Congo, for example, while Mazrui was still at Oxford, he wrote "Edmund
Burke and Reflections on the Revolution in the Congo," asserting that the
new nations of Africa, and particularly the Congo, needed to recognize that
legitimate government had to be anchored in an awareness and respect for
Africa's tribal history and traditions. "If it is something new that you are
constructing," he suggested to the leaders of Africa's newly independent
nations, "be sure to base it on what there is of the experience of what is old."

Mazrui taught at Makerere University, was a visiting professor at the
University of Chicago, and held a research fellowship at Harvard, all before he
defended his dissertation at Oxford University in 1966. While at Harvard he
coauthored *Protest and Power in Black Africa* (1970) with the political scientist
Robert Rotberg.

True to the fellowship program's expectations, Mazrui returned to Africa
to become a professor of political science and very quickly dean of the social
sciences at Makerere University in Kampala, Uganda. It took him only two
years to be promoted to full professor, skipping associate professor status
altogether. When the Makerere University Law School was first being created,
he was appointed its interim dean. His impact as a teacher was huge. His
political theory class at Makerere ranged from Plato to Nkrumah, and the

476E
Mazrui

THE ROCKEFELLER FOUNDATION

PERSONAL HISTORY AND APPLICATION FOR

A TRAINING AWARD IN _____

A SCHOLARSHIP IN **POLITICAL SCIENCE**

(Note: Please type or print all entries in English)

FIELD OF SPECIAL INTEREST **Western political concepts and institutions in newly-developing countries**

DATE **28th May, 1960.**

NAME IN FULL **Ali Al'Amin Mazrui** SEX **Male**

PRESENT ADDRESS **9 Mitford Road, Fallowfield, Manchester 14. England.**
(Street and Number) (City) (State or Country)

PERMANENT ADDRESS **P.O. Box 80** **Mombasa** **Kenya.**
(Street and Number) (City) (State or Country)

PLACE OF BIRTH **Mombasa, Kenya.** YEAR **1933** MONTH **February.** DAY **24th**

CITIZENSHIP **British Protected Person**

SINGLE, MARRIED, WIDOWED, DIVORCED **Single** WIFE'S NAME _____
(Form of customary legal signature)

DATE OF MARRIAGE _____ NUMBER OF CHILDREN _____ AGE AND SEX _____

_____ OTHER DEPENDENTS _____

PRESENT POSITION **Undergraduate, Manchester University** ANNUAL SALARY _____

WHAT PART OF SALARY AND OTHER INCOME WILL BE CONTINUED IF AN AWARD IS GRANTED? _____

FORM 497

81

audiences for his lectures in the Main Hall were always overflowing. He also traveled across Uganda to give public lectures.

Mazrui was on the faculty at Makerere for a decade before being forced into exile by the Ugandan dictator Idi Amin in 1972. He moved to the United States, where he took up a series of visiting professor positions and became a popular voice for Africa. In 1973 Mazrui joined the faculty at the University of Michigan, where he remained for the next 18 years. He served as director of the university's Center for Afroamerican and African Studies from 1978 to 1981. He served as president of the African Studies Association, vice president of the International African Institute in London, and vice president of the International Congress of Africanists. He then served as the Albert Schweitzer Professor of Humanities and Director of the Institute of Global Cultural Studies at Binghamton University, State University of New York; Andrew D. White Professor-at-Large Emeritus and Senior Scholar in Africana Studies at Cornell University; and Albert Luthuli Professor-at-Large, University of Jos, Nigeria.

Mazrui has authored more than 30 books, from *Towards a Pax Africana* (1967) to *The Politics of War and the Culture of Violence* (2008), and has even written fiction such as *The Trial of Christopher Okigbo* (1971). Every important newspaper in the world has carried his byline. In his 1986 book, *The Africans: A Triple Heritage*, he argued that postcolonial Africa had ignored the lessons of cultural continuities and was suffering from the curse of the ancestors, which was causing Africans to "multiply in numbers but not always have the food to feed your hungry children. Your political institutions will malfunction; your economic institutions will atrophy. Your warriors will ignore honour; your leaders will betray you; your trains will rust, your roads decay and your factories grind to a standstill." Based on this book he narrated a high-profile television series, *The Africans: A Triple Heritage*, for the BBC and PBS. The program has subsequently become a much discussed and shared YouTube staple.

Mazrui's work has even spawned its own collective noun – Mazruiana. Not surprisingly, then, Mazrui and his work are controversial. In *Islam: Between Globalization and Counter-terrorism* (2006) he explores, through the perspective of the rise and fall of civilizations, how Islam in the twenty-first century is caught between three interrelated forces—globalization, international terrorism, and the rise of the American empire—and looks at the way in which Islamic society is challenging the American empire.

Much of Mazrui's writing, however, seeks to "puncture universal theories about Africa" and to challenge Africans as well to see themselves differently. He has been critical of the economic, political, and cultural legacies of colonialism and has been described as Africa's leading theoretician on the concept of "cultural dependency." In the 1970s Mazrui suggested that African universities perpetuated Africa's cultural dependence on the West by giving slight attention to African history, culture, and language. He called for the "decolonization of modernization" by linking modernity to local culture and economic needs in Africa, diversifying the idea of modernization to include non-Western cultures, and promoting the influence of African culture on the West. "The full maturity of African education will come only when Africa develops a capacity to innovate independently," Mazrui wrote in 1975.

> "The full maturity of African education will come only when Africa develops a capacity to innovate independently."
>
> *Ali Al'Amin Mazrui, 1975*

The late Rupert Emerson, professor of political studies and international relations at Harvard, describes him: "One outstanding service which Professor Mazrui renders Africa is his readiness to ask inconvenient questions and to look under the rug to see what unpleasant matters may have been swept there. It is Africa's gain to have so persistent a gadfly as Professor Mazrui."

Mazrui's career is its own story of modern Africa. His effort to integrate Islamic history back into African history challenged the interpretation of Africa from a Eurocentric Christian perspective. His confrontation with Idi Amin and exile from Makerere highlighted the heroic efforts of the first generation of postcolonial African scholars to assert their intellectual freedom in the face of repressive political regimes. And throughout his career, he has exhorted readers to develop a more complicated understanding of the history of the continent and its relationship with the rest of the world.

AFRICA ADVANCING

I n August 1941 British Prime Minister Winston Churchill stepped aboard the USS *Augusta* for an extraordinary meeting with U.S. President Franklin Roosevelt. Britain wanted to secure American support in its fight against Nazi Germany, but Roosevelt wanted the world to know that American support would be based on certain basic principles.

The agreement reached by Churchill and Roosevelt became known as the Atlantic Charter. Its principal points included a commitment to renounce any territorial gains as a result of the war and to promote free trade and global economic cooperation. Most important to the people of Africa, the two leaders declared that their countries would "respect the right of all peoples to choose the form of Government under which they will live" and wished "to see sovereign rights and self-government restored to those who have been forcibly deprived of them."

Churchill told the members of the British Parliament that the Atlantic Charter applied only to European lands freed from German occupation. Nnamdi Azikiwe was appalled. The prolific editor of the *West African Pilot*, who had studied at Howard and Lincoln universities in the United States in the 1920s before returning home to Nigeria, noted that African soldiers were battling Nazi forces. "Are we fighting for the security of Europe whilst Africans continue to live under pre-war status?"

The Atlantic Charter helped define the terms of American participation in the Allied war effort and outlined a vision for the postwar world. Through its focus on the right to self-government, the Charter also gave hope to African nationalists that independence would come with the end of the war. (National Archives and Records Administration.)

THE Atlantic Charter

THE President of THE UNITED STATES OF AMERICA and the Prime Minister, Mr. *Churchill*, representing HIS MAJESTY'S GOVERNMENT IN THE UNITED KINGDOM, being met together, deem it right to make known certain common principles in the national policies of their respective countries on which they base their hopes for a better future for the world.

1. *Their countries seek no aggrandizement, territorial or other.*

2. *They desire to see no territorial changes that do not accord with the freely expressed wishes of the peoples concerned.*

3. *They respect the right of all peoples to choose the form of government under which they will live; and they wish to see sovereign rights and self-government restored to those who have been forcibly deprived of them.*

4. *They will endeavor, with due respect for their existing obligations, to further the enjoyment by all States, great or small, victor or vanquished, of access, on equal terms, to the trade and to the raw materials of the world which are needed for their economic prosperity.*

5. *They desire to bring about the fullest collaboration between all nations in the economic field with the object of securing, for all, improved labor standards, economic advancement and social security.*

6. *After the final destruction of the Nazi tyranny, they hope to see established a peace which will afford to all nations the means of dwelling in safety within their own boundaries, and which will afford assurance that all the men in all the lands may live out their lives in freedom from fear and want.*

7. *Such a peace should enable all men to traverse the high seas and oceans without hindrance.*

8. *They believe that all of the nations of the world, for realistic as well as spiritual reasons, must come to the abandonment of the use of force. Since no future peace can be maintained if land, sea or air armaments continue to be employed by nations which threaten, or may threaten, aggression outside of their frontiers, they believe, pending the establishment of a wider and permanent system of general security, that the disarmament of such nations is essential. They will likewise aid and encourage all other practicable measures which will lighten for peace-loving peoples the crushing burden of armaments.*

FRANKLIN D. ROOSEVELT

WINSTON S. CHURCHILL

August 14, 1941

he asked. In his response, Churchill offered no clear promise of independence, noting only that the Charter's principles were "not incompatible with progressive evolution of self-governing institutions."

Azikiwe hoped that the war would bring an end to colonialism. Many American leaders, including President Roosevelt, shared that hope, as did Raymond Fosdick, the president of the Rockefeller Foundation. And even as the nation waged all-out war, philanthropic leaders and public officials began to discuss ways in which the Foundation might contribute to Africa's future. One of the men involved in these discussions was an African-American scholar, intelligence analyst, and diplomat who had been Azikiwe's professor at Howard University in Washington, D.C., had participated in Malinowski's seminar, and had learned Kikuyu from Jomo Kenyatta.

East African soldiers served as an essential part of the British forces in Africa during World War Two. The war proved to be a turning point for African independence. It weakened the power of the British Empire and solidified nationalist sentiment among many Africans. (Library of Congress.)

Chapter Four: Africa Advancing

By any measure, Ralph Bunche was remarkable. Raised by his maternal grandmother in Los Angeles, the intellectually precocious Bunche, like many African-American students in the 1920s, was steered into the vocational education track in middle school. At the time, the influence of Booker T. Washington and the Tuskegee Institute model, which emphasized practical training for African Americans, was pervasive across the nation. Bunche's grandmother was furious. "This boy is going to college, and he must be ready for it," she told the principal, insisting that he be transferred into academic classes. Bunche graduated first in his class at Jefferson High School, and was valedictorian of his graduating class at the University of California, Los Angeles in 1927. Seven years later he became the first African American to receive a Ph.D. in political science from Harvard University.

In his dissertation, Bunche turned his attention to Africa and compared the systems of government in Dahomey (a French colony) and Togoland (administered by the French under a League of Nations mandate). Throughout his subsequent academic career he would focus on African issues, benefiting from and contributing to the development of institutions and scholarship supported by the Rockefeller Foundation or its grantees. The Julius Rosenwald Fund had already provided a scholarship to support field research in West Africa for his doctoral dissertation. After winning the Toppan Prize for the best political science dissertation at Harvard, Bunche received a two-year grant from the Foundation-supported Social Science Research Council to pursue postdoctoral research training in cultural anthropology at Northwestern University in Chicago, the London School of Economics, and the University of Cape Town in South Africa, and then to continue his research in South Africa. It was during his time at the London School of Economics that Bunche participated in Malinowski's seminar in social anthropology.

Ralph Bunche was an American academic and diplomat who would later join the Rockefeller Foundation's board of trustees. Bunche served with the U.S. State Department and the United Nations, where he dealt with issues affecting African colonies. In 1950 he received a Nobel Peace Prize for his efforts to negotiate a truce between Israel and Arab states in Palestine. (Los Angeles Public Library.)

In 1937 and 1938, Bunche traveled to South Africa to observe its emerging system of racial segregation first-hand. He stayed in the homes of African families and talked to many of the leaders of the black South African community, including the noted African physician Dr. Silas Molema. He visited Molema's nursing home and surgical clinic in Mahikeng, where Molema was licensed to operate on white patients but was not allowed to reside. Bunche visited black intellectuals, black newspaper editors, and traditional tribal chiefs. He traveled in the countryside and in black townships. The power of his travel notes consisted in his ability to stand back and observe the small, incidental events of daily life in South Africa—but, as he explained in a letter to his good friends Paul and Eslanda Robeson in London, his mind never wandered far from the big question: "I've been knocking around in South Africa trying to find out what sort of magic is employed to enable that handful of very ordinary pale-faces to keep the millions of black and colored so ruthlessly under the thumb."

At the University of Cape Town, the anthropologist Isaac Schapera, a colleague of Malinowski whose research in southern Africa had been supported

In South Africa and Kenya in 1937 and 1938, Ralph Bunche observed the lives of ordinary Africans, including miners working deep underground near Johannesburg. The trip shaped Bunche's opinions on the problems as well as the potential of an emerging postcolonial Africa. (Library of Congress.)

Chapter Four: Africa Advancing

by the International Institute of African Languages and Cultures (IIALC), encouraged Bunche to focus on the power and authority of native chiefs and launch a more expansive investigation of the "repercussions of South African government policies for black communities." After three months in South Africa, Bunche traveled to Kenya, where Kenyatta had arranged for him to meet with leaders of the Kikuyu Central Association.

Bunche spent only four months doing postdoctoral research in Africa, but his work made him one of the leading authorities on Africa in the United States. When World War Two erupted, Bunche took a position on the Africa desk at the Office of Strategic Services (OSS), the predecessor of today's Central Intelligence Agency, and in early 1944 he moved to the State Department. His boss at the OSS, the University of Pennsylvania historian Conyers Read, described Bunche as "perhaps the foremost authority in America on African problems. . . . His knowledge of Africa is unique, his diligence in research very remarkable, and his tact in personal contacts outstanding."

A Postwar Vision for Education in Africa

At the OSS, Ralph Bunche became aware of the war's profound impact on Africa. Like others, he foresaw the end of colonialism and with it a host of new problems as well as opportunities. In December 1942 he participated in a conference sponsored by the Institute of Pacific Relations (funded by the Rockefeller Foundation and Carnegie Corporation) at Mont Tremblant, Quebec, where he discussed the future of India and other Asian colonies with the highest-ranking British colonial authorities, including Lord Frederick Lugard, the IIALC's first chairman.

Bunche told the assembled leaders, "International machinery will mean something to the common man in the Orient, as indeed to the common man throughout the world, only when it is translated into terms that he can understand: peace, bread, housing, clothing, education, good health, and, above all, the right to walk with dignity on the world's great boulevards." He received a standing ovation. The conference anticipated the creation of the United Nations, and the agenda spoke directly to how the Allies might aid "in the establishment of conditions of racial, political and economic justice and welfare."

The British tried to finesse the primary *political* questions facing Asia. Colonial experts could agree that the future of India and Africa required self-government, but for the British Colonial Office and its allies among missionary societies, philanthropists, and academics, self-government and autonomy within the Commonwealth did not necessarily mean sovereignty and national independence.

Nonetheless, Bunche described the gathering as "the best international conference I've ever attended." He considered it so successful that he immediately began thinking about convening a similar event focused exclusively on Africa. He contacted a small group of American philanthropists to begin a discussion about the role of the United States in Africa's future.

As was his habit, Anson Phelps Stokes took the initiative. With Bunche's guidance, Phelps Stokes invited 30 people to a preconference at the Brookings Institution. Generally considered the first private think tank in the United States, Brookings traced its history back to 1916, when the Rockefeller Foundation helped to establish the Institute for Government Research (IGR). During World War Two, Brookings played a key role in researching international issues and was, therefore, a natural place to host a conference "to consider the possibility and desirability of organizing an African Institute [an American version of London's IIALC] and of arranging an international conference on the postwar future of Africa."

Phelps Stokes offered a preliminary agenda and posed key questions:
"(1) Is the formation of an African Institute both desirable and possible at this time? (2) Should the proposed institute be virtually restricted, as is the one in London [IIALC], to scientific subjects such as African Anthropology and Linguistics, or should it also consider Social, Economic, Health and Political problems, and Education—both in Africa and about Africa—interpreting these terms broadly?"

The Brookings Institution has served as a center of public policy research since it was founded in 1916 with support from the Rockefeller Foundation. In 1943 Brookings hosted a convening of influential philanthropists and academics to discuss the future of African colonies and American involvement on the continent, as well as a potential Institute of African studies in America. (Rockefeller Archive Center.)

The proposed agenda was rife with potential sources of conflict. The British were suspicious of American anti-colonial motives and nervous that a Mont Tremblant–style conference might focus on political questions that could only lead to a clash over the future of African sovereignty. By taking up questions of education, the Americans might also be intruding on the long experience and entitlement of British missionary societies. Indeed, representatives of the missionary movement advocated a narrower approach. They wanted no conference and no new institute. They supported a new survey of African educational problems that would focus on agriculture and missionary education strategies while steering clear of thorny political issues, and for the moment they seemed to have the upper hand.

Chapter Four: Africa Advancing

The list of invitees to the Brookings preconference included traditional voices of American philanthropy, many of whom had deep ties to the missionary movement. But the days when these traditionalists could dictate the approach to Africa were long gone. Bunche was not the only new black voice at the Brookings meeting. The renowned sociologist W.E.B. Du Bois was invited, as were Carter Woodson, the driving force behind the Laura Spelman Rockefeller Memorial's *Study of Negro Life in America*, and Francis Kwame Nkrumah, the young president of the African Students Association of the United States and Canada, who was studying education and philosophy at the University of Pennsylvania.

The powerful voices of Pan-Africanists such as Du Bois and Nkrumah set the tone of the meeting. Their call for an international conference on the future of Africa was supported by Edwin Embree from the Rosenwald Fund and Melville Herkovits, the director of the anthropology program at Northwestern University. Jackson Davis, however, reacted with caution. A voice of the old guard at the Rockefeller Foundation's General Education Board, he did not want to rile British colonial officials. "It was somewhat unfortunate," he noted, " that the *political aspects* of

W.E.B. Du Bois was an American sociologist and Pan-Africanist who argued for equal rights for African Americans and independence for African colonies. Du Bois was also a co-founder of the National Association for the Advancement of Colored People (NAACP) and the editor of the organization's journal, *The Crisis*. (New York Public Library.)

Africa in international relations was the chief interest of those who did most of the talking." Davis tried to steer the group away from politics. In notes written after the meeting, he cautioned that neither South Africa nor Great Britain would tolerate "outside interference" by Americans in Africa. Margaret Wrong, representing the International Committee on Christian Literature for Africa, concurred with Davis.

Ultimately, on March 10, 1944, the trustees of the GEB, which had become a virtual subsidiary of the Rockefeller Foundation, allocated $23,000 ($305,000 in 2013 dollars) to the Phelps Stokes Fund to underwrite a Commission on African Education. The commission reflected a very traditional approach to "practical" education for black Americans in the United States. Chairman Jackson Davis was a former principal and superintendent of schools in Virginia who specialized in education in the American South and interracial problems, as well as education in the Belgian Congo and Liberia. Commission member Thomas M. Campbell, a Tuskegee Institute agronomist and protégé of George Washington Carver, was a pioneer in the fields of agricultural education and extension work who had sought to bring modern agricultural methods to the rural African-American farmers of Alabama. The commission's third member, Margaret Wrong, came from a Toronto Anglican family with important links to church, state, and university. Working out of London, she had traveled tens of thousands of miles through sub-Saharan Africa on behalf of the International Missionary Council.

Davis originally included British East Africa in planning for the travels that would be part of the commission's work, but financial considerations, the difficulty of travel during wartime, and the length of time necessary to complete a continent-wide survey led him to shorten the trip. As a result, the commission limited its investigations to Liberia; the British West African colonies of Nigeria, the Gold Coast, and Sierra Leone; the French territories of Equatorial Africa and the Cameroons; and the Belgian Congo. The commission's findings were published in 1945 under the title *Africa Advancing: A Study of Rural Education and Agriculture in West Africa and the Belgian Congo.*

Africa Advancing

Africa Advancing argued that stability and continuity were essential for the development of educational and food resources in West Africa. Conceding that these countries needed to eliminate their economic dependency on colonial powers, the commissioners were nevertheless cautious, insisting that institutional and economic stability were essential if these countries wanted to attract large capital investments for projects that would support development. In the end, the commissioners concluded, Africa's only path was to cooperate with European policies that called for Christian education, gradual movement toward self-government, and economic integration. To the Pan-Africanists who had attended the meeting at the Brookings Institution, *Africa Advancing* was undoubtedly disappointing.

Historian E.C. Martin, who later reviewed the report in the IIALC's journal *Africa*, also expressed frustration with the final product. He suggested that the commissioners had evaded "the problem, which has had to be met over and over again, of how native enterprise is to be given adequate opportunity for expression while a final authority judges and controls." Indeed, Martin believed that the commission's work offered "little to distinguish the suggestions for African advance from equally well-meaning efforts of British authorities elsewhere which have led to passionate demands for the removal of European influence and control."

Martin conceded, however, that *Africa Advancing* did support a transition to self-government through education and agricultural development. These two goals were clearly linked in the commissioners' minds, since the report highlighted the value of education to the general well-being of African communities and specifically to effective farming practices and marketing of agricultural produce. Training African teachers would be essential. Overall, the reviewer recommended "a policy of the Three C's—co-operation, collaboration, and centralization," including the need for collaboration between government and missions and for co-operation between various missions in mission councils.

MOVING FORWARD

In the aftermath of World War Two, *Africa Advancing* did not lead to immediate action. There was too much political uncertainty, and the Foundation itself struggled to define its role in the postwar world. Nevertheless, the report brought to the forefront a number of important issues that would challenge and inspire U.S. philanthropy in Africa for the next six decades. The report also highlighted the role of media technologies (at the time, film and radio) in education, and especially the importance of educating women. Moreover, the creation of the commission brought new voices to the table. Ralph Bunche would become an important player inside the Rockefeller Foundation, where he would collaborate with a former colleague from his days in the OSS to support a fundamentally new approach to the Foundation's work in Africa. Meanwhile, Nnamdi Azikiwe and Kwame Nkrumah would soon play leading roles in shaping Africa's future.

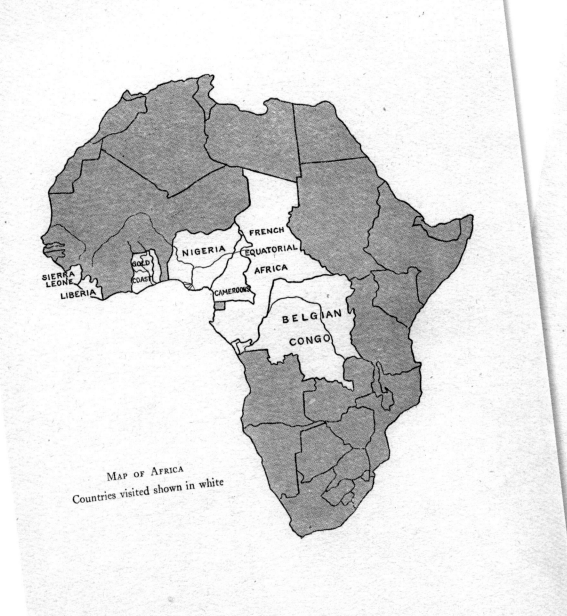

SIERRA
LEONE
LIBERIA

GOLD
COAST

NIGERIA

CAMEROONS

FRENCH
EQUATORIAL
AFRICA

BELGIAN
CONGO

MAP OF AFRICA
Countries visited shown in white

AFRICA ADVANCING

STUDY OF RURAL EDUCATION AND AGRICULTURE IN WEST AFRICA AND THE BELGIAN CONGO

BY

JACKSON DAVIS
THOMAS M. CAMPBELL
MARGARET WRONG

1945

In 1945 the Commission on African
Education, supported by the Rockefeller
Foundation, published *Africa Advancing*,
a report advocating a cautious approach
to African self-government. Commission
members determined that success would
be achieved through stability, investment,
and continued cooperation with Europe.
(Rockefeller Archive Center.)

"I would like to orientate my research on utilization of molecular biology for application in agronomy since this field of research is supposed to have a great impact in plant breeding and general knowledge on plant biology. I am very interested by the research … which deals with the identification of resistance markers to Rice Yellow Mottle Virus and aims at the production of transgenic plants which will be more resistant and adapted to African growing conditions. I am sure that this program will give me the benefit of modern biotechnology that I will be able to return to my national institutions."

Marie-Noelle Ndjiondjop
Fellowship Application, November 14, 1995

MARIE-NOELLE NDJIONDJOP:
HUMAN CAPITAL AND MOLECULAR BIOLOGY IN AFRICA

Cameroon is a nation of diverse landscapes and abundant potential where an estimated 70 percent of the population practices some form of agriculture, either at subsistence level or for export—or something in between. Fueled in part by agricultural production, the economy of Cameroon has experienced vast improvements since the mid-1980s, when a sinking economy forced the country to adopt austerity measures as well as a restructuring of its finances by the International Monetary Fund.

Marie-Noelle Ndjiondjop, a promising young science student, left Cameroon behind during that era, hoping to return with the tools to help create a better future. In France she earned an undergraduate degree at Université des Sciences et Techniques in Montpellier, where her continued study of the impact of climate on rice quality led to a Masters in Science. She then began work on her doctorate.

During her time at Montpellier, Ndjiondjop's interest in the science of agriculture evolved. As she spent more time in a laboratory setting she focused increasingly on the science of molecular biology and its potential to improve agricultural output and productivity. The science gave her insights to changes that affected not only her native Cameroon, but all of Africa.

The Rockefeller Foundation had helped to create the field of molecular biology, a term coined by Warren Weaver when he was head of the Foundation's Division of Natural Sciences. As the Green Revolution of the 1950s and 1960s developed and the Foundation recognized molecular biology's potential to improve agriculture in developing countries, it began offering financial support to research facilities as well as the scientists who staffed them. By the 1980s these programs had helped to shape a well-funded global network of research institutes that used advances in biotechnology to map genomes of plants and to create new strains of disease-resistant crops for use in the developing world (see Chapter Ten).

Ndjiondjop's research plans, as she embarked on her doctorate in 1996, coincided perfectly with the Foundation's desire to use science in propelling Africa forward. Proposing a project in the field of rice biotechnology, Ndjiondjop applied for a Rockefeller fellowship in 1995. In her earliest exchanges with Gary Toenniessen of the Agricultural Sciences Division,

NDJIONDJOP, M.N.

JHS JCB
NDJIONDJOP

THE ROCKEFELLER FOUNDATION

APPLICATION FOR A FELLOWSHIP OR TRAINEESHIP

Note: An unmounted passport size photograph of the applicant should be attached here.

(NOTE: Please type or print all entries in English and ANSWER ALL QUESTIONS.)

FIELD OF INTEREST Genetics, Molecular Biology, Biotechnology.

Date _____

Name in Full NDJIONDJOP NZENKAM Marie-Noëlle Sex F

Present Address Las Rebes 10. A. 556, Avenue Louis Ravas 34080 Montpellier
Phone: 67-54-67-65
Permanent Address B. P.   Yaoundé - CAMEROON.

Place of Birth Bertoua (CAMEROON) Year 1962 Month 12 Day 18

Citizenship Cameroonian _____ Country of Legal Residence _____

United States Social Security Number (if any) _____

Single, married, widowed, divorced Divorced _____ Spouse's name _____
                                                                  (Form of customary legal signature)
Date of Marriage _____ Number of Children _____ Ages _____

If single, are you engaged to be married? ___ No ___ If so, when? _____

Present Position _____

Monthly Salary ███████████
                                    (Identify currency)

Have you at any previous time filed an application with The Rockefeller Foundation for a grant for study or research? Yes ☐ No ☒

If so, give details _____

_____

_____

_____

If the grant was made, were you a candidate for a degree at an educational institution? Yes ☒ No ☐

Form 539 (Rev. 5 — 1974)

Ndjiondjop indicated her interest in mapping the genes resistant to rice yellow mottle virus (RYMV), the most damaging virus affecting African rice. She also wrote of her desire to return to Africa upon completing her studies in order to "join a research program on rice improvement through rice biotechnology."

On the strength of recommendations from the University of Dschange in Cameroon and her advisors at Montpellier, Ndjiondjop was awarded a Rockefeller fellowship for the duration of her doctoral studies in plant pathology and genetics. Over the next three years Ndjiondjop conducted research that mapped a major gene resistant to RYMV. The research was later used to improve strains of rice for African farmers. In 1999 Ndjiondjop successfully defended her doctoral dissertation, titled "Heredity, mechanism and mapping of marker linked to rice yellow mottle virus resistant gene in rice."

Ndjiondjop returned to Africa in 1999 to continue research that would better the lives of West African farmers. This goal brought her first to the Ivory Coast to begin a Rockefeller Foundation-supported post-doctoral fellowship at a research station sponsored by AfricaRice (formerly the West Africa Rice Development Association). Also known as the Africa Rice Center, AfricaRice is a leading organization devoted to rice research as a means of improving agricultural output and food security in Africa. Created in 1971, the Center has seen its membership grow from 11 to 24 African nations. Currently headquartered in Benin, the center operates research stations in Senegal, Ivory Coast, Nigeria, and Tanzania. AfricaRice is also a member of the Consultative Group on International Agricultural Research (CGIAR), founded by the Rockefeller and Ford Foundations. Originally a close-knit network of four agricultural research stations in the Philippines, Nigeria, Colombia, and Mexico, CGIAR is now made up of 15 independent stations around the globe. The scientists who work there remain committed to sharing their resources and research in an effort to increase agricultural productivity throughout the world, reducing hunger and poverty.

After completing post-doctoral research in 2002, Ndjiondjop continued her research at AfricaRice. She relocated to the Benin headquarters, where she became head of the center's biotechnology unit. Her research continued to focus on the genetic profiling and mapping of new strains of rice suitable for African climates and soil. Her most recent work, for example, seeks to identify rice genotypes that are tolerant to drought.

In addition to conducting her own research, Ndjiondjop has been tireless in her efforts to train Africa's next generation of scientists. Her team at AfricaRice has mentored numerous researchers and graduate students—the next generation of Africans who have the potential to transform African development. The goal, according to Ndjiondjop, is to strengthen the capacity of national agricultural research and extension systems in West Africa by developing modern breeders. "The hands-on experience gained by the students through their involvement in collaborative research, training programs, and

> "The hands-on experience gained by the students through their involvement in collaborative research, training programs, and technology transfer projects is very valuable."
> *Marie-Noelle Ndjiondjop, 2012*

technology transfer projects is very valuable," Ndjiondjop told *Rice Today* in 2012. Ndjiondjop's team has also helped to establish and equip new research laboratories in Burkina Faso, The Gambia, Guinea, and Mali, each dedicated to the science of molecular biology.

For all of these efforts, in 2012 Ndjiondjop was awarded the Robert J. Carsky Award, which honors outstanding contributions to rice research, training, and research support in Africa. Indeed, *Rice Today* has called her "the driving force behind molecular biology research at AfricaRice."

TURNING TOWARD
POSTCOLONIAL AFRICA

Throughout the pre-World War Two years, the Rockefeller Foundation's relationship with Africa had been shaped in complex ways by its historic association with the missionary movement, the existing framework of colonialism, pervasive and contested attitudes toward race, and the limits of its knowledge and understanding of the people of Africa. Within this context, the Foundation's accomplishments had been limited. Public health work in Egypt had provided some relief to the afflicted. The creation of the London School of Hygiene and Tropical Medicine provided an important training center for physicians who worked in Africa. A grant helped to establish what is today Kenyatta National Hospital, Kenya's first national referral tertiary facility. Meanwhile, the development of a vaccine to fight yellow fever, based on field research in Africa, helped prevent outbreaks among troops in Africa during the war; but because the vaccine needed refrigeration and was relatively expensive to make, it was not widely available in Africa in the early 1950s. All of the Foundation's initiatives helped to sow important seeds for change, but by 1952, after four decades of grantmaking, the Foundation had awarded only $1.9 million ($16.7 million in 2013 dollars) to African initiatives, or 1.3 percent of all the Rockefeller Foundation's foreign expenditures between 1913 and 1952.

Individual Africans had been able to travel to the United States to become physicians or nurses with support from the Foundation and its affiliated philanthropies. However, the Foundation's efforts to fund new institutions

for training black South African doctors and health care workers had been blocked by apartheid. Funding for academic institutions like the International Institute of African Languages and Cultures had, as Zachariah Matthews pointed out, created an opportunity for whites in South Africa, as well as Europeans and Americans, to gain a more complex understanding of African culture and institutions, but few people took advantage of this opportunity, and harsh racial attitudes shaped policymaking at every level of society.

Prior to World War Two, the Rockefeller Foundation's work in Africa was focused on public health. Members of the West African Yellow Fever Commission, pictured here in 1931, conducted important research in Nigeria to develop a vaccine for yellow fever. (Rockefeller Archive Center.)

The Rockefeller Foundation's inability to gain traction in Africa reflected a broader pattern in the emergence of international philanthropy and the role of non-governmental organizations (NGOs) in development. Prior to World War Two, most NGO activity in Africa was carried out by missionary organizations based in Europe or the United States. These efforts were primarily charitable or palliative in nature and not focused on systemic change. After World War Two, the social, political, and economic landscape in Africa began to change dramatically.

T he war had devastated Europe. Britain's economy was in ruins. Rebuilding the nation and at the same time managing a colonial empire became financially difficult and politically unpopular. In France and Belgium, the national government's ability to manage colonial states was equally distressed.

Meanwhile, independence movements in Africa gained steam. In Ghana (then known as the Gold Coast) Kwame Nkrumah emerged as the leader of the Convention People's Party, which sought immediate and full self-government for the country. In 1944 Nnamdi Azikiwe, Herbert Macaulay, and others had formed the National Council of Nigeria and the Cameroons (NCNC) to push for independence, a goal that Azikiwe would later describe as "my life's work." In East Africa, movements like the Kikuyu Central Association, which included leaders like Jomo Kenyatta, fought for African rights.

As interest in African affairs increased, leading African nationalists came to the U.S. seeking political support. Former first lady Eleanor Roosevelt met with Nnamdi Azikiwe, who would become Nigeria's first president, as well as K.O. Mbadiwe. The group also included African-American leaders Alain Locke, James S. Watson, and Clarence Holt. (New York Public Library.)

In the face of these movements, the government in Britain proposed a program of economic and social reform intended to lead to self-government, but within the British Commonwealth. This process depended on efforts to "Africanize" the colonial civil service by recruiting Africans who had received a western education—like Nkrumah, Azikiwe, and Kenyatta. But there were tensions within the colonial administration and the broader society among traditional leaders, labor movement organizers, and other African voices. As these movements for independence gained strength, various factions rivaled one another for popular support and influence.

As the colonial system in Africa began to fall apart, a host of new NGOs and multinational agencies—including the United Nations, the International Bank for Reconstruction and Development (the World Bank), and the International Monetary Fund—began to tackle issues in the developing world. In this new environment, the Rockefeller Foundation discovered new opportunities to promote the well-being of people in Africa.

New Leaders at the Rockefeller Foundation

As Africa was changing in the postwar years, so was the leadership at the Rockefeller Foundation. On the board, a new generation of trustees expressed increasing interest in the developing world. John D. Rockefeller 3rd, the grandson of the founder, had joined the board of trustees in 1932. After his father's retirement from the board in 1940, Rockefeller had become increasingly active. He believed that the newly emerging nations of Africa were critical to the future.

In 1948 Rockefeller traveled throughout Africa to deepen his understanding of the postwar environment. He met with French and English colonial officials; toured communities, schools, and hospitals; and talked with nationalist leaders. On the afternoon of September 22, for example, Rockefeller met with Nnamdi Azikiwe, whom he acknowledged as "the nationalist leader of Nigeria." The two men discussed Azikiwe's experiences and education in the United States, including Azikiwe's stay at the Rockefeller-funded International House at Columbia University. Azikiwe then shared his views on the future of West Africa.

John D. Rockefeller 3rd had a particular interest in the emerging nations of Africa. As chairman of the Foundation's board of trustees from 1952 to 1971, he was highly influential in supporting the Foundation's programs in the developing world.
(Rockefeller Archive Center.)

From Nigeria, Rockefeller went to the Congo and then on to South Africa, for talks with government officials. He also met with Alfred Bathini Xuma, the president of the African National Congress (ANC). Xuma had studied at the Tuskegee Institute and the University of Minnesota before obtaining a medical degree from Northwestern University in the United States. He had represented the ANC at the United Nations in 1946 and expressed the organization's opposition to South Africa's apartheid. In 1948 he was at the forefront of building an interracial alliance between South Africans of color in opposition to racial discrimination. In their conversation, Xuma told Rockefeller that black South Africans wanted five things: the right to vote, greater economic opportunity, a chance to own property, access to education, and health care. Xuma envisioned a future without color bars. As he told Rockefeller, "There is just one South Africa, not a European one and a native one."

From South Africa Rockefeller flew to Kenya, where he met mostly with colonial leaders. He was impressed with the country, but also deeply concerned about its economic future. He traveled to Ethiopia, where he talked with Emperor Haile Selassie. Like Xuma, Selassie stressed the importance of education to his country's future. By the time Rockefeller returned to the United States, he was deeply immersed in questions tied to Africa's transition from colonialism.

Rockefeller's election as chairman of the Foundation's board in 1952 coincided with the arrival of a new president who was also deeply immersed in issues related to decolonization. Dean Rusk had been born in the red-clay farm country of north Georgia in the United States, but he had come of age in a world of war, hot and cold, consumed by the global threat of nuclear holocaust, the challenge of international communism, the rise of nationalism in Europe's colonies, and the hopeful promise of international cooperation. Rusk had studied the rise of Nazi Germany as a Rhodes Scholar at Oxford. He had learned about Asia as an army staff officer on the China-Burma-India front during World War Two. He had witnessed the triumph of Mao Zedong and the People's Liberation Army from the Asia Desk of the State Department. He had also experienced the backlash from Senator Joseph McCarthy's anticommunist attack on Rusk's State Department colleagues who were charged with "losing China." He was Assistant Secretary of State for East Asian and Pacific Affairs when civil war broke out in Korea and the French went to war against the Viet Minh to save their colony in Vietnam. During his tenure as director of the State Department's Office of United Nations Affairs, he had also sponsored efforts to develop a long-range policy on emerging nations in Africa and around the world.

In 1948 John D. Rockefeller 3rd traveled throughout Africa meeting both with colonial officials and nationalist leaders. He recorded in a series of diaries his personal observations and the details of these meetings, which helped shape his perspective on the Foundation's work in Africa. (Rockefeller Archive Center.)

a result natives started own religious groups - not at all satisfactory, and do not offer the answer.

Still another partial answer to the detribalizing problem is the work of social welfare agencies such as the scouts, Y.M.C.A., etc. In these connection European leadership is needed and the natives are ready to accept it if they are not treated as inferiors or dictated to. They are ready to learn. The type of leadership is most important and the leader must understand the natives. One faces not only the racial problem in such relationships but also the problem of the different economic levels.

Muchohi Gikonyo - Trader and African member of Nairobi Municipal Council
E.M. Nyori - Assistant Superintendent in charge of native location.
Saul Sewe - Hospital Assistant - Charge under European supervision.
Joseph Katithi - Secretary of Kenya African Union (native political organization)

The main problem facing the African today is how to get more education for their children. There is a general demand for education among rural as well as urban Africans. However the facilities are so limited that only a relative few can be accommodated. Not only are many more primary schools required but all secondary schools and colleges. Education of the African is important to his advance and hence underlies everything else. Education of women is also much desired by the African as they are so im-

All of these experiences had made Rusk a tough Cold War internationalist, but they also cultivated a strong support for racial equality and convinced him that imperialism was dying. Former colonies in Latin America, Asia, and Africa, he believed, would emerge as independent nations in the near future. Those countries would need and deserve support. This support was vital to the interests of the United States, and it was also the right thing to do.

Rusk was the first Foundation president to come to philanthropy from government service. He had been a Foundation trustee since the spring of 1950. When he told President Harry Truman in 1952 that he was leaving the State Department to become the president of the Rockefeller Foundation, Truman responded, "Dean, you can have any job in my administration you want. Ambassador to Japan, whatever—I'd be delighted. But I will not stand in your way in taking the best job in America."

A Commitment to the Developing World

During his eight-year tenure as president, Rusk discovered that the boundaries between government policy and the Foundation's independence were not always easy to navigate. When John Foster Dulles accepted Dwight Eisenhower's appointment to be secretary of state, Rusk traveled often to Washington for private briefings. The relationship led Dulles to view Rusk, and the Foundation's work, as an extension of American foreign policy.

Rusk accommodated to some extent. With Dulles's encouragement, he participated in several informal but high-level foreign policy meetings "to discuss transatlantic frictions and solidarity of the western community." Dulles even went so far as to ask Rusk to lead a non-governmental advisory group to "undertake an examination of the 'colonial question' to see whether there was any way in which the west could get its relations with the non-west on a better basis." According to historian James Hubbard, as chairman of the advisory group, Rusk favored doing more for the nationalists and the independence movements in Africa. As president of the Rockefeller Foundation, he pushed the staff to look for ways to meet the needs of the people in these emerging nations.

Rusk was not interested in the nuances of anthropological research in Africa, or in the effects of a wage

During his tenure as president of the Rockefeller Foundation (1952-1961), Dean Rusk emphasized support for emerging nations in Africa and Asia. Agricultural assistance to promote economic and social development was a critical component of this strategy. (Rockefeller Archive Center.)

economy and urbanization on local culture. He bluntly announced his intention to deemphasize social science grants. He also challenged the Foundation's work in the natural sciences, announcing his intention to make agriculture the cornerstone of the new natural sciences program. Rusk and Rockefeller wanted to invest heavily in the emerging nations of the Third World, and they intended to use science-based agricultural assistance as a nonpolitical, pragmatic wedge.

Ralph Bunche (far left), United Nations Secretary General Trygve Lie (center), and U.N. official Wilfrid Benson (far right) met with Gold Coast officials Kwame Nkrumah (center left) and Kojo Botsio (center right) at the U.N. headquarters in June 1951. In 1957 the British colony of Gold Coast became the independent nation of Ghana. (United Nations.)

The Cold War complicated efforts to promote economic and social development in Africa. Foreign policymakers in the United States struggled to balance longtime relationships with allies like Great Britain and newly developing friendships with nationalist leaders. Trustees like Ralph Bunche and former U.S. Ambassador Chester Bowles were deeply aware of this tension. In 1955 Bowles traveled throughout Africa researching the book he would publish in the following year entitled, *Africa's Challenge to America*. The book highlighted the fact that the United States needed a more robust relationship with the people of Africa that anticipated

the eventual independence of Africa's colonies. These relationships, from the U.S. State Department's point of view, were particularly important in the context of Soviet expansionism.

    Some nationalist leaders campaigning for independence had visited or studied in the Soviet Union. While some of these leaders were socialists in the vein of the British Labour Party, others were dedicated communists. Still others were neutralists or authentic nationalists whose primary interest was the overthrow of colonialism rather than choosing sides in the global Cold War. At the same time, the United States, the Soviet Union, and, to some extent, China all vied for influence with these newly emerging nations, and foreign aid was often tied to implicit or explicit promises of loyalty to one side or another. As nationalist leaders, no matter what their personal ideologies, faced internal competition for leadership of their movements, the Cold War often weakened their ability to navigate their countries' development.

Hair braids worn by Fulani women in West Africa communicated marital and social status. In the 1950s the Rockefeller Foundation funded a number of influential studies in an effort to better understand the people and culture of Africa, including a study of the Fulani by the International African Institute. (Rockefeller Archive Center.)

Given the political uncertainty in Africa in the 1950s, the opportunities for constructive philanthropy often seemed extremely limited. The Rockefeller Foundation launched modest initiatives in the old tradition—enhancing Western understanding of Africa—as a way to explore how it might be successful. For example, the Foundation continued to support institutions and scholars focused on research *about* Africa. In the social sciences, new grants to the International African Institute (formerly the International Institute of African Languages and Cultures) helped underwrite an intensive study of the Fulani-speaking communities in West Africa. The Foundation also provided funding to the Royal Institute of International Affairs in London for studies of developing countries in Africa and other parts of the world. In 1959 a major ten-year grant of $250,000 ($2 million in 2013 dollars) to the School of Oriental and African Studies at the University of London helped support collaborative work by scholars from Africa, the United Kingdom, the U.S., and other countries working on African literature, languages, arts, religions, and history. Another $250,000 award provided matching funds for the construction of a new library.

Meanwhile, to help develop a better understanding of the emerging political environment in postwar Africa, the Foundation supported scholarship in this important arena. In 1952, for example, the Foundation awarded a grant to Gwendolen Carter of Smith College to visit South Africa and study the evolution of political parties and their relationship to racial problems. Carter's research led to the publication of *The Politics of Inequality* in 1958. A similar grant of $31,500 was given to Philip Mason at the Royal Institute of International Affairs "for a study of problems associated with racial conflicts in Central Africa and their implications for political developments in that area." Mason was an active member of a small group of British Africanists, a prolific author on race relations, and chairman of the Institute of Race Relations in London. He had developed an interest in the political consequences of apartheid in South Africa and Rhodesia (present day Zimbabwe). "This area was chosen," according to the 1954 annual report, "because it is the meeting place of two concepts of the political and social relationship between European and African races—partnership and apartheid." The theme of Mason's research was prescient, resulting in a two-volume epic—*The Birth of a Dilemma* (1958), about the origins of Rhodesia, and *Year of Decision* (1960), about the consequences of apartheid. All of these projects helped the Rockefeller Foundation and others understand the changing social and political context in various parts of Africa.

For decades the Foundation's primary work in Africa had been in the area of public health, related to the study of viruses and the environments in which they thrived. The Foundation continued this work in the 1950s, but it also launched tentative efforts to build on this base of knowledge. A grant to Cambridge University in 1953, for example, supported an innovative seminar on the "ecological problems arising from technical development of tropical and subtropical countries" in Africa. A grant to King's College at the University of Durham in Britain focused on improving environmental conditions in developing countries. The grant specifically sought to train West African students in public health engineering as part of a cooperative venture with Fourah Bay College in Sierra Leone. These initiatives provided benefits to specific communities, but they also gave the Foundation some limited insight into additional work it might do in the field of public health.

In the postcolonial era, many newly independent African countries would have an enormous need for professionals in health, agriculture, and education. In the 1950s, the Foundation gradually increased its investment in human capital in Africa in these arenas. It provided grants to physicians and other health workers to study health systems abroad. A doctor from the Blue Nile province in the Egyptian Sudan, for example, received a travel grant to North America to study public health administration. The Foundation helped an Egyptian professor of public health come to the United States and Canada to study public health teaching and administration. Meanwhile, a provincial medical officer from Kenya traveled to the Near East to observe new techniques, and a member of the staff of the Institute of Family and Community Health in Durban, South Africa, received a grant to study public health nursing and social work in the United States, Canada, Britain, and France. A grant to Nuffield College, Oxford, was designed to support the research of three professors and graduate students doing field work in Africa. The grant of $85,500 over three years was also meant to support Africans—especially those working in administrative positions or as teachers or researchers in new African universities or research institutes—to spend a year at Oxford as senior visiting scholars.

These fellowships helped prepare leaders who would play an important role after independence. Eustace Akwei, for example, who in 1934 was the second African from the Gold Coast to earn a medical doctorate from the University of Edinburgh, received support from the Foundation in 1954 to study the organization of medical and health services in the British West Indies, British Guiana, Puerto Rico, and the United States. The following year, as the Gold Coast transitioned to self-government, Akwei was appointed the chief medical officer to the Health Ministry in the Gold Coast by the country's new premier, Kwame Nkrumah.

All of these early grants in the postcolonial era provided the Rockefeller Foundation with ways to better understand the needs and priorities of emerging nations in Africa. The scholarship funded by the Foundation in the social sciences, the environment, and in medicine also underscored the challenges ahead. These projects did not yet lead to a coherent vision for the Foundation's future program in Africa, but they helped to convince Dean Rusk and the trustees that a much larger commitment was necessary.

A FUNDAMENTAL REALIGNMENT

In 1956 Dean Rusk noted that of the 81 members of the United Nations, no fewer than 19—with a total population of 6.5 million people—had become independent since World War Two. "The implications of these events are far-reaching," Rusk wrote in the Foundation's annual report. "Many of these nations are now attempting to build, some from the ground up, an administrative structure to take the place of one which has been swept away…. Their peoples are stirring with new hopes and expectations of economic and social improvement, the promised reward of independence." Rusk noted that many of these new nations faced challenges, but also enjoyed significant assets and opportunities. The leaders of many of these new countries had a long vision and a realistic view of the task at hand. "Rising expectations produce a new energy…. Pride in independence undergirds public morale and calls many to selfless and devoted service."

Given these changes and opportunities, the trustees of the Rockefeller Foundation had decided to approve "a sharp increase in Foundation expenditures in Latin America, Asia, the Middle East, and Africa." This more than doubled the funding going to these areas in the developing world—from $5.7 million to $13.7 million ($117.7 million in 2013 dollars). With a booming U.S. economy, the value of the Foundation's endowment had increased significantly, and Rusk and the trustees believed that the Foundation could afford to place this big bet at a crucial moment in history. Rusk acknowledged that these amounts were small "in relation to the total need," but the Foundation believed that if they were used to develop "professional leadership" they might play a critical role in the growth of new institutions in the developing world.

Rusk acknowledged that the Foundation's expanded program in Latin America, Asia, the Middle East, and Africa might develop unevenly. Much would depend on local circumstances. The Foundation itself, he said, "needs time to become acquainted with countries in which it has not had long experience." Over the next seven years, the Foundation would make a determined effort to better understand how it might make a difference in Africa.

President Jomo Kenyatta (second from left) welcomed African heads of state to Kenya in the mid-1960s. With the formation of the Organization of African Unity in 1963, the leaders of the newly independent nations of Africa sought

TRAINING HEALTH WORKERS IN SOUTH AFRICA AND THE CONGO

Having made the decision to significantly increase funding for projects in Africa and other parts of the developing world, the Rockefeller Foundation needed to understand where it could be most effective. As it had in the past, it sought to learn by gathering information and by making initial grants. And in keeping with a long-held belief that the best way to promote the well-being of humanity was by improving public health, the Foundation focused initially on health care initiatives. Two major efforts—one in the Congo and the other in South Africa—highlighted the continuing uncertainties of the postcolonial era.

A NURSING SCHOOL FOR THE CONGO

Under the control of the Belgian government since 1908, the Congo was considered Africa's richest colony by the time of World War Two. By 1959 it was producing 10 percent of the world's copper, 50 percent of its cobalt, and 70 percent of its industrial diamonds. Belgian missionaries and colonial governments had worked to build hospitals, clinics, and schools. Roughly 10 percent of the nation's children attended school, compared to 6 percent in India and lower percentages in most other African nations. But under colonial rule the Congolese people could not own land, vote, or travel freely. There were virtually no opportunities for Africans in the Congo to pursue higher education or professional positions.

During the colonial era, in the Congo and many parts of sub-Saharan Africa, schools for Africans were largely run by missionaries to train religious converts or by colonial officials seeking to train African workers. The oldest modern institution of higher education, Fourah Bay College, had been established in 1827 by the Church Missionary Society in Sierra Leone, but until the 1940s, it was the only institution of higher learning in West Africa that offered a college degree. After the war, the British government moved more aggressively to establish universities in its African colonies. Secondary schools in Nigeria, Ghana, and Uganda became the University College, Ibadan in Nigeria (1948), the University College of the Gold Coast (1948), and Makerere University College in Uganda (1949). In Sudan, the Gordon Memorial combined with the Kitchener School of Medicine to become the University College of Khartoum (1951). France also established universities in Africa, often affiliated with universities in France.

While children could receive free education at the grade-school level in the Belgian Congo, opportunities for higher education or professional training were severely restricted by colonial authorities. (United Nations.)

In the Congo, as the result of a 1906 agreement between King Leopold II of Belgium and the Vatican, the educational system was run primarily by the Catholic Church. Until the mid-1950s, these state-sponsored, church-run schools offered primary and vocational education to a limited segment of the African population. The first secondary schools were started in 1948. Then in 1954 Lovanium University opened in Kinshasa (Leopoldville) and was granted university status by the Belgian government two years later. The university initially offered courses in four fields of study—medicine, agriculture, pedagogy, and "social and administrative sciences"—under the stewardship of the prestigious Catholic University of Leuven in Belgium. Funds to construct the campus were provided by the colonial government of the Congo, the Mining Union, and private sources. But the slow expansion of the school's program and facilities, and the lack of educational opportunities elsewhere, frustrated many Congolese people. In 1958 they addressed petitions to a government study commission asking for "immediate improvement of education in quantity and in quality."

The Rockefeller Foundation was interested in helping to meet this need. As it began to explore opportunities to do more in Africa, Wickliffe Rose's vision of expanding medical and public health education around the world was still very much alive. The Foundation was also mindful of growing pressures for independence in the Congo. In 1956, in response to a Belgian call for a 30-year transition to independence, a group of moderate national-ist leaders published a manifesto in the *Conscience Africaine* calling for the Congo to eventually "become a great nation in the center of the African continent." Their evolutionary view of the transition to independence was challenged by more insistent voices, however, including leaders of the ABAKO party, who called for full political rights and unrestricted civil liberties immediately.

As these pressures for independence grew, the Foundation sent repre-sentatives to the Congo to explore the idea of working with Lovanium to establish a medical school serving the regional needs of French-speaking Africa. In conversations with university officials, the Foundation secured a promise from Lovanium to provide highly qualified European faculty and resources to match a proposed Rockefeller Foundation grant. The curricu-lum would be equivalent to that of Leuven University in Belgium. There would be no second-class degrees, no reduction of European standards. The association of Lovanium with an ancient and prestigious European univer-sity was essential to the Foundation's support, as was the founding principle that the university would be coeducational and would not discriminate on the basis of race, ethnic background, religion, or political beliefs.

These conversations provided the framework for a shared initiative, but within the Foundation a long-running debate resurfaced over the basic strategy for training health workers in underdeveloped regions. Since the days of Wickliffe Rose and Frederick Gates, Foundation officials had discussed the relative priorities for funding medical schools for highly educated physicians versus a more broad-based effort to train other health care workers, including nurses, public health engineers, and medical paraprofessionals. As the Foundation considered its strategy in the Congo, Virginia Arnold was the primary advocate for the training of nurses.

Arnold was a public health nurse who had served with the United Nations Relief and Rehabilitation Administration during the immediate postwar years in Egypt and Greece, where she helped to reorganize nursing services and training. She had joined the Rockefeller Foundation in 1956 as assistant

Lovanium University in Kinshasa opened in 1954. Two years later the Rockefeller Foundation began making grants to the school to improve the quality of education offered to its students. The Foundation tied its support to non-discriminatory policies. For most of the Congolese students pictured here in 1956, Lovanium offered the first opportunity to pursue post-secondary education in their own country. (Rockefeller Archive Center.)

director for Medical Education and Public Health. She believed that nursing was an essential component of social medicine, which emphasized decentralized, holistic approaches to supporting the health of communities. The proposal was consistent with the Foundation's thinking about the importance of nursing, going back to the Foundation's earliest work in countries like Thailand and South Africa.

Arnold proposed a grant of $75,000 to support clinical teaching facilities, faculty salaries, student scholarships, and construction of a dormitory for nursing students at Lovanium. She considered a nursing school to be a complementary part of the larger proposal to build a hospital and medical school, noting a report by the World Health Organization (WHO) that highlighted the shortage of qualified female nurses and midwives in the Congo. The report stressed the critical developmental role that nursing could play in nations that did not have the infrastructure or an immediate roster of qualified students to train as physicians. While the Congo could train five or ten physicians a year, it could train hundreds of nurses who would have direct relationships with families and mothers as well as the public health issues of entire villages, including pregnancy and birth, diet, and community sanitation.

As assistant director of Medical Education and Public Health at the Rockefeller Foundation, Virginia Arnold (left) was instrumental in securing funds to establish a nursing program at Lovanium University. Thomas Adeoye Lambo (right), the most eminent African psychiatrist of his generation, was chairman of the Rockefeller Foundation-funded Department of Psychiatry and later dean of Medicine and vice chancellor of the University of Ibadan. (Rockefeller Archive Center.)

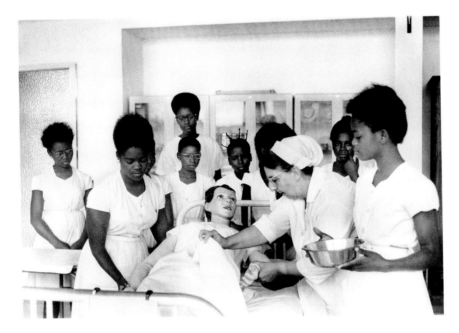

In 1958 the Rockefeller Foundation awarded grants to establish medical and nursing schools at Lovanium University. Four years later, these nursing students, from the Congo as well as neighboring African nations, were receiving essential training. (Rockefeller Archive Center.)

After local elections for communal council seats delivered a huge majority for ABAKO in December 1957, heightening the pressure for independence, Arnold also stressed the importance of educating women to play a role in an independent Congo. She cited social psychologists who worked in the Congo to defend the nursing initiative relevance to the overall preparation of the Congolese to govern their own country. On the eve of independence, only 8,200 girls throughout the nation were studying at any level of secondary school. By offering more opportunities to women to continue their education, nurse training could help transform the role of women in Congolese society.

Dean Rusk initially resisted the nursing proposal. He first wanted to see how the medical school would develop before committing to a broader educational initiative. With his support, the Rockefeller Foundation trustees awarded $230,000 to Lovanium University in the fall of 1958 for the construction and staffing of the medical school. The trustees did not approve a grant for nursing education, but Arnold persisted. "Nursing service is so intimately connected with medical care and with medical education that without a complementary developmental program in nursing, our program in medical education will necessarily suffer."

In the end, Rusk and the board of trustees were persuaded by Arnold's arguments. In December, the board approved a grant to add a nursing school at Lovanium. This was a bold investment in education and training fueled by the Foundation's vision for postcolonial nations' need for infrastructure and human capital. In his President's Review of 1958, Rusk cautioned that the Foundation operated under severe limits, and returned to the theme of supporting "individual competence at the more advanced levels." The Foundation would do what it did best: support scholarship and postgraduate training. "It cannot make large capital investments in support of general development; it cannot contribute significantly to the universal urge toward expanded and improved elementary and secondary education, although these are fundamental; it cannot justify the rapid liquidation of its resources through providing consumer goods and services to meet immediate emergencies. But it can assist in the preparation of competent men and women for roles of leadership."

The Foundation's investment reflected the guidelines articulated in Rusk's statement, but it was also a risky decision given the political uncertainty in the Congo. Weeks after the board's decision on the nursing program, rioting erupted in Leopoldville after colonial officials sought to repress ABAKO demonstrators. In the wake of the violence, the Belgian government announced that it would move to make the Congo independent in the very near future. Independence followed in 1960.

Agriculture was one of the earliest fields of study to be supported by the Rockefeller Foundation at Lovanium University, with funding that helped African students obtain advanced training in the field. In 1959 Pierre Lebughe Litite (right) was the first Congolese to receive a degree in agronomy. (H. Goldstein. Rockefeller Archive Center.)

In the face of the Congo's dramatic transition, the Rockefeller Foundation continued to invest in the training of nurses at Lovanium. The Foundation committed $100,000 in 1960, available through 1962, to support a WHO-sponsored center of graduate education for nursing instructors and administrative personnel in the 15 French-speaking countries of Africa. In 1963 it committed $133,570 for a two-year period to Lovanium University's Medical School and School of Agriculture. The Foundation continued to support staff and faculty development at Lovanium throughout the 1960s, until it became the University of the Congo in 1971.

In the course of supporting the new school at Lovanium, the Foundation had been forced to consider a complicated maze of problems that would be replicated in many parts of Africa and the developing world. During the Congo's transition to independence, the Foundation's officers had to negotiate with colonial administrators and nationalist leaders without ensnaring their humanitarian mission within the turbulent political environment. Given a context of minimal institutional development in higher education, they had to make hard choices about how to prioritize the Foundation's investments. Most importantly, they had to build relationships with people and institutions on the ground. These challenges had proved difficult in the last years of the colonial era in the Congo; they would be equally hard to navigate in the increasingly divided racial society in South Africa.

Returning to South Africa

As part of its postcolonial effort to help African countries meet their need for health care workers, the Rockefeller Foundation returned to its goal of training black physicians and nurses in South Africa with a project to create an innovative medical school in Durban. As in the 1920s, nothing was simple or easily accomplished in postwar South Africa. This was a country where the wealthiest and economically and scientifically most advanced society in Africa existed side by side with dire poverty, disease, and increasingly formal racial segregation. The epidemiological environment of the so-called native reserves and black townships remained as desperate as it had been when the Foundation first surveyed South Africa in 1924, with high rates of tuberculosis, venereal disease, and infant mortality. The internal tensions within white South African society—between European-style liberals who resisted racial segregation and conservative Afrikaner racialists committed to the principles of apartheid—created a pendulum that swung perpetually back and forth between the best hopes that economic development might improve the living conditions of all citizens and the harsh reality that whites

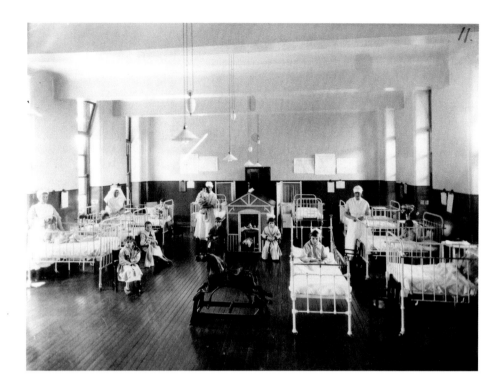

would not allow black Africans to share equally in the nation's wealth and government.

Despite the increasing racial polarization of South African society, the country's public health officials were at the frontier of social medicine in the late 1940s and early 1950s. During the decades since the discovery of the germ theory of disease, the fight against illness had focused on disease eradication and hospital-based disease management. But social medicine approached the problem of disease from an entirely different, holistic perspective. Lord Hailey, author of the famous *African Survey*, had touched on the themes of social medicine in 1938: "The first essentials for the prevention of disease are a higher standard of health, a better physique, and a greater power of resistance to infection. . . . [M]edical science must be in Africa increasingly concerned with the relations between nutrition and health, and with advising on the medical aspect of social policies bearing on the question of subsistence."

At the same time that South Africa was exploring ways to apply the principles of social medicine to a national public health system, John Black Grant of the Rockefeller Foundation was exploring the same questions in Asia. The son

The Rockefeller Foundation conducted its first health surveys in South Africa in 1924. While Foundation officers captured images of bright, well-funded facilities— like this children's ward at Witwatersrand University General Hospital— a very different reality in the black townships was marked by deplorable, unsanitary conditions and high rates of infectious disease. (Rockefeller Archive Center.)

of missionaries in China, Grant had attended medical school at the University of Michigan and then returned to China to join the faculty of Peking Union Medical College. By 1947 the Foundation had assigned him to travel the world in search of innovative approaches to social medicine. In South Africa, Grant met Sidney and Emily Kark, primary care physicians with a long history of trying to improve health services for the African population, and George Gale, the chief medical officer and secretary for health in the postwar government of General Jan Smuts.

Gale was also the son of missionaries. He had been raised among the Zulu and practiced medicine in rural Natal Province. For a brief time he had been on the faculty of Fort Hare Native College. As a government official he operated within the limits set by segregationist policies, but he was a participant in the Defiance Campaign, a civil rights initiative that advocated equal rights for all South Africans.

Gale and the Karks became the leading architects of a grand experiment in social medicine. They designed a universal health care system for the whole nation—black and white alike—based on hundreds of decentralized community health centers. Staffed by teams of physicians, nurses, and public health specialists, the centers would diagnose disease, perform surgeries, and deliver curative medical care. But they would also be intimately involved in the public health issues of the community: nutrition, maternity care, child development, working conditions, even fitness and recreation, and, most important according to Gale, public education.

When Grant arrived in South Africa, several dozen clinics were already in operation. He visited the Karks at the Pholela Health Centre in Natal, and was swept away. "Nothing in the whole world is more advanced" than what he had seen at Pholela, Grant reported. He quickly arranged for both the Karks and Gale to receive Rockefeller Foundation fellowships, in 1948, to refine their thinking.

Jan Smuts's wartime government primarily supported hospital-based private physician service, but committed enough public money to allow the Karks and Gale to expand their experiment in community-based social medicine. Like all proposals to improve social services for poor black Africans, the community clinic proposal represented a precarious balancing act. "The attraction of the health center idea for the state," it read, "was initially because it was seen as a low-cost way of dealing with rural health problems at a time when Africans were coming into hospitals in unprecedented numbers." If the system were fully implemented it would require 400 clinics nationwide—three-fourths in the sprawling black townships and rural areas—and thousands of black doctors, nurses, medical assistants, and public health specialists. The state would need another medical school. In 1951 the Durban Medical School was opened at the University of Natal with an innovative curriculum geared to public health and social medicine, and a mandate to train black doctors and nurses.

Smuts's government fell to the pro-apartheid Nationalists in the election of 1948. South African society quickly consolidated around formal racial segregation, and "the conservatism of the medical profession quickly reasserted itself and further subverted [the health center movement]," Shula Marks wrote. The Karks and Gale understood that community-based medicine would bring them into conflict with the Nationalists, and Gale soon lost influence at the Ministry of Health. He resigned his government position and became dean of the Durban Medical School. His original intent had been to accept any medical student who wanted to be exposed to the new approach, but the Nationalist government resisted the idea of an integrated medical school and he was forced to accept only black students. The Nationalist government also had no intention of supporting the school, and Gale's pay as dean was poor, but the Rockefeller Foundation agreed to supplement his salary with grants of $5,940 for three years while the school became established.

Sidney Kark and George Gale developed a plan to embed a Department of Social, Preventive, and Family Medicine in the new school. Under this plan, the Institute of Family and Community Health, which had been established by the Karks in 1946, was integrated into the Durban Medical School, and Sidney Kark became the first professor in the new department. The partners were pushing the envelope of government support. Gale frantically sought funding from the Rockefeller Foundation. "Those of us who are liberal in matters of Bantu advancement are fighting a desperate battle against reaction in various forms," he wrote to Warren Weaver, the director of the Natural Sciences division. The Foundation awarded $127,200 over five years ($1.1 million in 2013 dollars) to fund the department. According to the 1954 annual report, "The objective of the new department is to provide a setting for continuous training in preventive and curative medical care in the health centers and homes of the community."

But almost immediately the medical school and the family practice program were overwhelmed by South Africa's racial politics. While the Ministry of Health supported the new school, the Ministry of Education did not. The school became mired in controversy over its innovative curriculum and its funding. The Rockefeller Foundation was again criticized by conservatives for

Sidney and Emily Kark were proponents of social medicine, a holistic approach to health care that included treatment as well as preventative care and public health initiatives like proper nutrition and sanitation. Their work in South Africa attracted the attention of Rockefeller Foundation officer John B. Grant, who was influential in securing Foundation money that allowed the Karks to further develop their ideas and practice. (Rockefeller Archive Center.)

THE ROCKEFELLER FOUNDATION
INTERNATIONAL HEALTH DIVISION
PERSONAL HISTORY RECORD AND APPLICATION
FOR TRAVEL GRANT

Date __16/3/1948.__

Full __KARK   SIDNEY   LIONEL.__   Sex __MALE.__

Address __c/o NUFFIELD FOUNDATION: 12 MECKLENBURGH SQUARE   LONDON W.C.1. ENGLAND.__
(Street and Number)   (City)   (State or country)

ent address __Union Health Department. Box 2140. DURBAN   SOUTH AFRICA.__
(Street and Number)   (City)   (State or country)

of birth __Johannesburg. South Africa.__ Date of birth __22 October 1911.__ Race _____

ship __British__   Nationality __South African__

married __Married__   Wife's name __EMILY KARK.__
(Form of customary legal signature)

at position __Medical Officer in Charge. Training Scheme for Health Personnel. Union Health Department.__

you any constitutional disorder or physical defects? __NO.__

languages do you speak well? __ENGLISH.__

ose of Travel Grant __To study some aspects of health and medical care programmes, with special reference to methods of training of personnel — medical student, public health nurse and medico-social worker. in Social Medicine__

at type of work do you wish to see? __Health and Medical care service in Health Centres and hospitals illustrating team work of medical practitioners and auxiliary personnel mentioned above.__

hat places do you wish to visit? __In view of the necessarily short duration of my proposed visit it is suggested that most of my study be in one or few areas. The guidance of the Rockefeller Foundation would be appreciated in such selection of areas which might be of most value.__

ggested duration of grant __6 - 7 weeks.__

hat date do you wish to start? __April 24th or 25th (from England).__

MERGENCY ADDRESS: (Give name of nearest relative or other emergency address. The individual named will be notified by cable of your arrival.)

Name __Dr. EMILY KARK.__   Relationship __WIFE.__

Address __c/o NUFFIELD FOUNDATION: 12 MECKLENBURGH SQUARE   LONDON W.C.1. England.__

Form 405

Signature _____

Official Position ___Secretary for Health and Chief Health Officer for the Union of South Africa___

DR. G.W. GALE.

First and last years spent there	Degrees
1929 ___ 1936. (Away from University 1930 and 1931, returning in 1932).	M.B. B.Ch.

business, health)

Position	Years of Tenure
Surgeon, and Pediatrics	Dec 1936 - July 1938
) Nutrition Survey	1938 - 1939
Pholela Health Centre	1939 - 1945
Training	
Personnel.	1946 - to the present.

meddling in South African affairs. The South African Medical Association, which had supported the program of social medicine after the war, reversed course and put pressure on the government to restore the traditional medical school curriculum that was taught in the country's other three schools. Funding dried up, and the government announced plans to close the medical school. As the situation quickly deteriorated, Gale accepted an invitation in 1955 to become a professor of medicine at Makerere University in Uganda, where he established the Kasangati Clinic and continued his work in community-based medicine. "The cause of non-European higher education is not popular in South Africa," Gale wrote to Robert Morison, who had become the director of Medical and Natural Sciences at the Rockefeller Foundation. "I am in any case suspect as a liberal and a man with progressive ideas about the natives." Sidney Kark called Gale's resignation from the Durban School of Medicine "the end of a dream." Two years later, Kark himself resigned and took a position at the School of Public Health at the University of North Carolina.

The Foundation reluctantly withdrew its funding in 1960, and the Department of Family and Community Medicine closed. In 1975 the government of South Africa closed the Durban School of Medicine to black

When Sidney and Emily Kark, along with George Gale, failed to find support for universal social medicine in segregated South Africa, they began training black students at the Durban Medical School. Their program in social medicine came under fire from white conservatives. Unable to withstand the racial politics, the program ended in 1960. (Jeremy D. Kark.)

students. In the end, neither the South African government nor the medical profession was willing to invest in health care for the African population or a universal health care system, once the war was over and health services for whites were safely secured. Yet the principles at the core of the Rockefeller Foundation's work in Africa had proven to be sound, especially over the long term, as endowments through fellowships and networks brought truly innovative ideas to the Foundation's attention and enabled it to invest in an idea as big, at the time, as a medical training facility for black South Africans.

In the 1950s the Rockefeller Foundation supported a number of community-based health programs in Africa that focused on providing services in maternity care, child development, and public education. (Jeremy D. Kark.)

Indeed, for a while in the mid-1950s the Foundation made a real difference in the training of black South African doctors. At Durban, it had invested in both human capacity building and institutional development. It had sponsored critical fellowships, supported an innovative new medical school to train black African physicians and nurses, and figured out how to work with the South African government without precipitating a direct conflict over race. It had built its program solidly on the shoulders of respected local physicians and had supported a model for community-based health care that could be replicated throughout the world. Perhaps the project was not as elegant as the Foundation's original vision of a global network of modern, research-based medical schools connected to world-class hospitals, but it was a strategy better suited to the realities of Africa.

In the Congo and South Africa, the Foundation sought to address fundamental issues affecting the quality of health care in the African community in the 1950s. These innovative programs had been conducted within the context of very different social and political environments. In both situations, however, the strategy was designed to enhance the abilities of African leaders to shape the future of health care. In Nigeria, a similar effort to bolster medical education soon led to a more broad-based initiative to strengthen an entire institution of higher education.

ACADEMIC EXPLORATIONS

A s he rode the small elevator up to the offices of the U.S. consulate in Abidjan, Wole Soyinka thought about how to resolve his
predicament. With funding from the Rockefeller Foundation,
the 26-year-old Nigerian playwright had come to the Ivory Coast.
The day before, March 28, 1960, he had been able to arrange a meeting with
playwright Germaine Coffi Gadeau, a pioneer of Ivorian theater who had co-
founded Le Théâtre Indigène de la Côte d'Ivoire in 1938. But the conversation
had been frustrating; the two men did not share a common language.

Soyinka had grown up in a Yoruba family in Abeokuta, Nigeria. His
father was an Anglican minister and the headmaster of St. Peter's School. His
mother was a shop owner and a political activist. After two years of study at
University College in Ibadan (UCI), he went to the University of Leeds in the
United Kingdom, where he earned a B.A. and an M.A. in English literature and
worked with the Royal Court Theatre in London. He began writing plays that
combined European theatrical traditions with elements
of Yoruba culture. A two-year Rockefeller Foundation
grant from University College allowed Soyinka to return
to Nigeria; acquire a Land Rover, a tape recorder, and a
camera; and set out to complete a survey of West African
drama. "[T]hat vehicle became an extension of myself
through which I negotiated relationships with the overall
society," Soyinka would later write.

Efua Sutherland founded the Experimental Theatre Players (later Ghana
Drama Studio) in 1958. With Rockefeller
Foundation assistance, Sutherland was
able to write plays that she produced
throughout Ghana. Her work often
referenced traditional African stories
and myths. (Rockefeller Archive Center.)

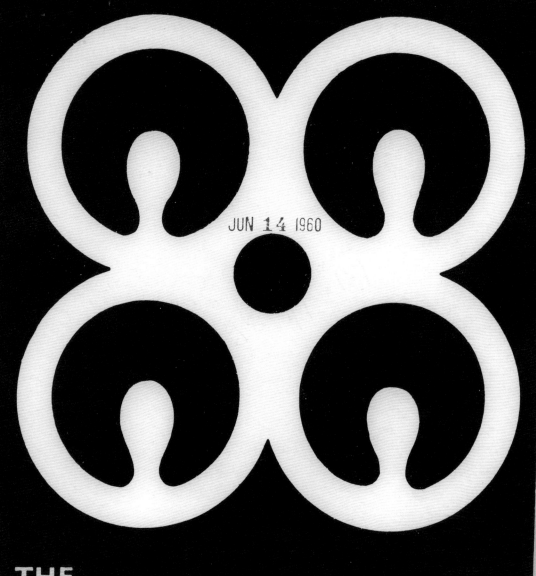

JUN 14 1960

THE EXPERIMENTAL THEATRE PLAYERS

Embarking on his travels in the last days of the colonial era, Soyinka was fascinated by the blending of African traditions with contemporary political expression and culture. Germaine Coffi Gadeau was emblematic of the moment. The author of eight plays, he also served as chairman of the Finance Committee of the Ivory Coast's Territorial Assembly and a minister of parliament. With his political rise, he was less involved with the theater, but was still deeply respected by younger, aspiring writers. Soyinka was disappointed that he had not been able to communicate more richly with Gadeau.

Located in the tallest building in Abidjan, the offices of the U.S. consulate smelled of wet plaster and reverberated with the labored sound of air-conditioners. Soyinka could see people in the open-air market below. Like Nigeria, the Ivory Coast was on the precipice of momentous change. In December 1958 it had become an autonomous republic within the French Community, and nationalists were campaigning for full independence, which would come in August 1960. Gadeau was deeply involved in this effort.

Robert July was assistant director of the Foundation's Humanities Division during a period of significant support for African academics and artists. July's work in Africa later inspired him to write a number of important books including *A History of the African People* and *The Origins of Modern African Thought*. (Rockefeller Archive Center.)

Soyinka had been hoping to find a translator at the consulate when suddenly he was surprised to see the familiar face of Robert July, the garrulous assistant director of the Humanities Division at the Rockefeller Foundation. In the early 1950s he had served as secretary of the Foundation's sister philanthropy, the General Education Board (GEB), while he was working on his Ph.D. in history at Columbia. He had been in charge of the GEB fellowship program, and made the internal switch to the Foundation in 1955. In the late 1950s and early 1960s he was traveling through Africa like a whirlwind, keeping a keen eye out for potential fellows, coaching them through their applications, and collecting research for future books on African intellectual history. He was meeting with hundreds of African intellectuals, authors, poets, playwrights, and artists who would be in the forefront of creating a new Africa and introducing it to the world. He was particularly impressed with Wole Soyinka, who would win the Nobel Prize in Literature 26 years later.

After Soyinka explained his predicament, the two men left the consulate to find Gadeau in his office at the legislative assembly. Gadeau had just returned from Paris with his troupe, which was scheduled to give a performance in Abidjan the following Saturday. With July acting as interpreter, the three men discussed the theater in West Africa. They talked of other West African playwrights, including Efua Sutherland, whom July had just seen in Accra. Sutherland had established the Experimental Theatre Players in Ghana, and she was working on a grant application that the Rockefeller Foundation would fund to provide the troupe with permanent space for rehearsals and performances. July urged Soyinka to visit Sutherland. Meanwhile, Gadeau and Soyinka shared their enthusiasm for an emerging theatrical tradition that combined African dance and mime with European-style dialogue. Both men were intensely interested in the ways in which humanistic traditions in West Africa might shape the future of their emerging independent nations.

Robert July and the Rockefeller Foundation shared this interest. Indeed, the Foundation's grant to University College in Ibadan, which supported Soyinka's research, was part of a broad experiment on the part of the Foundation and other American philanthropies to help develop a major university that would cultivate a new generation of leaders in an independent Nigeria.

Higher Education and an Independent Nigeria

Forging a common identity from disparate communities continued to pose a central challenge to Nigeria's future in 1960, as it did many other African countries during the postcolonial era. In 1914 British officials had combined historically different, and sometimes hostile, regions to create the colony of Nigeria. A new constitution in January 1947 had created a central Legislative Council at Lagos to tie the regions together—North, East, and West. Representation of black residents increased substantially relative to that of white colonists under this new legal structure. The new constitution also marked a significant milestone on the path to independence, but it also accentuated regional rivalries. In 1954 a revised constitution established the Federation of Nigeria, and national elections were held for the first time. Leaders like Nnamdi Azikiwe continued to push for independence, which finally came on October 1, 1960.

Nationalist leaders had already recognized the need for a strong university to train the professionals and administrators who would be needed to run the country. By the mid-1950s, Nigeria's oldest institution of higher education, University College in Ibadan had been in operation for less than a decade. In 1948, in response to nationalist demands and the recommendations of a special commission led by Scottish Member of the British Parliament Walter Elliot, colonial officials founded the institution as

a satellite of the University of London, with aspirations to make it an elite institution in Nigeria.

Nigerian playwright Wole Soyinka received a Rockefeller Foundation fellowship early in his career, and went on to receive a Nobel Prize for literature in 1986. (Keystone/Getty Images.)

The curriculum of the new institution was taken straight from London, however, with no effort to adapt it to the needs of Nigerian society. No courses were offered in fields like engineering, agriculture, economics, law, geology, or public administration.

When Soyinka was a student at the school in 1953, University College had 74 faculty members and 407 students, 18 of whom were women. There were also 49 medical students who had studied in the United Kingdom but were completing clinical work in Nigeria. This was at a time when several thousand Nigerians were enrolled in universities in the United Kingdom and the United States. Given the limited enrollment and Nigeria's growing need for professionals and leaders, nationalists like Nnamdi Azikiwe, Obafemi Awolowo, and Ahmadu Bellow, according to historian Ogechi Anyanwu, "rejected the 'elitist' and 'conservative' traditions of UCI and demanded radical changes in the institution's curriculum and admission policies to reflect the wishes and aspirations of Nigerians."

This Nigerian push for expanded educational opportunities combined with a growing interest among global private foundations and NGOs in the

Chapter Seven: Academic Explorations

mid-1950s to strengthen higher education in Nigeria. American foundations' interest in the issue reflected the philanthropic community's turn to a focus on Africa. In 1952, for example, when the Ford Foundation was beginning to emerge as the largest private foundation in the United States, it convened a conference to consider "the needs and activities of private American voluntary agencies" working in Africa. Following up on the recommendations of the conference, over the next six years Ford offered funding to African studies programs in the United States, helped establish an exchange program between Africa and the U.S., and expanded its Overseas Development Program to Africa, adding field projects to alleviate poverty, disease, and illiteracy.

At the Carnegie Corporation in New York, Alan Pifer, who managed its British Dominions and Colonies Program, was also focused on steering his organization's grantmaking in Africa toward education. He encouraged Nigerian officials to develop a plan, leading to the creation of the Ashby Commission, which issued its report in 1960. The Ashby Commission sought to provide a blueprint for the development of a large-scale system of higher education. According to Anyanwu, the plan was designed to "decolonize the elitist legacies of the British higher education system in response to the needs of postcolonial Nigeria" by expanding access, diversifying the curriculum, and engaging the private sector. It also sought to create an institutional environment that would help unite Nigeria's pluralistic societies.

Carnegie, Ford, and Rockefeller all agreed to provide substantial assistance to help the newly independent nation implement the Ashby Commission's grand strategy. Nigeria thus became an arena for them to learn collectively and individually about the issues facing a decolonizing Africa.

The Rockefeller Foundation in Ibadan

The Rockefeller Foundation first became involved with University College in Ibadan (UCI) in 1953, when it provided a $10,000 award to pay for equipment and expenses that would allow medical faculty staff to strengthen their groundwork. Well before the Ashby Commission report, the Foundation focused on strengthening and broadening the programs at UCI. Building on its strongest areas of historical expertise, the Foundation began with a focus on health care. In 1959 a growing epidemic of "kwashiorkor," a disease resulting from a combination of protein deficiency and exposure to acute illnesses such as smallpox, took the lives of many young children in Nigeria. The Foundation launched an innovative effort with the Faculty of Medicine to gather information on the incidence and causes of this disease at the village level. The pilot project created a study team lead by Dr. W.R.F. Collis, the head of the Department of Pediatrics. The team went into the Ilesha-Imesi area of Nigeria to collect vital statistics on health conditions, including village sanitation, nutrition, and medical care. University College researchers hoped to use this information to design intervention strategies and to train health care workers. As usual, the Foundation complemented this initiative by providing fellowships for UCI faculty members to visit and study facilities in other countries. Physiology professor John Grayson, for example, received a grant to study the laboratories at the University of the Witwatersrand in Johannesburg and Hebrew University of Jerusalem.

Unlike the grants that the Foundation made in the Congo and South Africa, grants to UCI supported the effort to strengthen the institution as a multidisciplinary center for learning and research, which included investing in the social sciences. With support from the Foundation, University College created a new department focused on Arabic and Islamic Studies to explore the influence of Islam over a period of several centuries in West Africa. This initiative also built on the Foundation's earlier grant for the study of Fulani peoples in West Africa.

The Foundation invested as well in the humanities and the arts, as a way to increase cross-cultural understanding in Nigeria. Prior to independence, Robert July had met with department heads at UCI to encourage their efforts to add courses in African literature and history. His most important contact was Kenneth O. Dike, the head of the history department, who came from Awka in eastern Nigeria. He had attended Fourah Bay College in Sierra Leone and then became the first African to earn a Ph.D. in history from the University of London. His dissertation on trade and politics in the Niger Delta during the nineteenth century set the stage for his future scholarship, a revisionist approach to history that made Africans, rather than colonizers, central to the narrative. Dike had returned to Nigeria to teach in the

Kenneth O. Dike (right), the first African to earn a Ph.D. in history from the University of London, became the principal of University College in Ibadan in 1960. Dike worked closely with Rockefeller Foundation officials—including John Weir, director for Medical and Natural Sciences (left)—to direct funds towards the university as well as local health projects. (Rockefeller Archive Center.)

Chapter Seven: Academic Explorations

UCI history department, and in the 1950s he recruited colleagues to collaborate on research projects that made Ibadan a pioneer in the new historiography of Africa. He became principal of the entire college in 1960.

July and Dike talked about the ways Rockefeller Foundation funding could help promising faculty and students at University College in a number of areas. Support for Wole Soyinka, for example, was linked to an interest in developing theater at the university. The Foundation also provided support for Fela Sowande, a pioneering jazz composer and ethnomusicologist.

All of these grants were made during a heady time not only in Ibadan but also in Nigeria. Independence seemed to promise a cultural as well as political renaissance under Governor-General Nnamdi Azikiwe and other nationalist leaders. But many people, including Soyinka, knew the path ahead would not be easy. Soyinka's play *A Dance of the Forests*, written during the time of his Rockefeller Foundation grant to mark Nigeria's independence, foreshadowed the timeless and universal temptations of political power and highlighted the legacies of colonialism that would have to be overcome. Some politicians in Nigeria were angered by Soyinka's play, but eventually it would be seen as ahead of its time, envisioning a new era when Africans would escape the colonial past by, as William McPheron has written, grafting the technology of the modern era onto the stock of Africa's own traditions.

UNIVERSITIES AND AGRICULTURE

Robert July believed in Soyinka's vision and in the idea that the intellectual climate cultivated by the modern university could help newly independent nations in Africa to prosper. July's work in Ibadan contributed to a growing belief among the staff and trustees of the Rockefeller Foundation that university development represented an important path for investment in Africa.

Foundation Vice President J. George Harrar, a leading agricultural scientist, had spent nearly 15 years helping the Foundation transform agricultural production in key regions of the developing world as part of what would become known as the Green Revolution. But Harrar also believed in the Foundation's commitment to education. As he explained in 1960, governments in the developing world were making enormous sacrifices to educate the next generation, dedicating "a proportion of the national budget five to ten times that which the citizens of the United States would find excessive." Meanwhile, families were making impressive sacrifices "to ensure the education of their children." A foundation that had consistently devoted well over ten percent of its resources to fellowships for advanced training abroad understood the value of international education. "But foreign training is looked upon as a supplement and not as an appropriate substitute for a satisfactory university education in the home country." In the abstract sense, knowledge was universal, but in its application it was extremely local.

Throughout its history the Foundation had been focused on developing local institutions of higher learning, especially in the field of health and medicine. In 1960, however, the Foundation began a major new initiative focused on agriculture in Africa. This innovative effort was initially focused on Kenya.

Siriba Training College, Kenya

The Rockefeller Foundation first came to Kenya to address medical and health care needs. According to historian Maurice Amutabi, the Foundation made a grant to help further medical education and endow a maternity hospital in Nairobi in 1924. The grant laid the groundwork for the King George VI hospital, later renamed Kenyatta National Hospital. As the Rockefeller Foundation sought to eradicate yellow fever and find a vaccine to prevent the disease, Foundation staff returned to Kenya to study mosquitoes and disease patterns. In the 1950s, however, as the Foundation looked for ways to engage more deeply in Africa, improving agriculture emerged as a primary interest.

After World War Two, African leaders in Kenya—including Jomo Kenyatta, the former president of the Kikuyu Central Association—lobbied the colonial administration for self-government and greater equity in rural land distribution and support. At the time, Kenya was still locked into the colonial economy established by Britain's conquest in 1895. On land taken from the Maasai, Luo, Kikuyu, and other peoples, white settlers used African labor to produce agricultural products for export—including wheat, maize, tea, and coffee—while importing finished goods from Britain.

In 1952 participants in the Mau Mau uprising, an anti-British movement in Kenya, fought for land reform and equal rights. When the Mau Mau rebellion broke out, Wangari Maathai—who became the first East African woman to earn a Ph.D. and would win the Nobel Prize for Peace in 2004—was a young Kikuyu girl whose father was a successful farmer. "The Mau Mau struggle," she later wrote, "was fueled most immediately by the sense of betrayal felt by soldiers returning to Kenya from the Second World War. Not only did they not receive any recognition or compensation for their service, but, to add insult to injury, their British colleagues were being showered with honors and even allocated land, some of it taken from the Kenyan war veterans, who were forcibly displaced."

When the British arrested Kenyatta in October 1952 as a leader of the Mau Mau, Rusk and the trustees of the Rockefeller Foundation had few resources with which to engage this new Africa, despite having contributed to its leadership. Kenyatta, after all (as described in Chapter Three), had received a European education and Rockefeller support through the International Institute of African Languages and Cultures. He had also participated in the Malinowski seminar at the London School of Economics. The other men who led the political movement that supported the Mau Mau guerrillas were also Western-educated advocates of the very principles that had been at the root of the American Revolution: equal rights, land rights, sovereignty, and relief from an oppressive, remote government. Eliud Wambu Mathu, for example, was the first black Kenyan to graduate from Oxford, and Peter Mbiyu Koinange did his undergraduate study in the United States at the Hampton

Many of the graduates from Siriba Agricultural College went on to become civil service officers in the Department of Agriculture and helped to develop postcolonial Kenya.
(Rockefeller Archive Center.)

Institute and Ohio Wesleyan University. Like Kenyatta, these men were members of the globally educated elite as well as revolutionaries.

Spurred by the Mau Mau rebellion, the British developed the Swynnerton Plan for land resettlement in 1954. Under the terms of the plan, the colonial government promised to strengthen and stabilize agriculture and raise the standard of living for black Kenyans. For the first time it allowed Africans, who had accounted for nearly 5.25 million of Kenya's 5.5 million people in 1948, to have title deeds to their land.

During the colonial period, when admission to the best Kenyan colleges was limited to white settlers, black Kenyans had to leave their homeland to seek out an advanced education. Siriba College provided the first opportunity for many to obtain an education at home that was not devoted only to vocational training. (Rockefeller Archive Center.)

As part of this effort the colonial government promised to provide black Kenyans with greater training opportunities in agricultural science. Since 1939 only white settlers had been able to attend Egerton Agricultural College to study farming. The lone parallel institution for black Africans was at Makerere College in Uganda. As part of the Swynnerton Plan and the British commitment to the "Africanization" of the civil service, the government planned to convert the Siriba Vocational School of Agriculture into a two-year agricultural college. The Rockefeller Foundation hoped it would become a model for other countries in Africa.

Chapter Seven: Academic Explorations

Siriba had been launched in 1950 to provide basic, rather than scientific, training in agriculture, veterinary science, and education. When John McKelvey Jr., an assistant director in the Foundation's Agricultural Sciences program, arrived in February 1959, he recognized that Siriba desperately needed support. African nationalists and the colonial government hoped that graduates of an upgraded program at Siriba would staff the government's agricultural extension service and work directly with farmers and herdsmen to raise agricultural productivity. To enable this transformation, the government, with the aid of a four-year grant of $171,000 from the Rockefeller Foundation in 1959, sought to build and equip new buildings on Siriba's Maseno campus, enlarge the faculty, and introduce a more advanced curriculum. Months later, the Foundation made an additional $60,000 grant for Siriba.

By the time Kenya became independent in 1963, with Jomo Kenyatta as the country's first prime minister, Siriba College was already playing a major role in the country's agriculture. Of the 288 diploma staff positions in the Department of Agriculture that year, 106 were filled by Africans who had trained at Siriba. The school graduated more officers than Egerton and Makerere University combined. According to Simeon Abulu, a former student interviewed by historian Maurice Amutabi, "Every African from secondary school who wanted to become an agricultural officer knew that they would have to pass through Siriba." As former colonial officials left the country after independence, these new graduates held the agricultural sector together during Kenya's transition to independence.

EXPANDING THE FOUNDATION'S WORK IN KENYA

These efforts to develop agricultural science in Kenya were complemented by new investments in crop development. The Foundation launched tentative efforts to improve wheat production in Kenya in the mid-1950s, when it provided travel grants to two researchers with the government's department of agriculture to visit Foundation wheat research stations in Latin America. These men had collaborated with Norman Borlaug, the head of the Foundation's Inter-American Wheat Improvement Project. In fact, as George Harrar wrote, genetic stock from wheat grown in Kenya played a critical role in the Foundation's development of wheat that was resistant to the virulent black stem rust. In 1960, however, Kenyan wheat crops were decimated by the disease. To help diagnose the problem, the Foundation provided $100,000 to the wheat breeding and research station at Njoro to support research into cereal rusts.

Harrar believed that the grants to these Kenyan institutions, along with grants supporting veterinary research in East Africa, would improve teaching and research in basic sciences while coordinating fundamental and applied research in agriculture and livestock production. "From among them," he wrote, "key institutions will emerge whose efforts, supported by the Foundation, will lead to removal of some of the critical obstacles now impeding agricultural development in Africa."

As the Foundation invested in training agricultural scientists and supporting research critical to the agricultural economy, it also returned to the field of public health. In Kenya, as in Nigeria, the Foundation funded an innovative effort to train paraprofessional health care workers and develop more detailed epidemiological information. One of the Foundation grants helped expand a health care center in Wangige, 30 miles from Nairobi, where students who had completed their studies could intern in the field.

> "Every African from secondary school who wanted to become an agricultural officer knew that they would have to pass through Siriba."
> *Simeon Abulu, 2003*

While much of this work in agriculture and health care was being monitored by the Foundation's scientists, the indefatigable Robert July made frequent visits to Kenya to assess the state of the humanities and the arts during a turbulent political era. In 1960, following July's recommendation, the Foundation provided a grant to support creative writing competitions sponsored by the East African High Commission. That same year, Ali Al'Amin Mazrui, a Kenyan who had recently graduated from Victoria University of Manchester, was awarded a Rockefeller fellowship to study in the United States, and Ugandan Bethwell Ogot received a fellowship to pursue graduate work in history in the United Kingdom.

All of these grants, in different fields and disciplines, reflected the Rockefeller Foundation's increasingly multifaceted approach to development in Kenya as well as Nigeria. Like Robert July, Foundation staff traveled across the continent throughout this period, talking to politicians, academics, and creative artists as newly independent nations in Africa developed their plans for the future. From these various initiatives and conversations, as described in the next chapter, a new strategy began to emerge that would continue to deepen the Foundation's work in Africa over the next two decades.

"The study of the History of Africa, like the study of other histories, is of great intrinsic interest. But it is also relevant for those occupied with present problems in Africa. To understand the present, it is necessary to know something about the past...East African History remains largely unexplored. The Study of the period between the Stone Age and the twentieth century is just beginning. To bridge this historical gap an integrated approach to the study of African History is imperative. The historian alone cannot do the task well. Anthropologists, archeologists, and paleontologists are needed....[and] to get a complete picture of the pre-European period of E. African history, it is essential that tribal traditions be incorporated."

Bethwell Allan Ogot
Fellowship Application, October 26, 1959

I n the late 1950s the young Kenyan historian Bethwell Ogot, studying
at the University of St. Andrews in Scotland, attracted the attention of
the Rockefeller Foundation's Robert July. Ogot was on track to finish an
M.A. in history and to graduate with top honors. He wanted to pursue a
Ph.D., but his research methods were considered controversial at the time.

Ogot believed that a complete history of East Africa could not be written
without relying on oral tradition, and that for too long the history of Africa
had been told from the point of view of its colonizers. Ogot insisted that
"tribal traditions be incorporated" into the narrative.

In October 1959, with July's encouragement, Ogot applied for a
Rockefeller Foundation fellowship to pursue a Ph.D. in history and
philosophy at the School of Oriental and African Studies (SOAS) at the
University of London. In the late 1950s SOAS was the center of African
historical studies, a new discipline still struggling for credibility in higher
education. Ogot's prospective academic advisor, Roland Oliver, who was
supported by a grant from the Rockefeller Foundation, was the university's
only lecturer in African history. In 1960 Oliver and John Fage, with another
grant from the Rockefeller Foundation, launched the *Journal of African
History* at SOAS.

Oliver and Robert July were excited by Ogot's proposal to construct a
history of the Luo people of western Kenya using oral histories in his native
language. The work would be interdisciplinary, relying not only on the
tools of history but also anthropology, political science, and sociology. It
would assert the primacy of the African voice in Africa's history. As Oliver
wrote, the project would be difficult because it reflected an emerging, but
fundamentally innovative, addition to historical methodology. "This will
require great qualities of perseverance."

The Rockefeller Foundation awarded Ogot a fellowship in December
1959. Over the course of the next few years, Ogot would find himself at the
center of one of the most intense controversies of his profession: Did pre-colonial Africa have a history separate from its engagement with Europe? The
question seems absurd today, but in his autobiography Ogot describes the
"uncertainty and the fears" that he and his graduate advisor felt during his
studies. "It was almost as if African history itself was on trial," he reported.

RWJ

47 7E

Ogot

THE ROCKEFELLER FOUNDATION

PERSONAL HISTORY AND APPLICATION FOR

A FELLOWSHIP IN **HISTORY**

DEC 18 1959

(Note: Please type or print all entries in English)

Field of Special Interest **AFRICAN HISTORY**

Date **26.10.59**

Name in Full **BETHWELL ALLAN OGOT**   Sex **MALE**

Present Address **MAKERERE COLLEGE, BOX 262, KAMPALA, UGANDA**
(Street and Number)   (City)   (State or Country)

Permanent Address **LUANDA SCHOOL, BOX 43, P.O. YALA, KENYA**
(Street and Number)   (City)   (State or Country)

Place of Birth **LUANDA SCHOOL**   Year **1929** Month **AUGUST** Day **3RD**

Citizenship **BRITISH**

Single, married, widowed, divorced **MARRIED**   Wife's name **GRACE AKINYI OGOT**
(Form of customary legal signature)

Date of marriage **3.10.59**   Number of Children **—**   Age and Sex **—**

Other dependents **—**

Present Position **TUTORIAL FELLOW**   Annual Salary ▮▮▮▮▮

What part of salary and other income will be continued if a fellowship is granted? **NONE**

Have you at any previous time filed an application with The Rockefeller Foundation? **NO**

If so, give details **—**

Have you at any time held a fellowship from any other American institution or agency or are you now an applicant for one? **NO**   If so, give details **—**

FORM 454

151

Indeed, in the early 1960s Hugh Trevor-Roper, an influential British historian, delivered a televised lecture that challenged the very existence of African history. "Perhaps in the future," he said, "there will be some African history to teach. But at present there is none; there is only the history of the Europeans in Africa. The rest is darkness, like the history of pre-European, pre-Columbian America. And darkness is not the subject of history."

In his work, Ogot rejected Trevor-Roper's point of view. At SOAS he emerged as a key figure among a new generation of African scholars. He became president of the Kenya Students' Association and worked with two men who would become leaders of post-independence Kenya, Tom Mboya and Oginga Odinga. Like many young African intellectuals, Ogot spent much of his spare time working on the politics of independence. As a student leader he wrote an open letter to Kenya's politicians, stating: "Political independence, we believe, is not enough. We must build, and build now, the social economic, moral and intellectual fabrics of our nation."

> "Political independence, we believe, is not enough. We must build, and build now, the social, economic, moral and intellectual fabrics of our nation."
> *Bethwell Ogot, 1960*

Ogot's apartment became an unofficial Kenya embassy in London. Ogot and his wife Grace Emily Akinyi Joseph, a devout Christian who was the first European-educated nurse from Kenya and a strong advocate for women's education, hosted leading intellectuals for conversations about the history and the future of Africa.

In 1961 Ogot participated in the Fourth International Africa Seminar in Dakar, Senegal, hosted by the International African Institute. He described this event as the first time African academic historians had the opportunity to meet and engage with one another. Ogot debated other African scholars, including Jacob Ajayi, Cheikh Anta Diop, and Joseph Kizerbo, all of whom would become important collaborators.

Before he had finished his Rockefeller-supported graduate work and research, Ogot joined the faculty at Makerere University in 1962 as a lecturer in the history department. At the time, Makerere University's courses looked very much like those offered at English universities. Ogot formed what became known as the "dissident group" to fight for an African-centered syllabus. He was also deeply involved with the Foundation-supported University of East Africa. With another grant from the Rockefeller Foundation, meanwhile, Ogot received a special lectureship at University College Nairobi that gave him time for research and writing to finish his dissertation.

In 1967 Ogot published the first volume of his *History of the Southern Luo: Migration and Settlement, 1500–1900*. Its impact on the history and historiography of Africa was significant and provided a basis for his continued efforts to Africanize the curriculum, first at University College Nairobi and later within the three-college system of the University of East Africa. He worked with the three departments of history at Makerere, Nairobi, and Dar-es-Salaam to establish the *Transafrica Journal of History*, which Ogot edited from 1970 to 1974.

Ogot has written that his early work prior was "largely nationalistic in spirit and Pan-Africanist in scope," but after 1980 he increasingly focused on "Africa's new place in the world." This transition reflected his dual role as a scholar and a public intellectual. He served the government on a number of important boards and commissions.

Over the next two decades, as Ogot rose to positions of power in the Kenyan university system, he pushed to transform Kenyan universities into African institutions. While teaching at the University of Nairobi, Kenyatta University, and Maseno University College, he wrote and produced curriculum and fostered opportunities for Kenyan students to be published. For almost five decades he has written about the history and politics of Kenya and the need for humanities education.

Ogot also played an important role in the development of public policy in Kenya. A member and officer of the UNESCO executive board for years, he also served as chairman of a number of state corporations including Kenya Posts and Telecommunications, Kenya Railways, and the National Oil Corporation. In 2003 he became chancellor at Moi University, and from this position he has continued to play a leading role in the development of higher education in Kenya.

CHAMPIONS OF HIGHER EDUCATION

On Tuesday morning, December 6, 1960, as the trustees from the Rockefeller Foundation gathered in historic Colonial Williamsburg in the state of Virginia, the headlines in the *Washington Post* captured the sense of a world in transition. In Moscow, a summit meeting of leaders from 81 nations had ended with a confident declaration that communism would triumph over the capitalist West, but without the need for war. Meanwhile, newly elected U.S. President John F. Kennedy, preparing for his inauguration, met with outgoing President Dwight D. Eisenhower to talk about the transfer of power, while down the street the U.S. Supreme Court struck down laws in the American South that segregated bus station restaurants by race. In the Congo, United Nations forces struggled to forestall an all-out civil war between troops loyal to Joseph Mobutu and those following former Premier Patrice Lumumba.

Robert July no doubt read these headlines. He had been in the Congo shortly before the country gained its independence in June. He visited with American Consul John Tomlinson as well as administrators and faculty at Lovanium University, all of whom were optimistic about the country's future. When he traveled farther into the interior, however, he found that many people were nervous about the transition. Now, nine months later and thousands of miles away, he undoubtedly worried about

Rockefeller Foundation trustee and U.N. Under Secretary for Special Political Affairs Ralph Bunche spent nine weeks in the Republic of the Congo in 1960 trying to prevent civil war and bloodshed following independence. Dismayed by the strife, he believed it was inevitable as the people of Africa "seek to satisfy their aspirations for freedom and independence." (Dennis Rayle. Rockefeller Archive Center.)

the fate of the people he had met and the future of the Congo.

July had been asked to speak to the trustees about Africa and to make the case for increasing the Foundation's investment in Africa's emerging nations. But this was a time of uncertainty for the trustees. Earlier in the week, a columnist in the *Washington Post* had noted that Rockefeller Foundation President Dean Rusk was among a handful of candidates that President-elect Kennedy was considering for secretary of state. One of the Foundation's trustees, Chester Bowles, was on the short list for the same position. And another trustee, Douglas Dillon, was being considered for secretary of the treasury. Meeting in Williamsburg—capital of the Virginia colony before the United States won its independence—contributed to a heightened awareness of both the past and the future. Its architecture and furnishings, carefully restored with funds provided by John D. Rockefeller Jr., recalled an era when Americans had clamored for equal rights as citizens within the British Empire, or, failing that, independence. July reminded the trustees of this fact as he began his talk.

"To the Africans, the United States offers great hope as an ex-colony and a liberal, wealthy nation, which has always espoused the cause of freedom," July said. But Africans, in all their diversity, were also leery of "the substitution of one type of yoke for another." Many harbored a

Grants to the University of Ibadan in Nigeria in the late 1950s helped the Rockefeller Foundation see the potential for a university development program that would train leaders for the soon-to-be independent nation. (Rockefeller Archive Center.)

Chapter Eight: Champions of Higher Education

suspicion that "our motives may be mixed with politics." And in 1960, as African Americans waged sit-ins and boycotts to end segregation, many Africans were also skeptical of the racial attitudes of American leaders.

Rockefeller Foundation President J. George Harrar (center) visited the University of Ibadan in 1970. Harrar hoped African universities, like land grant colleges in the United States, would provide technical assistance to farmers and rural communities and help promote economic development. (Rockefeller Archive Center.)

July summarized the history of U.S. relations with Africa. Since World War Two, he noted, American aid, given directly and through international agencies like the United Nations, had increased. International philanthropic agencies were also becoming increasingly involved on the continent. In 1960 there were 45 different organizations working in Africa, led by Carnegie, Ford, and Rockefeller. In addition, at least 30 American universities had launched African studies programs.

The Rockefeller Foundation, as July pointed out, had long recognized that, with independence, there would be more opportunity to work directly with Africans. Referring to the Foundation's work over the previous six years in the Congo, Nigeria, South Africa, Kenya, and a handful of other countries, he noted that grants had been made in the humanities, social sciences, natural sciences, medicine, and agriculture. The lessons learned from this work suggested to the officers that the Foundation could have significant impact.

July proposed a framework for action that reflected the officers' global planning and that reduced the risk of failure by not trying to achieve too much.

He recommended focusing on a handful of countries including Nigeria, Ghana, Uganda, Ethiopia, Liberia, and what were then Tanganyika and Rhodesia, adding that the Foundation should also consider the Congo if it was stable. He said the trustees should be willing to establish an operating program with resident staff working along interdisciplinary lines. He also suggested integrating this African program with institutions of higher education to address broad educational goals in the sciences and the humanities as well as specific development issues, including, for example, efforts to address diet deficiency among the African people.

A CONCEPT FOR UNIVERSITY DEVELOPMENT

The trustees were receptive to the officers' proposal as presented by Robert July, but many issues had to be resolved after President Kennedy selected Dean Rusk as secretary of state in January 1961. With Chairman John D. Rockefeller 3rd's strong support, the board named George Harrar as president of the Foundation. With a deep background in development issues, Harrar hit the ground running. Looking for a unified grand strategy for Africa that would build on the officers' recommendations presented to the board by July, Harrar turned to an internal staff memorandum written several years earlier by Norman Buchanan, the director of the Division of Social Sciences. Buchanan had argued that "explicit and major emphasis should be placed on the development of universities and institutes in developing countries." These modern universities could become the focal points of economic development and the conduit through which international aid might flow to new nations.

Buchanan believed that universities could become "key leverage points serving as citadels of protection for Third World scientists and scholars in their search for new knowledge and the study of important development problems." Buchanan also believed that these university centers of excellence would tend to radiate and diffuse ideas, especially in science and technology, to reproduce and generalize their excellence. This was a strategy that played to the Foundation's historic strength.

In 1961, drawing on Buchanan's memorandum, his conversations with July and other staff, and his own experience with agriculture in Mexico, Harrar asked the trustees to approve a university development program for developing nations in Asia, Latin America, and Africa. The program would take a holistic approach, providing support to select universities as essential centers of development. These universities would help to train leaders and be engines of economic innovation. The primary areas of funding would be in traditional core areas for the Rockefeller Foundation: health, agriculture, and the social sciences. To support this capacity building, the strategy would link universities in developing countries to American universities through graduate fellowships, staff development grants, and visiting faculty. Such a program faced real challenges in many African countries, not the least of which was the necessity for a strong local commitment to education so that primary and secondary schools could produce candidates for universities.

There was also a political reason to build African universities. A divide had already emerged between professionals educated in Europe and the United States, and indigenous political forces that had come to positions of power through the colonial military and police, traditional tribal affiliations, or local struggles for independence. People who had spent years in Europe or America were at times seen as elite outsiders. Quickly developing African universities could reduce the gap between scholarship and power.

 These goals could not be achieved through a series of long-distance grants. Instead, Harrar proposed that the Foundation embed its own operational staff in a number of select universities in the developing world. He envisioned that a small nucleus of Foundation staff members would, by agreement, become key faculty members in several sectors of each university, including medicine, economics, sociology, the humanities, and possibly agriculture. "The RF group would function as a regular faculty," he wrote, "but would also act as a coordinated RF unit under the general leadership of a senior staff member. This group would help to strengthen curricula [and] improve teaching and research training. Ultimately the RF group would be replaced by competent well-trained nationals." At the same time, these Foundation staff members would serve as a recruiting agency and financial sponsor for the best young American scholars, who would receive short-term contracts to serve as visiting professors in these emerging universities.

Visiting American faculty were expected to be defenders of high-quality standards, objective "disinterested" research, and a new meritocracy, but they had to avoid being seen as a new generation of cultural imperialists. There was eagerness in Africa to escape the existing model of the European university, which seemed irrelevant to Africa's pragmatic needs, while the American public university model—anchored in the tradition of land grant colleges that provided technical assistance to rural communities—held some appeal. But the Rockefeller programs could succeed only if they were invited, rather than imposed from the outside.

University building was clearly a long-term strategy. Harrar warned the trustees that it would take at least a decade, perhaps more. It would also re-quire a delicate balancing act derived from the need to commit for the long

THE KITCHENER MEMORIAL MEDICAL SCHOOL.
KHARTOUM.

term—to be prepared to stay through inevitable hard times—while operating day-to-day with the understanding that the Foundation would withdraw and turn over resources to Africans as soon as feasible.

In the summer of 1961, focusing on institutions that had already received grants, the Foundation considered four African universities, including University College in Nigeria and University College of East Africa. For the next two decades the University Development Program (UDP), with all its interdisciplinary character, its ethic of support for emerging African nationalism, and its organizational appeal to the best strengths of the Rockefeller tradition, became the focal point of Foundation activity in Africa.

The Kitchener Memorial Medical School, founded in 1924, merged with Gordon Memorial College after World War Two to create Khartoum University College. Governed by the University of London prior to independence, the institution became the University of Khartoum in 1956. Rockefeller Foundation grants helped the university expand its program and enrollments. (Rockefeller Archive Center.)

UNIVERSITY OF KHARTOUM

The earliest of the UDP's big commitments in Africa was to the University of Khartoum in Sudan, founded in 1902 as Gordon Memorial College and operated on a British model with an adjunct relationship to the University of London. Military leader General El Ferik Ibrahim Abboud had attended the school before enlisting in the Egyptian Army, and had appointed himself chancellor of the university in 1960. Its vice-chancellor until 1962 was Dr. Nasr el Hag Ali, a graduate of the American University of Beirut and a respected member of the Sudanese intellectual community.

Harrar was enthusiastic about a project in Arab-Islamic Africa but hesitant about working with Abboud's military government. Abboud was a strong-man. He had led a military coup against Sudan's first civil government and suppressed political parties, and the threat of civil war remained. But he was also anticommunist and committed to economic development.

Threats of war or political interference were worrisome, but not only was the University of Khartoum modeled after British universities, it was secular and independent. Every division of the Foundation had investments in the university, and perhaps most important in Harrar's estimation was the chance to support agricultural research in the arid regions of Africa where production was dependent on irrigation, one of the keys to the future of agriculture on the continent.

In December 1962 the Rockefeller Foundation trustees voted to extend their support of the University of Khartoum with a five-year grant of $500,000 ($3.86 million in 2013 dollars). The proposal was accompanied by a lengthy analysis by the Foundation's medical director, John Weir, who was enthusiastic about the potential of the university to become a developmental anchor in Islamic Africa. He saw Sudan as a nation

Agriculture students at the University of Khartoum in 1961 studied chemistry in laboratories supported by the Rockefeller Foundation. (Rockefeller Archive Center.)

committed to strengthening general education and
developing a university with high standards, staffed by
good Sudanese scholars. This was also a critical phase
for developing Sudanese staff, which was supported by
government funds for overseas and local scholarships to
encourage top Sudanese graduates to remain in the service
of the university. By 1959, 34 percent of the 158-member
faculty was Sudanese. There were 43 graduate students in
the university and 101 scholars studying abroad financed
by a Sudanese scholarship fund. When Dr. Nasr el Hag Ali retired in July 1962,
the deans of five of the eight faculties were Sudanese with strong academic
credentials. It therefore seemed possible for Weir to expect that well-trained
Sudanese scholars would comprise 80 percent of the faculty within ten years,
especially with Rockefeller Foundation support.

Animal husbandry and agricultural sciences at the University of Khartoum concentrated on the needs of pastoralists and farmers who inhabited Sudan's arid landscape. The Foundation also provided fellowships to Sudanese veterinary faculty to study microbiology and pathology in the United States and Europe. (Rockefeller Archive Center.)

With Rockefeller funding, the university announced a massive
infrastructure campaign to develop the capacity for hosting thousands of
new students in the coming decade. The government had also announced an
ambitious economic development plan that included massive investments
in secondary education, especially teacher training in the sciences, to feed
the university.

Chapter Eight: Champions of Higher Education

The Foundation's commitment to the University of Khartoum lasted five years (1962-1967) and represented a total investment of almost a million dollars. Twenty-one students also received Rockefeller Foundation fellowships. By 1967, however, the Foundation's officers were frustrated with the slow pace of institutional development at the University of Khartoum and the government's failure to provide a promised $17 million dollars for the project. Moreover, the political environment contributed to a massive exodus of the country's trained professionals in medicine and other fields, undermining the Foundation's efforts to strengthen the country's scientific and professional leadership. When Sudan and the United States broke diplomatic relations during the Arab-Israeli War in 1967, the Foundation chose to terminate the project.

Although the University of Khartoum project faced significant political and social challenges and the Rockefeller Foundation's total investment was modest by

Nearly 3,000 students were enrolled at the University of Khartoum in 1966. Rockefeller Foundation funding helped the university keep pace with rapid growth, especially in agriculture, veterinary science, the basic sciences, and the social sciences. The Foundation also helped strengthen the central library. (Marc & Evelyne Bernheim. Rockefeller Archive Center.)

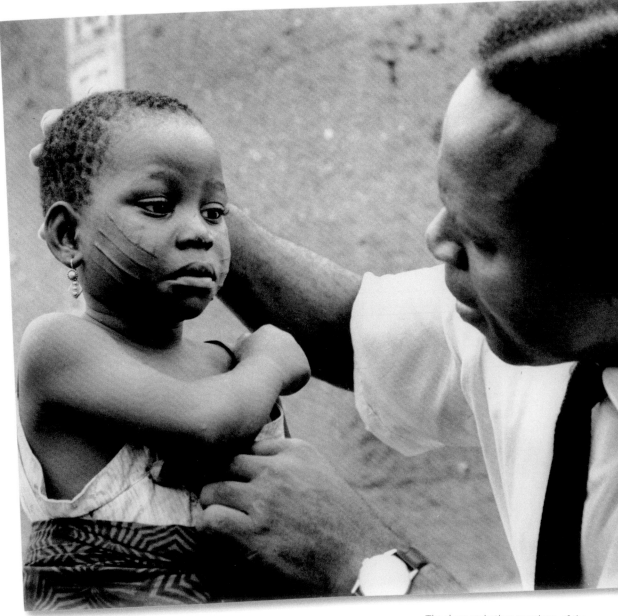

The dean and other members of the
medical faculty at the University of
Ibadan conducted research under
the aegis of the Institute of Child
Health, which had been established
with Rockefeller Foundation support.
(Rockefeller Archive Center.)

Chapter Eight: Champions of Higher Education

comparison with other UDP initiatives, the project left a legacy of strong local faculty as well as programs that weathered the changing political climate in Sudan for at least another ten years.

UNIVERSITY OF IBADAN

George Harrar had no inhibitions about launching a project at the crown jewel of African higher education, the University of Ibadan in Nigeria. According to James Coleman and David Court, who worked for the Rockefeller Foundation as program officers and later wrote a book about the University Development Program, "The university and the Nigerian government not only warmly welcomed but actively solicited Foundation assistance.... No single university in Africa or elsewhere seemed to offer in 1963 such a rare combination of promising indicators for a successful university effort."

The Foundation's efforts in Ibadan were designed to support the university's five-year plan for development. For nearly a decade the Foundation provided staff, resources, and expertise in collaboration with Nigerian leaders at the university. In health, for example, the Foundation helped establish a Department of Psychiatry, Neurosurgery, and Neurology in 1963—the first in Africa—under the department's charismatic founder, M. Olabode Akindele. Foundation grants and staff assistance also created a virology research unit to address a large number of undiagnosed "tropical fevers" that seemed to be common in West Africa. This new facility was affiliated with the Foundation's arbovirus laboratories in New York, which had continued to research tropical viruses and other diseases since the days of the Rockefeller Foundation's West African Yellow Fever Commission in the late 1920s. A year later, the Foundation provided another $200,000 to help establish a Department of Nursing.

The Foundation also helped the university reach out to the community. It granted more than $200,000 to support the creation of a new rural training and research center for health care administrators at Igbo-Ora, about 50 miles from Ibadan, which built upon an existing center and rural service run by the Western Region government. This innovative project sought to address public health needs by training midwives, sanitary officers, and other paraprofessionals to provide rural ambulatory medicine to communities lacking physicians. With funding from the Foundation, visiting staff from the London School of Hygiene and Tropical Medicine, as well as agencies of the United Nations, were able to share new procedures and technologies. In addition, the center collected demographic, epidemiological, and medical information to strengthen public health services. The Nigerian and international partners involved in the project hoped it would "become a model for future African health services."

Other grants to the University of Ibadan were made to strengthen teaching and research in agriculture and veterinary science. In addition, Foundation staff participated directly in the life of the university by serving as faculty. The Foundation also provided resident specialists in medicine, agriculture, and virology. These specialists helped with instruction as well as research in the field, collaborating with Nigerian maize breeders, for example, to hybridize local varieties with successful Mexican and Caribbean lines of maize. These programs focused on enhancing local expertise and associating Nigerian scientists with teams of agricultural researchers in other countries.

In addition to direct support for academics, the Foundation helped develop administration and infrastructure at the University of Ibadan, where a grant funded a study of accounting and administrative procedures. The Foundation also helped with the construction of faculty housing and paid for a librarian in the medical school. And by 1963 the Rockcfeller Foundation had awarded 27 fellowships to Nigerians, more than in any other African country.

The Foundation's investments in these efforts were substantial. In 1963 alone, as the University Development Program grew, funding for the University of Ibadan totaled more than $800,000. The Rockefeller Foundation had four staff members in Ibadan that year: one assigned to agricultural sciences and three to humanities and social sciences, including Robert July. A year later the Foundation's staff in Ibadan had grown to nine, with two in agricultural sciences, three in the humanities and social sciences, one in medical and natural sciences, and three in the virus research program.

Other philanthropic partners were also engaged in this effort. The Carnegie Corporation provided funding to the History Department at Ibadan. Led by Kenneth Onwuka Dike and Jacob Ade Ajayi, the department established a university press and enlisted other West African history departments in a two-year effort to create a common West African curriculum that honored the region's pre-colonial past, revealed the brutality of the colonial era, and insisted on continuity in African culture. The Ford Foundation also provided funding. The three donor organizations hoped that the University of Ibadan would become a model for other universities in West Africa.

The university went through all the growing pains that Nigeria went through in the two decades that followed independence. As revenues from oil production exploded in the late 1960s, increasing government investment helped the university expand. When oil revenues crashed in the 1970s, the university found itself overbuilt, overinvested in faculty and staff, and

surviving precariously day-to-day in an environment filled beyond capacity with competing publicly subsidized regional universities. During the civil war from 1967 to 1970, ethnic and regional tensions kept the university from achieving its idealized aspiration to become the national university of Nigeria. Prior to the secession of Biafra, for example, Ibo students made up 31.3 percent of the student body, and Ibo professors constituted 25 percent of the faculty. After war broke out, however, virtually all Ibo fled the university. Of the 766 incoming freshmen in the class of 1967, only 13 were Ibo. According to authors James Coleman and David Court, "The civil war threatened to transform the University of Ibadan into a largely but not exclusively Yoruba university." These tensions were aggravated by seizures of the government, which destabilized leadership and funding.

Students and faculty in agricultural sciences at The University of Ibadan in 1963 measured the growth of test plots of grass. Roderic Buller (right), a Rockefeller Foundation agronomist, was one of four Foundation staffers who worked at the university in 1963. (Rockefeller Archive Center.)

Despite the prolonged national crisis, the Rockefeller Foundation's commitment endured. By the time the Foundation ended the University Development Program in the early 1980s, it had invested $11 million dollars in Ibadan over 16 years, provided 157 fellowships, and subsidized 59 visiting scholars.

And despite the instability of the government, the University of Ibadan, which has been described as "an archetype of a British ivory tower colonial university," had become far more authentically Nigerian. This transformation, as Coleman and Court point out, had been anchored in the Foundation's early grants to creative artists and writers like Wole Soyinka and others, as well as to the rural life programs in Igbo Ora-Ibarapa and Badeku, which "contributed to the adaptation of the university to its Nigerian environment."

University of East Africa

In East Africa, the University Development Program had taken a more innovative and experimental approach. Largely at the encouragement of Tanganyika's charismatic president Julius Nyerere, the three emerging nations of Uganda (1961), Tanganyika (1962), and Kenya (1963) created a federated University of East Africa in 1963. The Rockefeller Foundation and other partners, including the Carnegie Corporation and the Ford Foundation, were already deeply invested in the individual universities that comprised the federation. Makerere University in Kampala, Uganda, was the oldest and most prestigious. It was founded in 1921 as a trade

At the Institute for Development Studies at University College Nairobi, students studied economics and the faculty conducted research on the Kenyan economy. (Rockefeller Archive Center)

school, slowly increasing its academic standing over half a century. It had trained the professional class of British Central Africa (including parts of present-day Malawi, Zambia, and Zimbabwe) for several generations, and had a strong agriculture school and medical faculty. The latter included an adjunct community health center at Kasangati, where Sidney Kark had brought his theories of community-based social medicine after he left South Africa. The newest college was University College in Dar es Salaam, Tanganyika (Tanzania after 1964), where administrators hoped to build the first regional law school. Royal College in Nairobi, Kenya, was the third partner (renamed University College Nairobi in 1964), where administrators sought to create a world-class veterinary school to serve the pastoral agriculture sector of East Africa.

The key idea behind the new University of East Africa was that each national college would maintain its core faculty in arts and sciences, but highly specialized professional faculty would be dispersed among the three schools in a way that increased efficiency and quality. "The economizing rationale of having expensive professional faculties serve a larger region was most persuasive," Coleman and Court argued, "particularly for the donors."

In 1963 the Rockefeller Foundation convened a conference of donors at its Bellagio Center in Italy, and immediately became the largest single donor to the University of East Africa within a network of eight philanthropic partners. The project was immensely popular and, according to Coleman and Court, benefited from "the high quality interim expatriate leadership and emergent cadre of indigenous leadership, as well as a climate of uncritical receptivity for foreign assistance." Within a decade the number of partners had grown to 21. The Foundation and its partners appreciated the ability to begin from the beginning, without being shackled to the rigid British model of a university, and the Rockefeller commitment was large. Beginning with a $3 million investment in 1963, the total grew to $20 million by the time the UDP was terminated in 1983.

The university was characterized by flexibility and an innovative atmosphere, but as predicted by Julius Nyerere, the demands of nation building tested the university's ability to survive. In Kenya, for example, ethnic rivalries and student protests perpetually swept the campus. In her memoir, for example, Wangari Maathai told her own story of how her academic career was affected by tribal rivalry in 1966. Appointed as a research assistant and then informed that the job had been given to someone else, as Maathai later described in her memoir, she was ultimately able to enter a doctoral program in Germany. She returned to Kenya in 1969, completed her dissertation, received a Ph.D. from University College Nairobi, and took a post on the faculty of the School of Veterinary Medicine. She was the first woman in East or Central Africa to have received a doctoral degree.

In the end, the University of East Africa lasted only seven years, dissolving into its three constituent parts in 1970. Each of the institutions continued to receive independent support from the Foundation, although it was dramatically reduced in the late 1970s. Between 1964 and 1970, however, the growth of all three participating universities had been spectacular. The number of East African members of the academic staff had increased from 49 to 661. Sixty percent of the academic staff had received financial support or fellowships for advanced training from the Rockefeller Foundation, including Bethwell Ogot, who became chancellor of Moi University in Kenya, and world-renowned postcolonial scholar Ali Al'Amin Mazrui.

Return to the Congo

Under different conditions the Foundation might have launched its efforts to develop universities in Africa in the Congo. It already had a long history with Lovanium University in Kinshasa, with a large existing commitment of close to one million dollars in the medical school and nursing program as well as an investment in the agriculture school. Lovanium was also academically rigorous, its student body was diverse, and it played an important regional role.

But the transition from Belgian rule to independence had been violent and unstable. Rockefeller trustee Ralph Bunche had returned exhausted from a United Nations assignment to independent Congo that involved trying to help stave off civil war. The experience had almost killed him, and he confessed his frustration with the Belgians along with his despair over the Congo's emerging leaders. Everywhere from Kisangani to Kinshasa, the intrigue of the Cold War caused suspicion and hostility.

The Foundation had therefore decided it would not include Lovanium as a first-round participant in the UDP. Taking a second look in 1967, the trustees authorized a three-year grant of $160,000 for academic staff development, then watched cautiously as the Congo became Zaire, and as Lovanium was swept into a nationwide reorganization of higher education. In December 1971 the trustees appropriated another $150,000 to study the feasibility of a university development program at Lovanium.

Over the next decade the university and the Foundation would meet the challenges of political upheavals in Zaire. In April 1969 student unions based at Lovanium made demands on President Mobutu Sese Seko for a role in university administration. Demonstrations became violent, and students were

killed by the police. When students tried to recognize the two-year anniversary of the demonstrations in June 1971, another round of violent clashes occurred. Mobutu closed Lovanium and conscripted its students into the army. The campus—along with the Protestant Free University of Congo in Kisangani and the State University of the Congo in Lubumbashi—became a partner campus of the National University of Zaire (UNAZA) under the control of Mobutu's party, the Popular Movement of the Revolution (MPR).

Makerere University College in Uganda was one of three institutions associated with the University of East Africa in the 1960s, all of which received support from the University Development Program. (Rockefeller Archive Center.)

The reorganization assigned both the medical school and the agriculture school to remote campuses, which created unforeseen problems. The influential Faculty of Social Sciences at the old Lovanium campus at Kinshasa, however, grew quickly under the stewardship of its dean, M. Crawford Young, a Rockefeller-embedded professor of political science from the University of Wisconsin who was widely respected as the leading Zaire expert in the United States. Young's leadership lasted only two years before Mobutu appointed a new dean, a man tied to Zairian internal security.

In general, the strategy of embedded visiting faculty and the rapid preparation of indigenous staff through the Foundation's fellowship program simply did not work in Zaire because none of the New York officers directly involved in the UDP at that time spoke or understood French. Nor did any of them have an experiential basis for a sense of identity with francophone Africa. The fellowship program could not fully take into account the volatile problems associated with ethnic diversity and gender bias, and fellowship selection often unintentionally reinforced old patterns of "haves" and "have nots," according to Coleman and Court. "None of the 27 Zairian fellows were female, while only two women were among the 91 Zairian *stagiaires* (staff development fellows)."

For eight years the Foundation struggled to keep the social science program alive and to develop the medical school and the agriculture program on the old, abandoned Belgian experimental farm at Yangambi. But the Zaire government failed to provide promised matching funding, and the experiment foundered. In addition, the Belgian government and expatriate faculty abandoned the national university, while many Zairians assumed there was a link between Foundation policy and U.S. support for Mobutu.

During his 1975 trip to Zaire, Foundation President John Knowles confronted both the university administrators and Mobutu concerning the corruption, ethnic cronyism, and lack of financial support for the universities. This had no impact on Mobutu, and in 1980 the Foundation "finally, in frustration and with regret," wrote Coleman and Court, ended its commitment. The compelling lesson of the Foundation's program in Zaire was that institutional development was impossible in a university inescapably tied to autocratic rule.

The End of University Development

By the close of the 1970s, many people in Africa and in the philanthropic community had come to recognize the limits of the university-led model for development. Efforts to cultivate elite talent seemed to have produced limited benefits for the continent as a whole. In hindsight, this was hardly surprising. But in the 1950s and early 1960s Americans and Europeans in the donor community had believed that they could transplant institutional models from the developed to the developing world to help African or Asian countries become more like Western nations. Economic growth would be the measure of success. In many countries, however, economic growth did not reduce poverty or unemployment. Often it led to growing inequality, which often seemed to be perpetuated by the elite nature of universities.

After a review of the successes and disappointments of their programs, USAID and the Ford Foundation ended their university development programs. The British Government and the World Bank, meanwhile, decided to refocus their support for education on the needs of the poor in the developing world. The World Bank produced a study questioning the rate of return on investments in higher education in Africa, though the report was later disavowed by the bank.

James Coleman had worked closely with the Foundation's University Development Program in Africa for 12 years. A Harvard-trained Ph.D., Coleman was the founding director of the African Studies Center at UCLA. From 1965 to 1978 he had been a professor of political science and an administrator at Makerere University in Uganda, the University of Nairobi, and the University of Dar es Salaam. For 11 of those years he had also been an associate director of the Rockefeller Foundation. Appraising the successes and failures of the initiative, he noted that donors became particularly frustrated that universities had not, in fact, developed strong relationships with development efforts.

Donors did not withdraw from university support altogether. Rather, they began to focus on those elements within universities that had a strong development orientation, including agriculture, economics, and health. This new focus, as Coleman pointed out, led the Rockefeller Foundation to change the name of the UDP to Education for Development Program (EFD) in 1973. Other donors followed a similar course. Under this new concept the idea of a "developmental university" emerged, an institution in which the curriculum and degree programs were adapted to the needs of the local culture and society. A greater emphasis was placed on practical, applied learning with in-service training incorporated into the curriculum. But even with this new focus, university development continued for only a few more years.

The Rockefeller Foundation terminated the Education for Development Program in 1983, believing it had achieved its goals to the extent possible. Indeed, concerted collaboration between African institutions and American and European faculty and experts had helped to build strong universities. Enrollments at African universities increased 20-fold between the 1960s and 1985. These institutions had helped to train a generation of African leaders. And within two decades, the Foundation and its partners would renew their commitment to higher education in Africa with a multimillion dollar partnership. (See pages 240-241.)

Despite the political and social changes that besieged the continent in the decades after independence, many of these universities weathered the storm and would play a critical role in Africa's development in the twenty-first century. Indeed, the Foundation's emphasis on building capacity, especially human capacity, through the UDP/EFD as well as the fellowship program meant that, as it returned to different projects in Africa, both within and outside universities in the 1990s and beyond, the Foundation could find well-qualified and committed experts in the fields of health care, agriculture, and demographics who had ideas, plans, and energy for future efforts.

FELLOWSHIP PROGRAM

AN INVESTMENT IN HUMAN CAPITAL

The Rockefeller Foundation fellowship program has been a key element in the Foundation's longtime effort to build a global network of exceptional individuals united by the principles of science and humanism. For nearly a century, the fellowship program emphasized the Foundation's core principle of pursuing knowledge at the extreme edge of creativity and innovation. Foundation President Raymond Fosdick once wrote that these fellows "are among the unifying forces at work on an international basis, sending their ideas along the highroads of the world, raising their voices across geographical boundaries and barriers of racial hate."

The first two African fellows were white scientists from South Africa, selected in 1924; the first black African fellows were selected in 1958. After 1958 the number of fellowships awarded to Africans increased dramatically. At its peak in 1970, the African fellowship program supported 129 Africans studying abroad on postgraduate fellowships.

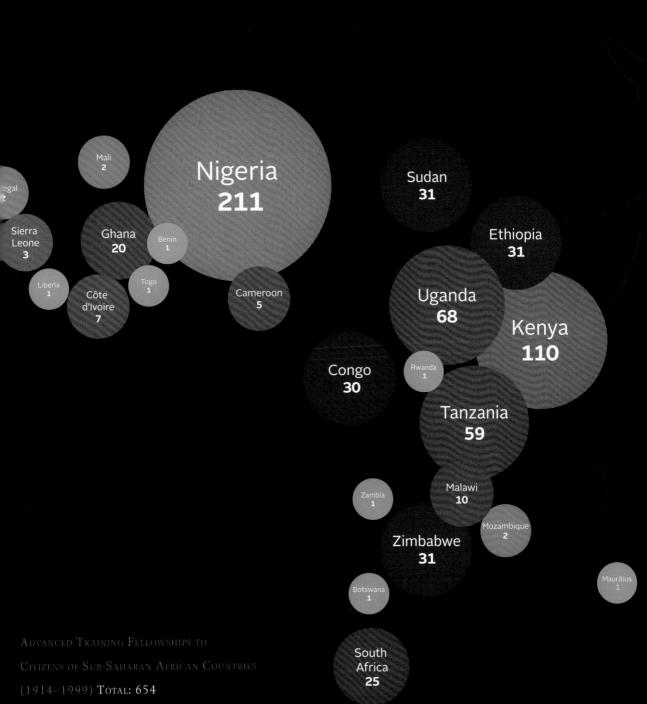

Mali
2

Sierra
Leone
3

egal

Ghana
20

Benin
1

Liberia
1

Côte
d'Ivoire
7

Togo
1

Nigeria
211

Cameroon
5

Sudan
31

Ethiopia
31

Uganda
68

Kenya
110

Congo
30

Rwanda
1

Tanzania
59

Zambia
1

Malawi
10

Mozambique
2

Zimbabwe
31

Botswana
1

Mauritius
1

South
Africa
25

Advanced Training Fellowships to

Citizens of Sub-Saharan African Countries

(1914–1999) Total: 654

APARTHEID AND
SOUTH AFRICA

By the 1970s the Rockefeller Foundation was well-established as a major international donor and agent for change around the world and in Africa, but developments at home and abroad challenged the Foundation's ability to sustain the momentum behind its initiatives. In Africa, Idi Amin, who had risen to power in Uganda in 1971, gutted the Foundation's efforts at Makerere University and forced faculty such as Ali Al'Amin Mazrui into exile. Mobutu Sese Seko had tightened his grip on Zaire. In South Africa, the Nationalist government had imposed more draconian apartheid laws and regulations, suffocating not only the protests of its citizens but their development. All across southern Africa, guerrilla wars challenged white authority. In the United States, the Watergate scandal, the Vietnam War, student protests, and the civil rights struggles of African Americans undermined the nation's faith in government and major institutions, and this climate of self-doubt affected the Foundation as well. In addition, the OPEC oil embargo and runaway inflation were eroding even the Rockefeller Foundation's ability to expand its programs in developing nations and at home.

Faced with investment losses in a tumbling stock market, Foundation President John H. Knowles asked the trustees to begin comprehensive reviews of all programs with the object of retrenching. The review

By the mid-1970s, many Americans were increasingly uneasy with the U.S. government's unwillingness to challenge South Africa's system of apartheid. Under President John Knowles, the Rockefeller Foundation considered forming an independent commission to study U.S. policies toward South Africa. (United Nations.)

process was completed in May 1974 with the publication of *The Course Ahead*, which proposed substantial cutbacks across the Foundation's programs. Despite the changing landscape of humanitarian work, Knowles never proposed that the Foundation spend itself out of existence. "Grim as things look today," he wrote, "the worst is likely yet to come—and with it exceptional opportunities to be of service."

Knowles was 35 when he came to the Foundation from Massachusetts General Hospital, where he had been the youngest general director in its history. In 1969 he had been nominated by President Richard Nixon to become Assistant Secretary of Health, Education and Welfare, but his nomination had been thwarted by the American Medical Association on the grounds that he had been a critic of private medicine and an outspoken advocate of Medicare. Unlike Dean Rusk or George Harrar, Knowles was not an internationalist. In some ways he evoked the early days of the Foundation, when research-oriented physicians dominated its culture. And yet Knowles was aware that his interests were at odds with the momentum of history. "We are passing from an era of hard science," he wrote, "into a time that is more concerned with the social sciences and human behavior where there is a paucity of measurement and control."

For Africa, the biggest effect of the trustees' review was a decision to reduce the Education for Development Program's operational staff and gradually phase out the program itself. The news was disappointing to the staff, who sensed that the trustees had not understood the progress that had been made.

Despite the decision to retrench, the Foundation did add one new program, the Conflict in International Relations program, which reflected a sober recognition that the Cold War policy framework that had led the United States into Vietnam was no longer a useful way of viewing the world. Understanding conflict in regions around the world depended on a new paradigm. The new program did not seek to staff the foreign ministries of emerging nations. But it did reflect the continued influence of foreign-policy experts on the Foundation's board of trustees. Knowles brought Mason Willrich to the Foundation in 1976 to direct the program. Willrich was a law school professor at the University of Virginia who had served as the assistant general counsel for the United States Arms Control and Disarmament Agency. According to writer Waldemar A. Nielsen, Willrich accepted the appointment on the basis of an explicit understanding with Knowles and the chairman of the board that he would take an activist approach emphasizing policy studies. This new program would have important consequences for Africa.

Chapter Nine: Apartheid and South Africa

Under the aegis of the new Conflict in International Relations program, the Rockefeller Foundation began to look at how it might help ease tensions in southern Africa and contribute to the end of apartheid. From some points of view, South Africa was the most destabilizing nation on the continent. American foreign policy in southern Africa seemed woefully behind developments taking place on the ground, and the Foundation began to look for a way to help clarify the issues and American interests in the region.

According to one of the Foundation's consultants, "The framework [of U.S. policy] that did exist [for southern Africa] was drawn up in 1969 and proved to be weakened by false premises. It assumed, in the language of a U.S. National Security Council memorandum, that whites were in South Africa to stay and that U.S. policy would be tailored to this reality. In 1976, when Secretary of State Kissinger, who served under President Richard Nixon, began to readjust U.S. policy to reflect the new realities of an independent Mozambique and Angola, he found his efforts jeopardized by diminished U.S. credibility in the region." Existing American policy, such as it was, also made it difficult for the United States

Elected in 1976, President Jimmy Carter believed the United States should do more to address racial injustice in southern Africa and to promote peace in the Middle East. In meetings with President Anwar Sadat, Carter brokered an agreement between Egypt and Israel. His administration antagonized officials in South Africa by openly opposing apartheid. (Warren K. Leffler. Library of Congress.)

In 1978 demonstrators protested South Africa's refusal to withdraw from Namibia and allow free elections. Namibia, formerly known as South West Africa, was one of several African territories that had been colonies of Germany prior to World War One. After Germany's defeat, it was supposed to be managed under a League of Nations (later United Nations) mandate. South Africa, instead, tried to annex the territory. (Alon Reininger. United Nations.)

to influence the wide variety of militant movements for independence in southern Africa, and ceded the ground of national liberation to the Soviet Union.

Nixon's successor, President Jimmy Carter, was determined to break from Cold War orthodoxy and make human rights a centerpiece of his foreign policy. His promise to increase U.S. attention to Africa seemed to offer an opportunity for the Foundation to provide constructive assistance. As James P. Grant, the president of the Rockefeller Foundation-funded Overseas Development Council, a Washington, D.C. think tank, pointed out, "Although the Carter administration seems prepared to make rather far-reaching changes in U.S. policy toward Africa it cannot take these steps without public support. The government needs a sounding board to test its ideas on Africa policy, and may find it useful to have a private organization able to develop support for new policies on Africa."

Decades earlier, in the 1920s and the 1940s, the Rockefeller Foundation had tried to help promote health training and educational opportunities for black South Africans, but it had been thwarted by the country's racial policies. The Foundation had operated a virus laboratory in Johannesburg in collaboration with the South African Institute for Medical Research for many years. And in the mid-1970s, it had invested $145,000 for six

Chapter Nine: Apartheid and South Africa

fellowships and sponsored a conference on southern Africa, but it was new territory for the Foundation to consider playing such an overt role in the formulation of American policy.

Knowles asked Terry Myers, an independent foreign relations expert, to assess the pros and cons of Foundation sponsorship of a national commission to review American policy on behalf of the Carter administration. "For the last decade and a half, the United States has had no clear policy towards Africa," Myers reported. "It has been a policy of fits and starts." A policy review by an independent commission could be very valuable, but Myers was cautious about how to proceed. A commission whose recommendations favored "black nationalists supported by the frontline nations" by advocating a strong trade or arms embargo of South Africa could upset traditional American allies, including Great Britain, Iran, and Israel, all of whom had relations with South Africa. "It might also prove unacceptable, domestically, to adopt a policy that would appear to abandon white interests in South Africa, and it might—if it isolated South Africa—create a pariah nation, uninterested in following U.S. interests on questions such as nuclear proliferation and arms sales."

Nevertheless, as Myers advised, the larger historical context required involvement. South African apartheid was anathema to American values, and the civil rights movement in the United States was demanding action. Moreover, American industry needed stable access to South African minerals and security for ships passing the Cape of Good Hope. South Africa had also made itself a rogue nation by developing nuclear weapons and taking an interventionist approach that threatened its neighbors. Perhaps the most powerful historical agent was the increasing militancy of the South African black community, which had moved far beyond the civil rights demands of inclusion to a formal program of national independence and guerrilla warfare.

With Myers's report in hand, Knowles recommended to the board of trustees that the Foundation move forward. In June 1977 the trustees appropriated $250,000 for an "initiative to establish an independent national commission on U.S. policy toward Africa." The trustees were explicit about the purposes of the commission: "to identify and assess the opportunities for and limitations of the U.S. role in southern Africa; to increase public understanding of the changes occurring within the region and the implications of alternative U.S. courses of action; and to provide the U.S. government with an independent assessment of these alternatives."

The trustees were ambivalent, however, about how the Foundation would be involved in this work and how the Study Commission on U.S. Policy Toward Southern Africa would interact with the U.S. government. According to the resolution establishing the group, "The commission would be—and must appear to be—independent and balanced. But it is essential that the group have encouragement and cooperation from the highest levels of the U.S. government." The trustees even expected that President Carter or Secretary of State Vance should be ready to "invite a distinguished American to form the commission."

The most serious concern about getting directly involved seemed to be the very real possibility that the Carter administration's policies and the events in Africa were evolving so quickly that they would make a thoughtful commission report irrelevant by the time it was published. But the commission would also face challenges building credibility with different racial groups in the United States, Africa, and the rest of the world.

Forming the Commission

After weeks of internal review, Knowles turned to Franklin Thomas to conduct a "feasibility study" for the project and to make a formal proposal to the Foundation. Thomas, a graduate of Columbia Law School, had been deputy commissioner of the New York City Police Department and the Bedford Stuyvesant Restoration Corporation. In the middle of his work on the proposed commission, Thomas would be selected as the first African-American president of the Ford Foundation.

As Thomas planned a schedule and developed a budget, while collecting nominations for potential commission members, he and Knowles fielded concerns from staff and trustees. The commission would push the Foundation deeper into African affairs at a time when actual program investments were being withdrawn because of budget pressures. One advisor cautioned Thomas, "Foundation funds might be more usefully applied in southern Africa through other strategies, such as fellowships and institution building."

A remarkable number of outside comments also flowed into Knowles's office. Henry Kissinger supported the idea of the commission. Outgoing Ford Foundation President McGeorge Bundy, who had served as national security advisor to U.S. presidents Kennedy and Johnson, told Knowles, "South Africa policy symbolized by apartheid is not only morally repugnant but both murderous and suicidal." Bundy argued that the commission report could be very valuable. A report that started from the "proposition that apartheid is inescapably destructive will so startle the center and the right that RF will not, on balance, be seen as false to its own convictions."

There was a definite pattern to the comments and suggestions. Individuals with real experience in Africa, who were aware of how quickly events were moving, recommended that the Foundation take action. Donald Woods, the

exiled South African journalist who had been a friend of the Pan-Africanist militant Steve Biko, was a Nieman Fellow at Harvard University in 1978. He encouraged Knowles to make sure the commission reached out to the liberation movements. "Put bluntly, the main need of the U.S. is to make up a lot of ground lost to the Russians in Africa during the Nixon-Ford years."

Richard Sklar, a political scientist from the University of California, Los Angeles, who had been a young professor on assignment at the University of Ibadan during the University Development Program, argued that President Carter's desire to reconsider American policy in southern Africa "implies nothing less than an American commitment to the cause of racial equality." He detailed the stakes: $1.6 billion in U.S. investments in South Africa, loans totaling $263 million, and 350 American corporations with a presence there. But Sklar was skeptical that the United States could control events in the region. Among the liberation movements, he argued, race and socialism were fused. To be credible, he recommended, "The membership of the commission, therefore, should include individuals who are associated with liberation support activities in the United States in addition to individuals from the spheres of business, religion, national security studies, and Africanist scholarship."

Perhaps the most aggressive voice was that of Dunstan Wai, an Oxford-educated Sudanese scholar holding a visiting research fellowship with the International Relations Division of the Foundation. Wai's book *Interdependence in a World of Unequals* had just been published by the Foundation. In a lengthy memorandum to Deagle and Thomas, Wai described conditions all across Africa as "desperate," but he argued that the proposed commission should keep its focus exclusively on southern Africa, which he described as the most pressing problem on the continent. Wai was critical of existing U.S. foreign policy in the region. "Black African countries are unanimously agreed on one issue, that Africa will not be at peace with the world until the southern Africa crisis is resolved. . . . It is widely believed in Africa that the U.S. actively supports the South African regime. . . . It is also believed that if the United States simply stands by as it had done in the last two decades, white racism and repression will deepen, Black resentment and revolt will eventually spread and there will ensue a violent confrontation with ominous implications for U.S./African relations and for U.S. international standing." Wai concluded by bluntly warning the Foundation that "the United States cannot design blueprints for Africa's development. It can only work effectively if it seeks cooperation with African governments in behalf of their development. In other words, the problems of independent Africa are going to be decided by Africans in Africa."

John Stremlau of the international relations staff wrote to Thomas in July 1978, worried that the Carter administration had already moved far ahead of the commission, putting its work in jeopardy. The debate over the role of the commission had shifted dramatically in two years. In early 1977 the commission had been seen as a proposal to give cover to President Carter's plans to move in a new direction. By the second half of 1978 the staff warned that "the establishment of a Rockefeller Foundation supported national commission risked being construed as the 'establishment's' reaction to Carter's new Africa policy and might easily become a brake on the administration." John Stremlau noted that "After neglecting the problems of poverty and underdevelopment in Africa for so long it struck some as regrettable that the escalating violence in southern Africa should now be rewarded by greater attention from the American foreign policy establishment and there was concern expressed that this would be seen in Africa as another indication of white America's preoccupation with kith and kin and protection of the status quo."

Fundamentally, staff and trustees at the Rockefeller Foundation recognized that there were major risks involved in launching such a commission. In his concept report to the Foundation, Thomas identified a key concern: A consensus commission would work to the middle and stifle voices and ideas on the margin. In situations where "fringe" or "leading edge" voices had had ample time to promote their ideas and try to win supporters, a consensus-driven approach was appropriate. In South Africa, according to Thomas, "leading edge views [were] just beginning to emerge" and had not had sufficient time to enter the mainstream of debate. A commission might cut short this conversation.

There were other risks as well, including the possibility that the commission would have little impact, if any, or that it would find itself at cross-purposes with the U.S. government. There was also a possibility that commissioners chosen for the diversity of their points of view would become factionalized. Throughout its history, however, the Foundation had tackled projects that faced overwhelming odds—efforts to eradicate disease or to increase the food supply and feed hundreds of millions of people. As one reviewer concluded, a Foundation-sponsored commission on U.S. policy in southern Africa was likely to be highly original while offering significant potential for influencing the policies of the U.S. government, private American businesses, and NGOs.

Moving Forward

On December 4, 1978, the trustees deepened their commitment to the concept of the commission by authorizing $600,000 to support its initial work. Progress was delayed, however, because John Knowles had been diagnosed with cancer. The prognosis was not good, and he died in March 1979. While the trustees worked to choose his successor, Sterling Wortman, a long-time Foundation officer, served as acting president. He announced the grant and the creation of the commission in August 1979.

The eleven-person Study Commission on U.S. Policy Toward Southern Africa included two corporate executives, the presidents of the Ford Foundation and Carnegie Corporation, a representative of the AFL-CIO, several strong civil rights voices, and the presidents of two universities. It also included one scholar with direct experience in African affairs (Constance Hilliard), but no one who had direct contact with the liberation movements as Richard Sklar had recommended. The commission relied on a staff of 14, three advisors, 79 consultants, and 13 editorial consultants.

The commission devoted the next two years to research—including study trips to Africa—and dozens of commission meetings. Its substantial report was published by the Foreign Policy Study Association in 1981 under the title *South Africa: Time Running Out*. Released in May, the report was broadly distributed to policymakers and news organizations in the United States, Europe, and southern Africa. Copies were sent to the governors of all American states, to Congressional leaders, and to the CEOs of Fortune 500 companies as well as the 350 companies with operations in South Africa.

As the review in *Foreign Affairs* noted, the commission's report was replete with facts and figures, but also "lifted by a moving series of interviews with a cross section of South Africans." It provided a rich insight into the movements and forces shaping the growing crisis, but the review also said that a desire to find consensus among widely different points of view "muffles significant insights."

The report underscored the need for an activist U.S. policy toward South Africa. It called for strengthening the arms embargo to include subsidiaries of U.S. companies; a nuclear embargo designed to contain South Africa's development of nuclear weapons; and a policy of withholding diplomatic recognition and economic aid from the independent homelands created by apartheid policy until such time as the black majority in South Africa had obtained "an effective share in political power." The report recommended that American corporations not expand their operations in South Africa and that those not already in-country make no new investments. It did not embrace the perspective of people seeking the most dramatic and immediate changes in U.S. policy, including disinvestment.

While the study commission's impact on U.S. policy would be limited, in large part due to a new administration in the White House, its report generated a number of editorials in leading newspapers in the United States. The *Chicago Tribune* called it "an unusually thoughtful study." The *Los Angeles Times* agreed with the report's main thesis, that widespread bloodshed was inevitable if whites in South Africa continued to perpetuate the status quo. In South Africa, newspapers took note of the report. The *Rand Daily Mail* suggested that it was likely "to spark off a heated debate in American business circles" regarding investment policies.

Mfanafuthi Johnstone Makatini, the African National Congress's representative to the United Nations, testified before a U.N. special committee in March 1981 as the U.N. prepared for an international conference on sanctions against South Africa. The Study Commission's report was released as this conference convened in May 1981. (Saw Lwin. United Nations.)

When *South Africa: Time Running Out* was published, Ronald Reagan had already replaced Jimmy Carter. After submitting copies of the report to the White House, Thomas received cordial thank-you notes from several members of President Reagan's staff—including Edwin Meese, Michael Deaver, and Chief of Staff James Baker—but he was never able to meet with the president to present the commission's findings. Jeffrey Gayner, the director of Foreign Policy Studies at the Heritage Foundation, wrote Thomas to express his disappointment at what he called the commission's "narrow perspective" on the topic and suggested that for this reason it would be "much less useful to the Reagan administration than it might have been." Indeed, Reagan retreated from the Carter reforms and returned to the "constructive engagement" policy of the late 1960s. He refused to pressure the South African government on civil rights reforms.

Still, the Foundation learned valuable lessons. When the Conflict in International Relations program was launched, Knowles argued that the initiative was in the Foundation's self-interest. "The realization of other Foundation objectives will depend to a large degree on the development of a more stable world order," Knowles wrote in the 1973 President's Review. Knowles had hoped that the program would "be directed toward the support of measures for the anticipation, avoidance, and resolution of conflicts that are likely to disrupt the international community, and the development of international institutions with greater capacity for dealing effectively with emerging issues of global interdependency."

While the work of the commission could not have this kind of substantial impact on foreign affairs, it helped focus thinking at the Rockefeller Foundation and elsewhere regarding philanthropy's role in southern Africa during the height of apartheid. To leaders at the Foundation, the experience with the commission revealed that the Foundation's historic efforts to focus on the basic needs of people for food and health were most effective at the grassroots. Whatever was going on in the world, it seemed to become clear that the Foundation needed to do what it did best, which was develop human and structural capacity to meet the challenges of life, education, health, and equality faced by African communities every day. As the Foundation began to develop a fundamentally new approach to work in the developing nations of Africa, it would give partnerships and collaboration a renewed priority as the way to build capacity not only within local communities but also entire nations.

AFRICA AND
THE GREEN REVOLUTION

The financial crisis that hit many charitable organizations in the 1970s, caused by dramatic inflation and a prolonged decline in the value of stocks and other assets, led to a profound shift in the Rockefeller Foundation's strategy. It also marked the beginning of a third major era in the Foundation's work in Africa. The first 40 years had been defined by frustration. Research laboratories and study teams had gathered information and developed recommendations for programs. But efforts to promote public health and medical education for black Africans had been stymied by colonial authorities or the racial policies of white leaders in southern Africa.

In 1956 the second major era in the Foundation's work in Africa began when President Dean Rusk and the board of trustees made a major financial commitment to the developing world. With the global expansion of work in agriculture, which became known as the Green Revolution, and the creation of the University Development Program, the Foundation moved "from the library and the laboratory into the fields and streets." By 1965 the Rockefeller Foundation had 22 staff stationed in four African nations working in agriculture, humanities, social sciences, university development, medical education, and public health. It was indirectly funding dozens of scholars and visiting faculty at universities throughout the continent. This direct engagement contributed to a major increase in the Foundation's worldwide field staff, from 57 employees in 1955 to 148 by 1967. With the financial crisis of the

The Rockefeller Foundation promoted research on maize in association with institutions in Egypt, Uganda, and Nigeria in the mid-1960s as part of the International Maize Improvement Program. (Marc & Evelyne Bernheim. Rockefeller Archive Center.)

1970s, however, the Foundation could no longer sustain this level of operations. Under President John Knowles, the Foundation reduced its field staff dramatically, to 49 people by 1980.

Money was not the only reason for reducing field operations in the developing world. As Knowles's successor, Richard Lyman, acknowledged in 1981, "There has always been at least ambivalence, if not antagonism toward outside experts on the part of the population being served." Rockefeller Foundation officer Joyce Moock, an anthropologist who had been the Foundation's assistant director of social sciences, echoed Lyman's insights. In an analysis of the history of the Foundation's field staff operations, she pointed out that developing countries were no longer tolerant of highly visible expatriate staff in key positions within their national institutions. Neither were they willing to allow foreigners to bypass normal administrative channels or cut through bureaucratic red tape to launch new initiatives.

Other factors were also driving the need for a new strategy in Africa and other parts of the developing world. The Rockefeller Foundation and other non-governmental organizations (NGOs) were increasingly disenchanted with the big ideas that had fueled development theory during the first two decades after World War Two. As Moock would later point out for the Foundation's trustees, "Even where spectacular economic growth has been achieved, some of the fundamental and dramatic effects—upon income distribution, class stratification, land tenure and inheritance systems, human rights, gender roles, urban congestion, traditional values, forms of governance, and political stability— were not anticipated, nor were they well understood."

Lyman recognized what had been missing from the Foundation's approach to Africa for 60 years when he wrote that "Third World perspectives have seldom been incorporated into the formulation of development theory. Concepts have usually been articulated in the industrial North and exported, as a package, to the South." A new strategy demanded a greater emphasis on collaboration with other foundations and NGOs, and most of all with the people of Africa.

American Botanist Homer LeRoy Shantz conducted research in Africa. A member of the Rockefeller Foundation's education commission in 1925, he studied and praised African farming techniques. (University of Arizona.)

All of these critical insights led to a new approach that marked the beginning of a third era in the Rockefeller Foundation's work in Africa, one that reflected a new philosophy of practice. But as the next four chapters in this book highlight, new programs were built upon the experience of previous explorations and initiatives. In agriculture, population sciences, education, and health care, the Rockefeller Foundation's track record and expertise allowed it to bring to the table collaborators from different backgrounds and disciplines to frame innovative ways to address the opportunities and challenges facing Africa at the end of the twentieth century.

In the case of agriculture, some of the most useful insights for this work had been offered half a century earlier.

Learning from African Farmers

Homer LeRoy Shantz understood the importance of agriculture for development in Africa. A respected American botanist who had earned his Ph.D. from the University of Nebraska, Shantz was a member of a Rockefeller Foundation-funded commission on education in Africa in 1925. He took detailed notes on the flora and fauna of East Africa, studied farming techniques, and developed a deep respect for African agriculture.

"The agricultural methods of the Natives in Africa have often been condemned as shiftless, wasteful and destined to decrease the productivity of the country," Shantz wrote. "These statements, in a way, reflect the attitude of the European toward the Native, the assumption that since he does not follow our methods and our practices he must be essentially wrong. But there are many testimonies in the literature to the effect that the Native is an excellent agriculturalist." Shantz described the local methods of allowing land to lie fallow and regenerate. He described the diversity of small farms, the farmers' opposition to "continuous cropping" of a single crop, and their use of cattle manure to fertilize and restore the soil. "Natives, by their method of abandoning the land and taking a new piece, accomplish what the European, with all his staff of scientifically trained men, has not yet satisfactorily accomplished."

During his travels in East and Central Africa Shantz observed African agriculturalists breaking new land; cutting and burning timber or brush; and planting, weeding, protecting, and harvesting their crops. He was impressed that African farmers worked their land year round, often producing multiple harvests. He admired the ways in which African farmers selected and rotated land for cultivation to ensure new, rich soil, free from harmful bacteria, fungi, and insects, "thereby avoiding the two greatest problems of modern agriculture, the maintenance of soil fertility and physical condition and

When Homer Shantz visited South Africa, Fort Hare College was one of the only educational institutions that offered advanced training in scientific agriculture to black South Africans. The school began offering a diploma in Agriculture and Business Proficiency beginning in 1916. (Rockefeller Archive Center.)

the avoidance of plant diseases." Unlike Europeans and Americans, Shantz stated in his report to the commission, Africans often planted a diversity of crops to create ecological synergies. They avoided planting monocultures in repeated seasons.

Shantz studied the unique characteristics of different farmers. The Wachagga were growing coffee on the slopes of Kilimanjaro "and have small plantations of [coffee] trees excellently cared for, and have shown considerable ingenuity in pulping and handling a new crop." The Tutsi living in the present day country of Burundi planted crops along rivers and lowland streams during the dry season, and "utilize the available streams for irrigating and show engineering skill in diverting streams and constructing aqueducts."

Shantz made several recommendations about agricultural education. He suggested that Africans did not need to be told how to prepare land or when and what to plant, but, like most American farmers, they would benefit from a greater knowledge of natural science. He also suggested that schools needed to recognize and build on the central role of women in agriculture.

In 1925 Shantz concluded that African villagers were quite capable of feeding themselves. But he cautioned that integrating African agriculture into global markets would distort landholding patterns and disrupt tribal life. He was critical of the impact of tribal reserves in South Africa—where large populations were forced onto lands with poor soil—and the expanding settler plantations in Kenya and Uganda. His greatest concern was the potential for

European plantations and export-based agriculture to reduce African farmers to cheap labor on white plantations. "If this country is developed as a white man's country, it will result in pushing back the Native population or making them laborers on white plantations. It would soon break down the Native tribal rule, remove the Native from the land as a producer and result in the complete domination of the country."

Shantz's report was prescient, but it represented only a small portion of the commission's larger study of education in Africa. Against the backdrop of colonial rule in 1925, the Foundation was unable to identify a promising strategy for work in this arena. But Shantz's insights would echo over subsequent decades as the Foundation looked for ways to help African communities feed their populations.

The Green Revolution

In 1943 the Rockefeller Foundation launched an experimental program in Mexico designed to increase agricultural yields. The project focused on improving the seed varieties cultivated by farmers, increasing fertilization, diversifying crops, limiting soil erosion, and improving irrigation. Measured by the increase in the volume of food produced, the experiment was enormously successful. In the 1950s the program was expanded to other Latin American countries and then to Asia and Africa. Retitled the Conquest of Hunger program, the results were dubbed the "Green Revolution" in the 1960s.

In Mexico and other countries, the Green Revolution played a key role in expanding food production. In Africa, however, the Rockefeller Foundation's agricultural scientists and their local partners faced unique challenges. Under the colonial regime, a two-tiered land policy encouraged large-scale expropriation of the best agricultural lands by white farmers who were engaged in the export economy. Meanwhile, black farmers were forced to cultivate marginal lands for subsistence. This situation gave rise to intense political conflict in a number of countries. The Mau Mau rebellion in Kenya, for example, reflected a fierce fight for land equity and self-determination. Prior to independence, these issues made it difficult for NGOs to push for a cooperative approach to development.

As African countries became independent, the Rockefeller Foundation sought to replicate its model for agricultural development in Africa. Through the University Development Program (as described in Chapter Eight), the Foundation supported the development of agricultural sciences at leading universities and funded agricultural research stations. In Kenya, for example, the Foundation, Oxfam, and other NGOs helped spark what became known as

"the little green revolution," leading to increased wheat and maize production. This work helped inform a second major phase in the development of the Foundation's Conquest of Hunger program.

In the 1960s President George Harrar also launched a presidential initiative to build a network of international research institutes designed explicitly to work on broad agricultural themes as well as individual crop improvement. This effort had the potential to transfer discoveries by agricultural scientists to fields and farms around the world. In addition the institutes would make it possible to leverage the Foundation's prestige as the original sponsor of the Green Revolution to involve a wider variety of funding agencies. The Rockefeller and Ford Foundations, for example, worked together to create the International Rice Research Institute in the Philippines in 1962 and the International Maize and Wheat Improvement Center (CIMMYT) in Mexico in 1966. In 1968 the Foundation opened the International Center for Tropical Agriculture in Colombia.

The institutes were experimental, but they had tremendous potential to create an international network of agricultural scientists offering easy access to their research. They also created an opportunity for scientists to move beyond research on single crops to integrate strategies for soil management or the control of insect pests and plant diseases common to all tropical regions. Wheat research provided by CIMMYT in Mexico, for example, was used in 19 nations and was instrumental in saving India from imminent famine. High-lysine corn research from CIMMYT helped many nations, including Kenya.

In 1967, with the launch of the International Institute of Tropical Agriculture (IITA) at Ibadan, Nigeria, this new institutional approach was expanded to Africa. A stable school of agriculture at the University of Ibadan played a key role in the selection of the University of Ibadan as the site for the new institute.

Partnerships with governments and other funders, especially the Ford Foundation, were critical to the strategy for developing these institutes. In 1971 these partnerships led to a long-term plan for management of the institutes. The World Bank, the United Nations Development Programme, the African Development Bank, a wide variety of other funding agencies, 13 nations, and the Rockefeller, Ford, and W.K. Kellogg foundations joined forces to create a new Consultative Group on International Agricultural Research (CGIAR). Together, these funders provided a block grant of $35 million to launch the new framework.

The CGIAR, in turn, helped launch additional new entities in Africa, including the International Laboratory for Research on Animal Diseases (ILRAD) in Kenya and the International Livestock Centre for Africa in Ethiopia. Additionally, the Foundation funded a network of smaller research institutes, including the East African Veterinary Research Organisation, the East African Agriculture and Forestry Research Organization, and the plant breeding research station at Njoro, Kenya, which supported critical research into sorghum and millet production.

The International Institute of Tropical Agriculture at Ibadan opened in 1967. It was part of a network of international research institutes launched by the Rockefeller Foundation and other funders to improve agriculture in developing countries. (Rockefeller Archive Center.)

The Foundation continued to make various grants to CGIAR network of international institutes. The International Institute of Tropical Agriculture in Nigeria, the West Africa Rice Development Association (WARDA) in Liberia, and the International Laboratory for Research on Animal Diseases in Kenya all received large grants in the 1980s, and a senior Rockefeller Foundation staff member served as interim director of WARDA when it experienced management difficulties in 1985.

The evolving partnership that helped create and sustain CGIAR and the other agricultural institutes provided a path to sustainability and stimulated enormous investments by others in the development of agriculture in the developing world and especially in Africa. With support from the World Bank, various international agencies, and NGOs, CGIAR was able to invest $185 million in 1985 alone. Indeed, the lessons learned from the creation of these institutions would provide a powerful model for the Foundation's work in agriculture and other arenas in Africa that would continue to evolve over the next several decades.

SEARCHING FOR A NEW STRATEGY

When the Rockefeller Foundation reduced its field operations, it searched for a new strategy to sustain its work in agriculture. Various grants supported the exploration of new approaches in the mid-1980s, including $20,000 for the Equator Foundation in Hartford, Connecticut, "to support the creation and expansion of a marketing plan for a chicken farm in Zambia (1986)"; $500,000 of support "to institutionalize a social science research support unit to the International Centre of Insect Physiology and Ecology in Nairobi (1987)"; $100,000 "toward a study on cassava and maize research needs and priorities in eleven coastal countries of West Africa (1987)"; and $360,000 for the International Fertilizer Development Center in Muscle Shoals, Alabama, used to study soil fertility in Africa (1988).

Throughout the 1980s, periodic droughts led to widespread famine in parts of Africa, even as the birthrate rose to three percent per year. As a result, Africa was the only continent to experience a decline in per capita food production. Policymakers worried that Africa faced the prospect of acute and continuing food shortages. The Foundation sought to train a new generation of agricultural scientists in demography and human health as well as food production. One such project placed African social scientists in postdoctoral fellowship programs with international research centers. These ten annual fellowships hoped to train a "future generation of African social scientists versed in multidisciplinary research and sensitive to the human and social complexities inherent in the agricultural transformation process." The Foundation also explored the possibility of expanding its assistance for scientific training to the pre-doctoral level for young Africans, enhancing its effectiveness and relevance in a region with relatively few scholars trained to the doctorate level. All of these explorations confronted the fundamental challenge of trying to increase the available human capital in the field of agriculture.

After the Foundation restructured its Agricultural Sciences Division in the mid-1980s, the postdoctoral fellowship program was expanded and focused increasingly on "application of technology" by "strengthening the often fragile linkages between research centers and country efforts." A new, more cohesive strategy toward Africa was developed in 1985 that included Improving Family Food Production Systems.

This new program sought to strengthen national agricultural research systems to improve the food-production strategies of farming families in sub-Saharan Africa. The project supported both individuals and institutions, and emphasized biological as well as socioeconomic research on crops such as roots and tubers that were the "nutritional mainstay of much of the population." The Foundation provided support to two institutions funded by the CGIAR, for example, to study cassava, a shrubby

Immunologist Keith Banks and Jane Ngaira at the International Laboratory for Research on Animal Diseases (ILRAD) in Kabete, Kenya studied bovine white blood cells in an effort to prevent insect-borne diseases. ILRAD was part of a network of research institutes launched by the Rockefeller Foundation and other NGOs in Africa. (Marion Kaplan. Rockefeller Archive Center.)

plant grown for its edible root that was widely cultivated by the "very poor in sub-Saharan Africa" and provided at least 50 percent of the calories consumed by nearly 200 million Africans. With over $2 million from the Rockefeller Foundation, researchers in nine African countries examined a wide range of issues, including the growing, processing, consumption, and marketing of cassava. African agricultural graduate students also received support to work on the cassava project as part of their doctoral research, and the Foundation funded a social science research unit at the International Centre of Insect Physiology and Ecology in Nairobi, Kenya. This unit aimed to evaluate "farmers' needs, wants, and the appropriateness of new technology for pest control." All of these initiatives began to suggest a new way to use agriculture as part of an integrated strategy for development.

I
n the mid-1980s President Richard Lyman had convened a trustee task force to look at the Foundation's historic commitment to science and technology. Like many of his predecessors, he was concerned that political and social issues often undermined the promise of new technologies. He wondered whether the Foundation should focus more on these obstacles to development. The trustees, however, "concluded that science and technology born of scientific advance remain tremendously important and that progress in these areas is indeed a necessary, although not sufficient, condition of improved living standards in poor countries." The trustees also decided that "in the search for that elusive prize, 'comparative advantage,' ours lay in continued work in these fields."

To improve the use of this technology and promote interdisciplinary thinking, the Foundation created the International Program to Support Science-Based Development in 1986. This new program operated on the "premise that scientific advance and technical innovation can serve the cause of international equity by helping to reduce the incidence of poverty, disease, malnutrition, unwanted pregnancies and illiteracy in developing countries, and thereby advance the well-being of their peoples." The program sought to distribute scientific knowledge and technology more equitably across the world. It also made agricultural science just one of many tools designed to promote food security, as part of a holistic paradigm of development that included health and population control. Acting through third parties and partnerships, the Foundation promoted scientific research and technology in the laboratory, but sought to disburse this learning to those "neglected" regions that needed it most.

The Foundation's strategy paralleled the work of others in Africa. In 1985 the member countries of the Organization of African Unity resolved to devote 20 to 25 percent of their national budgets to agriculture by 1989. As Thomas Odhiambo, the director of the International Centre of Insect Physiology and Ecology in Nairobi, put it, "What we are trying to do is see how to move Africa out of its present problems in agriculture. We believe an extremely important part of that is to strategically use agricultural research as a motor or engine for that development."

In the early 1990s the Foundation provided additional resources for an interdisciplinary approach by creating an African Initiatives program to address the needs of the continent. The Foundation also added new personnel, hiring economist John Lynam to run its East Africa programs. It recruited Malcolm Blackie, former dean of agriculture at the University of Zimbabwe, to lead the

Foundation's southern Africa programs. And it supported local professional development. In 1989, for example, the Foundation cooperatively funded Zimbabwe's Agriculture Faculty to develop a graduate program to train the country's future research and extension staff, and to form ties with the small farm community.

Expanded funding was also directed toward diversifying crops. With support from the Foundation, Washington University in St. Louis, Missouri, applied biotechnology techniques used on tomato and tobacco plants to improve cassava. This project became the starting point for supporting a modest international research network for new biotechnology research on cassava that eventually became critical to the Foundation's agricultural work in Africa. New blight-resistant varieties of cassava were introduced in 30 African countries in the late 1980s. The Foundation also funded a cooperative project with Makerere University and the Uganda government to increase banana productivity. Another project supported maize research to help small farmers in Malawi.

At the same time, the Foundation supported research related to environmental issues affecting agriculture in Africa, especially as they related to soil fertility, water management, and livestock. The Foundation's Global Environmental Program, launched in 1989, provided grants to study continuous cropping systems and cultivation strategies based on an understanding of ecological systems to enhance soil productivity and sustainability. Meanwhile, through the Tropical Soil Biology and Fertility Programme (TSBF), scientists in Kenya, Zambia, and Zimbabwe studied the biological processes in tropical soil to improve crop yields.

All of these research projects aimed to solve immediate problems and also to increase the capacity of African scientists and institutions to formulate and address critical issues in agricultural science in Africa. In the mid-1980s one World Bank official had estimated that Africa had only about 2,500 agricultural researchers, but needed about 25,000. The Foundation endeavored to help increase this supply of human capital, supporting the Forum on Agricultural Resource Husbandry, for example, which worked to strengthen graduate education in Kenya, Malawi, Uganda, and Zimbabwe. By providing competitive grants for master's degree students to study soil- and crop-management field research with an eye on policy and farmers, the forum functioned as a research network linking more than a dozen institutions in eastern and southern Africa.

The Foundation's programs in Africa were specifically designed to support low-income, small-holder farmers. In Malawi, for example, a program started in the late 1980s aimed to increase maize production among small-holder

farmers by looking at soil, agro-forestry practices, weeding, and pest and disease damage measurement.

Even where Foundation-funded projects were successful, however, they were overshadowed by a looming food crisis in Africa. Some compared the situation to India in the 1960s. Policy reforms and investments by governments and NGOs had resulted in only limited improvements in agricultural productivity. Periodic droughts in East Africa and other parts of the continent led to food shortages and crises. The situation discouraged policymakers in Africa and in the NGO community. At the close of the 1990s, under the leadership of a new president, the Foundation once again began to look for a more effective approach to African agriculture.

To help maintain the soil, Rockefeller Foundation advisors in 1967 recommended planting nitrogen-fixing cowpeas with tall crops like millet. For Hausa women in Nigeria these protein-rich legumes were a staple of the family diet. (Rockefeller Archive Center.)

The specter of imminent famine in Asia in the 1960s had propelled the first Green Revolution. The mandate had been to increase yields, and the scientists had done a spectacular job by any measure. But when Gordon Conway was selected to lead the Foundation in 1998, he faced two equally pressing problems. First, the techniques of the Green Revolution had never been successfully transferred to Africa. Population continued to outpace improvements in agricultural productivity and marketing. Africa's complexity seemed to daunt the initiatives of the Foundation and other NGOs working in agriculture. The Foundation cited a host of reasons, including "complex weather conditions, limited government capacity, scant infrastructure, and markets for both inputs and crops that remain concentrated in cities and coastal areas." The second major problem Conway faced was related to Africa's wide variability of soils, weak finance and marketing systems, its vast array of crops, the presence of myriad crop diseases, its land tenure systems trapped between small-scale subsistence farms and large-scale industrial farms, and its widespread poverty. The combination of these factors precluded the irrigated monoculture models of the original Green Revolution and made it difficult for national agricultural systems to benefit from narrow research in commodity crops. Western governments and the NGO community also shared some responsibility for the situation as aid commitments for agriculture declined or became increasingly unstable.

Conway and others at the Rockefeller Foundation recognized that the Green Revolution depended on the heavy use of synthetic fertilizers and irrigation, which created unintended environmental consequences. Furthermore, the high cost of inputs and machinery favored large landowners, which did not further the Foundation's goal of promoting greater income equality and stability among the poor.

Africa needed a new Green Revolution adapted to the realities of Africa. In some sense, it demanded a return to the vision articulated by Homer Shantz 80 years earlier, anchored in the expertise of small African farmers but complemented by science.

The Rockefeller Foundation's new president in 1998 understood this vision. Before coming to the Foundation, Conway had conducted field research in various locations in Asia and the Middle East on behalf of the Ford Foundation, World Bank, and USAID. He was known for pioneering Integrated Pest Management in the 1960s and for articulating the concept of sustainable agriculture in the 1970s. He seemed to blend pragmatism and idealism in his vision for development and agriculture.

Under Conway, the Rockefeller Foundation restructured its programs to focus on four core program themes: Food Security, Creativity and Culture, Working Communities, and Health Equity. "Cross themes" promoted interdisciplinary and integrated strategies. These themes and cross themes aimed to help the world's poor in an integrated and interdisciplinary fashion, grounded in focused regional activities in Africa, Asia, Latin America, and the West Coast of the United States.

The new Food Security program was more deliberately focused on the needs of the poor than any previous Rockefeller Foundation agricultural program. Moreover, it explicitly subsumed agricultural science under food production, acknowledged the shortcomings of past work, and made Africa a top priority. Grants were awarded in several well-defined categories. "Enabling Farmer Participation" involved small farmers in both the process of defining research needs and implementing innovations based on research discoveries. Grantmaking focused on involving farmers in "setting priorities for and conducting plant breeding, developing seed production and distribution systems, and improving agronomic practices." "Applying Science and Technology" grants sought to promote further cooperation between local scientists and farmers with scientists in the fields of biotechnology, plant breeding, and agroecology. A third grant category, titled "Strengthening Policies and Institutions," emphasized professional development and institution building to strengthen local organizations and influence key policymaking in the interest of food security. In all three categories, grants were focused especially on sub-Saharan Africa and Southeast Asia. At the same time, the Foundation offered a series of grants designed to help nations in Africa and other developing countries wrestle with issues related to the application of new technologies to agriculture. The Foundation gave grants to promote "Global Dialogue on Plant Biotechnology," for example, to help communities and nations address concerns about plant biotechnology and shape policies to cultivate a more stable policy environment for research.

As international interest in promoting African development increased in the early years of the twenty-first century, the Rockefeller Foundation worked with other philanthropies to support higher education across sub-Saharan Africa. Many of these efforts targeted food security and agriculture. The Rockefeller Foundation forged a new partnership with the Carnegie Corporation and the Ford and MacArthur foundations, which came together in 2000 as the Partnership for Higher Education in Africa. The partnership pledged $100 million over five years to support African universities. By 2005 the William and Flora Hewlett Foundation, the Andrew W. Mellon Foundation, and the Kresge Foundation had joined the partnership and it redoubled its initial

investment with a commitment to spend an additional
$200 million. As a part of this initiative, the Rockefeller
Foundation's work with Makerere University was tailored
to the specific needs of regional agricultural research.

As biotechnology became an
increasingly important tool in
agricultural science, the Rockefeller
Foundation created a new grant
program entitled Global Dialogue on
Plant Biotechnology to help developing
nations in Africa and elsewhere address
public concerns. (Jonas Bendiksen.
Rockefeller Foundation.)

African leaders welcomed this new investment, as
well as new interest from the private sector. In 2002,
on the eve of the G8 meeting in Canada and the World
Summit on Sustainable Development, South African
president Thabo Mbeki suggested that "a great moment is
at hand: a chance for developed countries to make a sound investment while
helping to break the cycle of African underdevelopment." Mbeki suggested
that a new "partnership of equals," modeled after the Marshall Plan for Europe
in the wake of World War Two, would raise living standards in Africa, return
profits to investors, and might also "rekindle that humanism that should lie at
the foundation of global relations."

Reflecting its deepening commitment to Africa's progress, the Rockefeller
Foundation opened two regional offices in Africa during this period. Since
1966, the Foundation had maintained an office in Nairobi. After field operations ended in the mid-1980s, the staff was reduced, but its long-time director,
political scientist David Court, remained as the Foundation's representative in
Africa. In 1992 Court was joined in the Nairobi office by Katherine Namuddu,

a senior scientist who worked on education initiatives. In 2000 the Foundation restaffed the Nairobi office under the direction of Cheikh Mbacké, and opened an office in Harare, overseen by Akinwumi Adesina (who was appointed Nigeria's Minister of Agriculture in 2010). Mbacké was a Senegalese population scientist who had received his Ph.D. from the University of Pennsylvania. He had joined the Foundation in 1992 as a senior scientist in the Population Sciences division. Adesina was an agricultural economist from Nigeria who had earned his Ph.D. at Purdue University and worked at several CGIAR-sponsored agricultural institutes in West Africa before joining the Rockefeller Foundation in 1998. With Namuddu, Mbacké, and Adesina on board, the Foundation began a historic shift toward a more African-led staff.

The National Agricultural Research Organisation (NARO) in Uganda was established to promote science-based market oriented agriculture. With grants from the Rockefeller Foundation, NARO research has studied the potential effects of climate change on East African agriculture. (Jonas Bendiksen. Rockefeller Foundation.)

Under this new leadership, the Foundation supported a number of important agricultural initiatives, including the Agricultural Productivity and Food Security Task Force in Zimbabwe, the Maize Productivity Task Force in

Malawi, and the Sustainable Community Oriented Development Programme in Kenya. The Foundation also funded the National Agricultural Research Organization of Uganda to distribute new maize varieties with improved disease resistance and more efficient nitrogen utilization. These new varieties were developed specifically so that farmers could save seed from their harvest for the next planting.

These projects were part of a larger effort to promote more holistic, systemic development that would "build the capacity of African institutions and strengthen their commitment to serving smallholder farmers." At the same time, the Foundation began to make good on Conway's intention to promote local input and responsibility and to cultivate agricultural prosperity by working with the natural environment. Rooted in decades of engagement and learning by doing, these grants fueled progress in African agriculture. Against the backdrop of a growing population, however, an atmosphere of crisis persisted in Africa. As former U.N. Secretary General Kofi Annan pointed out, Africa was the only continent that failed to grow enough food to feed its people. In the twenty-first century, the Rockefeller Foundation's deep experience in Africa was combined with new leadership and the passion of new partners to launch a grand initiative to create a green revolution in Africa.

A Green Revolution in Africa

In the first years of the twenty-first century, the Rockefeller Foundation and its partners in Africa were increasingly interested in working with small farmers and small businesses to ensure food security by stimulating market forces. The Foundation funded and invested in a network of small businesses to develop, package, and distribute seeds, fertilizers, and other materials for small farmers and to create outlets for larger harvests, hoping that market forces would help develop distribution networks for seeds and soil nutrients. Likewise, the Foundation provided grants to cereal banks to help farmers work together to store and sell their produce to get a better return. In keeping with the value it placed on local input and sustainable development, the Foundation offered grants to enhance "resident expertise" in agricultural sciences, on both the individual and institutional levels.

Although many of these initiatives helped build institutional capacity within Africa, Judith Rodin sensed the need for a bolder and more integrated approach after she was named president of the Rockefeller Foundation in 2005. Rodin came to the Foundation from the University of Pennsylvania, where she had been the first woman to head an Ivy League institution. A prominent research psychologist and an accomplished university leader,

she was particularly focused on taking a systems approach to development issues. And she understood the importance of partnerships.

Soon after Rodin became president, she led the Foundation's development of an ambitious partnership with the Bill and Melinda Gates Foundation to launch the Alliance for a Green Revolution in Africa (AGRA). The goals of AGRA were bold. The project sought to fund 40 national seed breeding programs every year with the objective of developing, in five years, 100 new and improved crop varieties suitable to the niche soils and weather of different African regions. It also aimed to provide 200 graduate-level scholarships to train a new generation of African crop scientists. Finally, AGRA aimed to create a network of 10,000 agro-dealers—small businesses to distribute seeds, fertilizers, chemicals, and, most important, the technical knowledge that small farmers would need to make the transition from traditional farming to modern farming. The Rockefeller Foundation's goal over the longer term was to "develop 400 new crop varieties and to eliminate hunger and poverty for tens of millions of people within ten years."

A research psychologist and former president of the University of Pennsylvania, Judith Rodin became president of the Rockefeller Foundation in 2005. Under her leadership, the Foundation launched major pan-African initiatives including the Alliance for a Green Revolution in Africa. (Rockefeller Foundation.)

Chapter Ten: Africa and the Green Revolution

The AGRA partnership focused substantial resources on improving African agriculture. While the Foundation had spent nearly $150 million on Green Revolution work in Africa in the seven years leading up to 2006, for example, AGRA received that much in its first grant appropriation—with $100 million coming from the Gates Foundation and the remaining $50 million from the Rockefeller Foundation—to be distributed over five years.

The partners created the Program for Africa's Seed Systems (PASS) to implement AGRA's goals, and set up an office in Nairobi to monitor and evaluate its results. PASS funded research to develop improved crop varieties. AGRA also focused on improving the distribution of seeds to farmers, and helped develop a network of African agro-dealers. In its first years, AGRA also funded nearly 30 organizations in eight African countries for training African crop scientists at African universities to work within their communities. In addition to providing funds, the Rockefeller Foundation provided two experienced program officers to AGRA—Joe DeVries to lead the work on seeds and Akin Adesina to lead the work on building markets.

In 2007 former United Nations Secretary General Kofi Annan became the first chair of the Alliance. Under his leadership, by 2010, AGRA worked in 13 countries, pursuing a "system-wide approach" to stimulate gains in the quantity and quality of food crops in sub-Saharan Africa. Rockefeller and Gates made significant additional multimillion dollar grants to launch the soil health and markets programs, as well as to focus on policy and innovative financing mechanisms for African agriculture. Its Soil Health Program helped farmers improve the fertility of their fields and its Market Access Program resulted in greatly increased income and decreased food insecurity for farming families. In a speech that year, Annan underscored the importance of AGRA in the context of declining international support for agriculture. In 1980, he pointed out, 18 percent of all development aid was focused on agriculture, compared to only three percent in 2008.

Strategically, the Alliance concentrated investment in the "breadbasket region" of four main countries: Ghana, Mali, Mozambique, and Tanzania. It also supported work in South Africa, Malawi, Zambia, Uganda, Kenya, Ethiopia, Rwanda, Nigeria, Niger, and Burkina Faso. Reflecting the historic pattern of the most successful Rockefeller Foundation initiatives, AGRA's core funding expanded to include resources provided by governments as well as other agencies and international institutions. AGRA was an independent organization and by 2012 it had a board and governance structure whose "approach and leadership are uniquely African."

By 2010, when the first evaluations of the program began to emerge, AGRA leaders reported that researchers had developed 332 improved varieties of maize, wheat, beans, banana, sweet potato, cassava, sorghum, millet, cowpea, and rice adapted to the conditions of Africa. Of those, 183 varieties had been commercialized and were being sold by hundreds of small agro-dealers or distributed by NGOs. AGRA revised its 2006 goals and committed itself to the creation of 750 improved varieties by 2020, as well as doubling the income of 20 million small farmers and cutting food insecurity in half in 20 countries.

AGRA and the Rockefeller Foundation worked together to help African farmers prepare for the growing challenges posed by climate change. Between 2010 and 2012, the Foundation gave $1 million to the United Nations World Food Programme for its Climate and Disaster Risk Solutions (CDRS) unit to partner with the African Union Commission to establish the African Risk Capacity project, a sovereign risk-management system for providing natural disaster assistance to African countries. Foundation grants also supported other innovative projects to promote resilience and food security in sub-Saharan Africa, including a crop and livestock insurance program in Kenya and the Oxfam America Horn of Africa Risk Transfer for Adaptation (HARITA) project. Meanwhile, with support from the Foundation, the Rwanda Meteorological Service and the Walker Institute for Climate System Research of the University of Reading in the United Kingdom began work on climate risk modeling to create a national

Small scale rural agro-dealers in Kenya represent the type of entrepreneur that the Rockefeller Foundation sees as a crucial link between research, improved seeds, farming techniques, and the smallholder farmer. With support from the Foundation, many agro-dealers have received training to help small farmers with cultivation strategies. (Jonas Bendiksen. Rockefeller Foundation.)

Chapter Ten: Africa and the Green Revolution

climate change risk map that will allow researchers to evaluate adaptation strategies. These efforts aimed to build farmers' resilience to climate change and variability to minimize the harmful effects on food security.

As a part of its overall effort to increase agricultural yields in Africa, AGRA funds research in Uganda to develop new seed varieties that will result in hardier and more productive crops. (Jonas Bendiksen. Rockefeller Foundation.)

Overall, the Foundation's new initiatives and partnerships in Africa built upon years of experience. Lessons learned in previous decades—during the University Development Program and the Green Revolution—provided important insights about the unique challenges of African climate, soil, ecology, and social systems that ultimately led to breakthroughs in research and implementation strategies. To be sure, more work needed to be done in Africa, to build on local expertise and leverage the powers of scientific research, as Homer Shantz had recommended in the mid-1920s. By 2013, however, AGRA had established a "credible, promising beachhead" in parts of the continent, from which it was "breaking out." It had helped to reduce the hardships of subsistence farming and address the chronic risks of shortages and starvation faced by farmers. Meanwhile, AGRA and the Rockefeller Foundation continued to seek a "more expansive vision" and promote innovation that would strengthen market systems and improve infrastructure. The success of these efforts, however, would depend on stabilizing the explosive growth of Africa's population.

POPULATION
AND WELL-BEING

The last two decades of the twentieth century marked an important transition for Africa during which the continent experienced new highs, such as the first democratic elections in South Africa and Namibia, and great lows, including the devastating 1994 Rwandan genocide. Population continued to grow at a rapid pace throughout this era, outstripping increases in food production. In the face of a looming crisis, the Rockefeller Foundation, along with other NGOs and national governments, looked for ways to stabilize Africa's growth.

For half a century the Foundation had been a global leader in understanding the relationship between the Green Revolution and population stabilization. The Foundation's longtime chairman, John D. Rockefeller 3rd, had created and funded the Population Council, a research and educational organization focused on issues related to human reproduction and health. He had labored for a decade to push the issue into the top tier of the Foundation's agenda. But President Dean Rusk and the trustees had resisted, afraid that opposition to "population control" from Catholics as well as the Soviets would undercut programs in the developing nations that Rockefeller believed would most benefit from population policies. Meanwhile, population in the emerging nations was growing exponentially, doubling every 30 years in many parts of Africa.

With George Harrar in the 1960s, Rockefeller finally found a partner who shared his view of the essential dynamics of population. Harrar had never

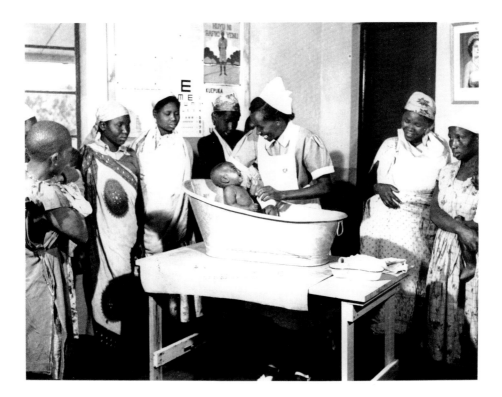

looked upon the increases in crop yields at the heart of the Green Revolution as a technological "fix" to the problem of overpopulation. "Clearly measures must be taken now if the world is to retain any sort of balance between nutrition and numbers," he told a meeting of the American Philosophical Society. "Acceptable ways must be found to decrease population growth rates and, simultaneously, to increase world food supplies. These are the two fundamental and interrelated elements of the modern dilemma."

Rockefeller Foundation President George Harrar understood that population studies, along with agricultural sciences, were essential to Africa's development. To help manage population growth in Kenya, the Foundation supported programs at local health stations to educate women in family planning and in maternal and child heath. (Rockefeller Archive Center.)

Harrar understood runaway human population growth the way a natural scientist would, as a matter of limited resources in an ecosystem, beyond the subjective influence of religion or culture. "No greater challenge faces mankind than the stabilization of population," he warned in his 1963 President's Review. "All must one day understand that no ethically oriented society can survive the erosion of overwhelming numbers of disadvantaged people. Uncontrolled increases in population without consideration of the carrying capacity of the world's natural and man-made resources will render life less and less meaningful."

In their 1963 review of the Foundation's programs, the trustees had placed an emphasis on population science, which became one of five core themes in the "Plans for the Future" report that drove Foundation strategies for the coming decade. But the Foundation's understanding of the population imperative in Asia was dramatically different from its understanding of the issue in Africa, where missionaries had reported that population might actually be declining before World War Two. Even as anecdotal evidence suggested that new governments should be worried about demographics, no countries had accurate census data to determine what was happening with their populations. The idea that African populations would grow as a result of improved health care and nutrition was a widely discussed theoretical proposition, but no one knew by how much.

Harrar's initial instinct was to embed population studies in regional research universities and community-health centers, as part of the growth of medical and social sciences. But turning population science into an academic pursuit created problems of its own. It meant that the most intimate,

Initial efforts by the Rockefeller Foundation to slow population growth in Africa focused on making population science a program of study in African universities. (Rockefeller Archive Center.)

private dialogue between men and women was being studied in the abstract at universities far removed from the daily lives of families and the choices they make. In 1967, however, the Foundation gave the medical school and the school of public health at Makerere University a grant to study the social aspects of family planning with an emphasis on child spacing, improving maternal and child health, and the benefits of smaller family size. This study helped the Foundation to realize, as Harrar noted in 1970, that "achieving an about face in attitudes toward fertility was as problematic as the development of a safe, cheap, and universally acceptable contraceptive."

By the mid-1970s the Foundation had decided that it needed to do more. It frankly admitted that it had "dragged its feet in getting started with the promotion of active family planning programs and practical contraceptive research, and that the delay was costly." Indeed, while not yet overpopulated, many African countries faced exponential population growth that meant children and youths outnumbered working adults, putting enormous pressure on education and health care systems as well as on individual families.

The task of reversing this trend exacerbated an old conflict within the Foundation. At the intersection of the natural sciences and the social sciences, government officials and the public invariably preferred the quick-fix "magic bullet" of scientific discovery and technological innovation to the slow, tedious process of community change. "The agriculturalists and nutritionists could demonstrate concrete, short-term results; with family planning, both ends and means seemed dubious," the Foundation noted, but "the advantages of having fewer children or of stabilizing the national population were much harder to get across."

The Foundation had begun to pour resources into the Population Council to develop contraceptives. In the late 1960s, the council had begun working with universities in Africa to help them improve training in demographics and research. The Rockefeller Foundation complemented this initiative in the 1970s by supporting fellowships in demography and providing small grants to African universities to study labor migration. It funded efforts, for example, to develop acceptable ways to communicate family planning in Nigerian rural communities. Foundation-funded researchers also studied the demographic consequences of polygamy and women's roles in family planning. But, with the exception of Kenya, work on population remained marginal in African public policy. By 1980 the realities of population growth were all too apparent in Africa, where the number of people had doubled to 480 million in just 30 years.

With this growth in mind, the Rockefeller Foundation redoubled its efforts. In the 1980s it awarded an increasing number of grants to projects in

Africa that integrated health care for children and families with research on demographic shifts. It spent almost $3 million in 1987 and 1988 to support population work. The Centre for Development and Population Activities (CEDPA) in Washington, D.C., used a Foundation grant to organize a Nairobi conference on "Options for a Better Life for Young Women" in 1988. A major long-term grant of $300,000 was awarded to the University of Pennsylvania to train African demographers. In Tanzania and Uganda, Foundation grants helped local governments to improve child nutrition and immunization coverage and to research the best means of intervening in the AIDS crisis, all of which were starting to be understood as essential to the projects concerned with population changes. This intersection of health care for children and families with research on demographic shifts would become increasingly important with the Foundation's later work on HIV/AIDS.

DEMOGRAPHIC TRENDS

In 1991 the directors of the Rockefeller Foundation Division of Population Science and the Population Council published a commentary in the *New York Times* and other national newspapers to celebrate a remarkable milestone. "A contraceptive revolution—a remarkable success story—has gone largely unnoticed in the West," wrote Steven Sinding and Sheldon Segal. "It is as impressive as agriculture's green revolution, and perhaps equally important in averting widespread famine in many developing countries. Third-World women are averaging 3.9 children, and more than 50 percent of the women use some form of contraception, according to estimates of the United Nations. This is a stunning change from the 8 percent who used contraception in 1965 when they were averaging more than six children." Basing their commentary on a population survey by the United Nations, Sinding and Segal singled out a handful of countries for special attention. Thailand, Indonesia, Mexico, Colombia, Brazil, and even Bangladesh were all countries where the Foundation had long histories of partnership with strong central governments.

Their conclusions about Africa were less optimistic, but still offered a sense of progress. "There are still Third-World states, primarily in sub-Saharan Africa and the Islamic world, where the use of contraception remains low and fertility remains high. But even in several of these—Kenya, Egypt, Zimbabwe—the acceptance of contraceptives seems to be growing." Kenya was the biggest success story of sub-Saharan Africa. The Rockefeller Foundation had helped the new government develop a population policy in 1966, only a few years after independence. Kenya had a very high baseline of

8.1 births per woman in 1970, and by 1990 the rate was down to 6. But it was still far higher than the 3.9 that Sinding and Segal celebrated for all of the Third World in 1991.

In Kenya and around the world, however, population scientists were beginning to realize that they were looking only at the front end of the demographic transition. Where women were educated, where the economy provided food security and opportunity, and where medical technology provided the means to conquer disease, couples began to make personal decisions to limit their family sizes—assuming, of course, that they had access to safe, affordable, reliable contraception. Foundation leaders had long understood the relationship between these core elements of economic development and lower birth rates. The complex associations among food, disease, education, and economic security that made the demographic transition possible were always at the core of the Foundation's programs. If Africa was slow to reduce its birthrates, there were two key issues that had to be addressed.

First, the demographic transition required stable government and stable civil society. Second was a more practical problem discovered by researchers in the late 1980s. All across the developing world, including Africa, demand for safe, affordable contraceptives far outstripped their availability. Field studies indicated that couples were not inhibited from using contraception by culture or religion or tradition. In many cases, even when the institutions of civil society seemed weak, couples were ready to reduce their family sizes and women were ready to have fewer children. But they had no access to birth control technologies.

In their commentary in the *New York Times*, Sinding and Segal outlined the challenge. The World Bank estimated that developing countries spent a total of $3 billion yearly on family planning and related activities such as demographic surveys and public information campaigns. Other nations provided about $600 million of this total. "If the U.N. projection of a world population of 6 billion by 1999 is not to be exceeded,"

Women in Kenya in the 1960s could visit a local clinic for advice on family planning and primary health care. Rockefeller Foundation population programs helped policymakers coordinate their efforts to slow population growth. The relative success of these efforts led the Foundation, in the 1980s, to provide grants to support similar initiatives in other nations. (Wendy Stone. Rockefeller Archive Center.)

Sinding and Segal wrote, "the people in developing countries will require 44 billion condoms, 9 billion cycles of oral contraceptives, 150 million sterilization operations and 310 million intrauterine devices or Norplant insertions. This means the annual cost of family planning programs in the Third World will triple, to about $9 billion; contraceptives alone will cost $400 million to $500 million a year."

No sub-Saharan country could afford such an investment, so even where political will existed and national policies were in place (as in Kenya), implementation of family planning strategies lagged far behind Asia and Latin America. African countries struggled in a vicious cycle. An exploding population prevented nations from consolidating gains from economic development. In the face of economic insecurity and a dearth of contraceptive resources, couples continued to have large families. In the absence of strong government programs, the gap between demand for contraception and availability continued to grow.

New Investments

With the beginning of Peter Goldmark's presidency in 1988, the Foundation had begun to search for a new approach to Africa and population issues. As Vice President Kenneth Prewitt explained, population stabilization would depend on the ability of African governments to develop an internal capacity "to assess the economic and political payoff of the wise use of science and technology." The Foundation could help with this effort by linking its Science-Based Development initiative with population issues, but it would need to reestablish its field presence in Africa. "There are simply too few institutions which can effectively operate as intermediaries linking RF funds and program goals to grant opportunities in Africa."

Prewitt suggested that this staff and new programs would be problem-driven. "Science-based development starts from a particular problem and then engages in training and institution building

A major component of Rockefeller Foundation funding in the population sciences has been research on contraception. Among the projects that received support was this Norplant clinic and research project run by Dr. Japheth Mati (pictured). A remarkable example of resourcefulness, this Kenyan clinic ran without the aid of electricity or running water. (Rockefeller Archive Center.)

as necessary to mount an attack on that problem." Within this paradigm, the accelerating fertility rate was the problem, not the scarcity of biomedical scientists or demographers. As with agriculture, the new strategy would stimulate partnerships and linkages to leverage the Foundation's resources.

Throughout the 1990s, the Rockefeller Foundation poured resources into all three critical components of population science. It supported research in reproductive biology, research in contraceptive technology to develop longer-lasting and safer forms of birth control, and studies of population policy.

In keeping with the Foundation's tradition, grant makers looked at the problem of human capacity. Demographers barely knew how many people lived in each country. They understood little about the transition from rural village life to urban life, or how local cultures and economies influenced family planning decisions. They did not fully understand the relationship between the academic achievement of girls and the age of marriage, birth spacing, and family size. Africa needed well-trained demographers and scientists with expertise in population policy.

At all of the universities that had participated in its University Development Program (UDP), the Foundation provided grants to African scientists to support population policy research. This was made possible by the institutional capacity that had been developed in association with the UDP during the 1970s. The grants and fellowships ranged from narrow technical issues—such as Oyewole Adeyemo's research into the "molecular biology of the sperm protein(s) involved in egg-sperm binding during fertilization"—to broad sociological investigations like C.L. Wechungura Kamuzora's work on "high fertility and women's life circumstances in rural Tanzania." Scientists at the University of Ibadan studied "the safety of Norplant contraceptive implants for use by women with sickle cell anemia," and researchers at the University of Nairobi received a grant to research "women's status and fertility levels in Kenya."

African scientists by the hundreds went into the villages and urban communities of Africa and laid a foundation for population policy, but the process was painfully slow. The cornerstone of the Foundation's demographic research effort was an ongoing grant to the University of Pennsylvania to train Ph.D.-level African demographers. For two decades, African graduate students, supported by the Rockefeller Foundation, passed through the University of Pennsylvania Population Studies Center.

Demographers had long argued that large families were an essential part of the economic structure of subsistence-level families in rural countries. More children meant more labor as well as more security for parents as they approached old age. But as the Foundation and its partners began to engage

women, and as demographers began to ask questions about family life, they arrived at a new insight: large numbers of women wanted smaller families and access to contraception. "We have discovered that a great deal of child-bearing of poor people, especially women, is unintended and unwanted," Sinding told a conference on population and development in 2009. "Seeing children as a net resource is a distinctly male construct. Thirty years of household surveys, in scores of nations, have now shown us extremely high levels of unmet need for contraception which, if satisfied, would result in considerably lower levels of fertility, by as much as a whole child in much of Africa."

In the 1990s the regional office staff in Nairobi increased to support the Rockefeller Foundation's expanded grantmaking in Africa. New initiatives reflected innovative approaches to long-time areas of concern in population, agriculture, health, and education. (Rockefeller Foundation.)

Sinding's conclusions reflected decades of investment in population research and programs aimed at stabilizing population growth in developing countries in Africa and elsewhere around the world. They also led to a simple but profound idea. Elevating the status of women and improving their limited access to education had to be at the heart of any solution to rampant population growth. "No factor is more important than female education when it comes to reducing female fertility," Sinding argued. Indeed, with this insight, the Foundation had already been working for more than a decade to help women in Africa who were stepping forward to lead a quiet social revolution.

While demographers had long believed
that Africans produced large families
for the purposes of available labor and
economic security in old age, in more

"Greatness is not made by man. You cannot plant greatness as you plant yams or maize. Who ever planted an iroko tree—the greatest tree in the forest? You may collect all the iroko seeds in the world, open the soil and put them there. It will be in vain. The great tree chooses where to grow and we find it there, so it is with the greatness in men."

Ogbuefi Odogwu, the Elder
No Longer at Ease, Chinua Achebe

CHINUA ACHEBE: THINGS FALL APART

I n 1960 Chinua Achebe had just published his first novel, *Things Fall Apart*, to international acclaim and he was also a rising star at the Nigerian Broadcasting Corporation. To the Rockefeller Foundation's program officers, Achebe had the potential to play a significant role in the development of modern Africa.

As a child in his father's ancestral village of Ogidi, Achebe learned both the traditional ceremonies of an Ibo village and Christian hymns at his father's Sunday services. He was an honor student. Like many precocious young Africans of his generation, he enrolled in the first class of University College, Ibadan in 1948. Though he began as a pre-medical student, Achebe soon discovered a passion for writing and storytelling. He crafted his experiences and insights of growing up in the era of transition between European colonialism and African independence into a widely acclaimed trilogy: *Things Fall Apart* (1958), *No Longer at Ease* (1960), and *Arrow of God* (1964). He was awarded a six-month Rockefeller Foundation fellowship in 1960 to study "the conflict of cultures." Achebe once asserted that the fellowship was "the first important perk of my writing career."

Achebe was first noticed by the Foundation at a meeting of midlevel staff at the Nigerian Broadcasting Corporation in 1958. Robert July, the assistant director of the Humanities Division, was surprised by the quiet reserve of the three Africans in his meeting and finally concluded that their response "was partly due to their lack of preparation for any possibility of outside help in cultural fields." They did not know the Rockefeller Foundation and the Foundation did not know them. July met with the young author several times over the following two years. "During our long conversation I was again struck with Achebe's maturity and intelligence," July wrote in his diary on February 14, 1960. July invited Achebe to apply for a Foundation fellowship and encouraged the Nigerian Broadcasting Corporation to sponsor him. Achebe was interested in visiting East Africa, a place he had never seen. July suggested that he travel to the West Indies and the United States as well. "This would be helpful in getting him the sort of literary and publishing contacts he ought to have."

Achebe's fellowship application proposed an exploration of his own continent with a practical goal for venturing into the British colonies of East Africa, very much in the spirit of what July and the Foundation wanted to see from the African fellows. With independence from Great Britain only months

RWJ

497E

Achebe

THE ROCKEFELLER FOUNDATION

PERSONAL HISTORY AND APPLICATION FOR

A FELLOWSHIP IN _____

AUG 24 1960

(Note: Please type or print all entries in English)

Field of Special Interest ___CONFLICT OF CULTURES___

Date ___10 JUNE 1960___

Name in Full ___ALBERT CHINUA ACHEBE___ Sex ___MALE___

Present Address ___BROADCASTING HOUSE___ , ___ENUGU___ , ___EASTERN NIGERIA___
                    (Street and Number)   (City)   (State or Country)

Permanent Address ___"___ , ___"___ , ___"___
                    (Street and Number)   (City)   (State or Country)

Place of Birth ___OGIDI___ , ___Nigeria___ Year ___1930___ Month ___Nov.___ Day ___16___
                    (City)   (State or Country)

Citizenship ___NIGERIAN___

Single, married, widowed, divorced ___SINGLE___ Wife's name _____
                                                              (Form of customary legal signature)

Date of marriage _____ Number of Children _____ Age and Sex _____

_____ Other dependents ___Old parents and brother in England___

Present Position ___CONTROLLER___

Annual Salary ███████

What part of salary and other income will be continued if a fellowship is granted? ___One quarter (¼)___

_____

Have you at any previous time filed an application with The Rockefeller Foundation? ___NO___

If so, give details ___—___

Have you at any time held a fellowship from any other American institution or agency or are you now an applicant

for one? ___NO___ If so, give details ___—___

FORM 454

229

away, and the Nigerian Broadcasting Service planning to broadcast through-out the continent, Achebe wanted to build a network. He wanted to meet the writers, social critics, and cultural leaders of the continent. He wanted to broaden his perspective. Achebe was not just trying to reach beyond the Ibo villages of his novels; he was trying to reach beyond independent Nigeria to the idea of modern Africa, an idea that existed mostly in the imaginations of young Western-educated African intellectuals.

In his book *The Africans*, Mazrui explained the significance of Achebe's journey: "What Africa knows about itself, what different parts of Africa know about each other, have been profoundly influenced by the West....What Nigerians know about Kenya, or Zambians know about Ghana, is heavily derived from the wire services of the Western world transmitting information across the globe." Achebe set out "with high hopes and very little knowledge of real Africa." What he discovered was the implacable, elaborate system of racial inequality and segregation in East Africa on which imperialism had "sharpened its iron tooth."

"The West seems to suffer deep anxieties about the precariousness of its civilization."
Chinua Achebe, 1975

Face to face with a Kenya that was struggling to overcome the legacy of British repression of the Mau Mau rebellion, Achebe wrote a letter to Robert July about the destabilizing undercurrents in Kenyan society on the eve of independence. "Here politics means racialism—European, Asian, African. On top of this racialism there is also tribalism, which does not come as a complete surprise to a Nigerian!" In Nigeria Achebe had grown up understanding the oppressive paternalism of colonialism. But during his travels he discovered oppression of an entirely different cast—the color bar. "The chief problem was racism," he bluntly explained.

If Achebe represented the future of Africa, in Robert July's perspective, he also represented the future of the Rockefeller Foundation's fellowship program in Africa. July wanted to broaden the traditional parameters of the fellowship program. Achebe did not do postgraduate research into Afri-can literary themes. His fellowship was not strictly academic. Achebe was exploring Africa to make himself into a global leader. Nigerian independence overwhelmed Chinua Achebe's fellowship after only six months, and he never made it to the United States until years later.

On February 18, 1975, the by then celebrated novelist delivered the Chancellor's Lecture at the University of Massachusetts, Amherst, where he held a joint appointment in the English and African American Studies departments. Achebe was only 45 years old at the time, but he was an international cultural celebrity. His life spanned the rise of great expectations, yet-to-be-realized hopes, and uncertain futures in Africa. "The *Heart of Darkness* projects the image of Africa as 'the other world,'" Achebe told his audience. "The antithesis of Europe and therefore of civilization, a place where man's vaunted intelligence and refinement are finally mocked by triumphant bestiality." Instead of accepting this view, Achebe asserted that "the West seems to suffer deep anxieties about the precariousness of its civilization and to have a need for constant reassurance by comparison with Africa. If Europe, advancing in civilization, could cast a backward glance periodically at Africa trapped in primordial barbarity it could say with faith and feeling: There go I but for the grace of God."

Achebe's point was clear. For a century, Europeans had explained Africa to the world, and even to itself, and gotten away with it. For a century, Africans had had no voice in the conversation about Africa. In 1975, with help from the Rockefeller Foundation, a new generation was coming to center stage to project their voice to the world.

For the next three decades, Achebe provided the inspiration to this new generation. He launched two literary magazines, *Okike* and *Nsukkascope*, to showcase emerging African writers. Displaced by the civil war in Nigeria, Achebe moved to the United States where he taught at the University of Massachusetts, Amherst. He later returned to Africa to teach at the University of Kenya and the University of Nigeria. His 1987 novel *Anthills of the Savannah* was a finalist for the Booker Prize. In the 1990s, after being seriously injured in an automobile accident, Achebe returned to the United States where he taught at Bard College and later Brown University.

Shortly before his death in 2013, Achebe celebrated the publication of his memoir *There Was a Country*, which chronicled his life during the Nigerian Civil War between 1967 and 1970. He argued that the war, with its roots in the arbitrary boundaries drawn during colonialism, foreshadowed future conflicts in Africa. As a result, "The Biafran war changed the course of Nigeria. In my view it was a cataclysmic experience that changed the history of Africa." Indeed, the book highlighted abiding themes in Achebe's work, especially in its celebration of African traditions and its concern for the legacies of colonialism.

EMPOWERING WOMEN

When the Forum for African Women Educationalists was established in 1992, women in Africa struggled with poor access to land, credit, health care, and education. They bore the brunt of poverty, violent conflict, and social and environmental disasters. Girls were taken out of school before their brothers if money was scarce or labor was necessary. Girls and women in many sites of conflict in Africa were beaten and raped, then often marginalized by their families due to the shame of the violence or a resultant pregnancy. And women, with less access to transportation and more domestic responsibilities, struggled to get access to humanitarian aid when disaster struck. But things were beginning to change.

The United Nations Decade for Women, launched in 1976, had marked the beginning of a new era in global efforts to promote the advancement of women by opening a worldwide dialogue on gender equality. This included a key objective: the integration and full participation of women in social and economic development. For NGOs and many philanthropic organizations, the 1980s had been a time of reflection as they thought about how their programs and strategies had shaped the environment for women and girls.

Women had not always been integral to philanthropic interventions. The interrelated beliefs that public and private spheres were separate, especially in Africa, and that the influence of women did not extend outside the home led policymakers and leaders at global philanthropies to

underestimate the fundamental roles women played
in agriculture, fertility, and household management,
as well as in the broader economy and trade in African
communities. Maasai women in Kenya and Tanzania,
for example, were certainly responsible for child rear-
ing, but they also had important rights over livestock
that affected land tenure, marriage responsibilities of
extended kin groups, and community structures. By not recognizing these
relationships, development programs drawing on colonial understandings
of gender relations often ultimately disenfranchised women from rights
and privileges that should have benefited them.

In 1976 the United Nations declared
a Decade for Women. International
conferences, like this one in Copenhagen
in 1980, rallied philanthropic
organizations, including the Rockefeller
Foundation, to women's issues related to
development. (United Nations.)

At the Rockefeller Foundation, a belief in the importance of female
education had deep roots in the organization's culture. The original Phelps
Stokes Commissions in the 1920s and 1940s, funded in part by the Foundation
and its related philanthropies, had gone village to village, missionary school
to missionary school, preaching the virtues of female education. "All school

systems should make a special effort to bring to their schools a full proportion of the girls of the community," wrote the author of *Education in Africa* in 1925. Two years later, in a second report, the commission devoted an entire chapter to "The Education of Women and Girls." But by the early 1980s gender was not a critical framework for the Foundation's development strategies.

While philanthropic efforts in Africa in the 1920s stressed equal education for girls, teaching them became a low priority as the century progressed. By the 1960s scenes like this, in which girls are being taught the basics of science in a Nigerian classroom, were often the exception rather than the rule. The 1980s saw renewed efforts to improve the status of women through education. (Rockefeller Archive Center.)

In 1981 Rockefeller Foundation President Richard Lyman created a Task Force on Women's Programming to stimulate new thinking. The task force reported that the Foundation's "male-dominated program activities" did not adequately involve women in competitions for grant and fellowship awards. To address this deficiency, the task force recommended increasing the number of grants directly concerned with women's activities and ensuring that women were involved as participants in activities aimed at accomplishing broader objectives. It also said the Foundation should evaluate the impact of its grants on women, especially where the effects might be negative. With these goals in mind, the Foundation launched a new grant program focused

Chapter Twelve: Empowering Women

on women's issues. In 1983 and 1984 the Foundation appropriated $750,000 in grants to "a systematic effort to improve the understanding and recognition of changing gender roles in the work place and within the family."

As the relationship of gender issues to development gained greater attention, Joyce Moock in the Foundation's office in New York and Katherine Namuddu in Nairobi coordinated an effort to incorporate a new approach to the empowerment of women in Africa. The female education (FEDMED) program, anchored in conceptual work by Namuddu and Anna Obura, sought to leverage between $150-200 million from various donors. This initiative led to a confluence of ideas relating to development, population growth, and women's education that powered one of the most influential breakthroughs of the 1990s for both the Foundation and philanthropic work globally.

Bringing women and their roles in society to the forefront of philanthropic agendas required profound changes in the way foundations operated. The Rockefeller Foundation's long history of work on population growth and contraception, however, helped guide the Foundation to important new insights. As Moock told the board of trustees, the same dynamic was at work with women's education as with contraception. Young women wanted to go to school, and in many cases their families wanted them to go to school, but poverty and the lack of local facilities often made it difficult for these girls and families to realize

Women like this chemistry student at Cuttington College in Liberia were at the vanguard of a movement to increase the participation of women and girls in education in Africa in the 1980s. (Rockefeller Archive Center.)

their ambitions. Foundations could and should help. Indeed, Moock suggested that women's education might be the "single most influential investment that can be made in the developing world." As she explained, "unfulfilled demand by parents for female education exists, as it does for reduced fertility, if conditions are appropriate."

To make a difference in this arena, as the Foundation had learned in agriculture and population, it would need to bring others to the table and, most importantly, it would need to work with women in Africa who were already pressing for change. After the Manchester meeting of Donors to African Education (described in the Introduction), the Foundation recognized an important opportunity. In Nairobi, Eddah Gachukia, a well-respected educator and founder of the Riara Group of Schools, prepared a concept paper for a women's advocacy group for education. Gachukia and Katherine Namuddu, from the Rockefeller Foundation's staff, then traveled to Zimbabwe to meet with Fay Chung to begin organizing. They invited 12 women who were leaders in education in sub-Saharan Africa to meet in Nairobi in May. At this meeting, the group adopted a name for their group—Forum for African Women Educationalists (FAWE)—and began planning a major summit to launch the organization in the fall.

LAUNCHING THE FORUM FOR AFRICAN WOMEN EDUCATIONALISTS

When leading African educators came together in the fall of 1992 at the Foundation's Bellagio Center on Lake Como, Italy, the five women who had met the year before at Manchester—Vida Yeboah, Paulette Missambo, Alice Tiendrébéogo, Simone de Comarmond, and Fay Chung—made a powerful case for a new initiative on behalf of girls' and women's education in Africa, which led to the formal establishment of the Forum for African Women Educationalists (FAWE). They were joined by women from other African nations, including Agathe Uwilingiamana, the prime minister of Rwanda.

FAWE's primary strategy was to promote individual empowerment, in this case through educating girls and linking them to a growing pan-African network of educated and ambitious women. With the leadership of FAWE's African women ministers, the project was rooted in the structures and needs of local governments and administrations. FAWE embraced a continental challenge by adopting specific and collaborative models focused on local situations and demands. FAWE worked directly with governments and policymakers, providing a unique forum through which countries with fewer resources could take advantage of regional skills and materials. The Rockefeller Foundation provided critical support and helped to enlist other donors. Eddah Gachukia served as executive director, working initially out of the Foundation's Nairobi office. By 2000 the Foundation had awarded more than $15 million through 28 grants, which FAWE channeled to national initiatives.

FAWE's success was evident in countries like Rwanda, where its Centres of Excellence were able to influence governmental policymaking to increase opportunities for girls to study at universities. New opportunities inspired girls to dream. According to one Rwandan student, interviewed by Josefine Arlesten and Sofia Leijon for their book on FAWE, "They say that the girls are the future leaders.... [W]hat FAWE has done is to encourage girls to become job-creators. We learn how to create jobs.... We have the vision 2020, our target is development and FAWE helps us reaching that target."

Fay Chung was one of five African educators who were instrumental in founding the Forum for African Women Educationalists (FAWE), which connected African women throughout the continent in an effort to increase the number of educational opportunities for girls. Between FAWE's founding in 1992 and 2000, the Rockefeller Foundation provided $15 million to FAWE initiatives. (Rockefeller Foundation.)

The FAWE initiative helped drive systemic change. As a Rwandan teacher told Arlesten and Leijon, "with the beginning of schools like FAWE we train children in sciences. They attend to different universities and they are doing different jobs. And the gospel spreads.... These are girls who are going to get families and once you educate the woman, you educate the family and the whole society."

Outside of Rwanda, other African governments adopted gender-positive policies as a direct result of FAWE's advocacy, including free primary education, re-entry policies for adolescent mothers, scholarships for needy girls, and gender-responsive pedagogy. The governments also began to appoint more women teachers.

In 2009 the Rockefeller Foundation renewed its support of FAWE by awarding it a $150,300 grant for a two-year research project on "African Women in Institutions of Higher Education: The Case of Universities in sub-Saharan Africa." The grant memo argued that it would enable FAWE to "reaffirm its position as a promoter of gender equity" and make it possible for "FAWE to re-examine the results of this work and develop new advocacy and training tools that are needed in order to deepen academic women's professional development and nurturance for lifelong careers in academia and management at university." The grant was made "in the light of a 2005 UNESCO report which revealed that in 90% of African universities the majority of senior management is men, even in institutions where 50% of the staff are women."

FAWE was uniquely positioned to take on the challenge of lowering the key barriers to women's full participation in university leadership, since the organization was already collaborating with the Partnership for Higher Education in Africa (PHEA), helping it to broaden its advocacy work on behalf of women. The Rockefeller Foundation had helped to launch the Partnership for Higher Education in Africa after a number of leading universities, including Makerere in Uganda, began to reshape their curriculum and financial strategies in response to market demand. These moves helped to revitalize these institutions and provided evidence that despite the political and social challenges of the 1970s and '80s, which had contributed to the end of the Foundation's University Development Program, the investments of the 1960s had created abiding capacity within these institutions. To support the new strategies developed at Makerere and elsewhere, the Rockefeller Foundation and the Carnegie Corporation worked together to recruit other major donors who believed that strong, equitable universities were critical to the development of Africa. In September 2000 these partners launched the new organization and pledged $100 million over five years (a pledge that was renewed in 2005 for another $200 million).

The Rockefeller Foundation grant to FAWE supported the efforts of the Partnership for Higher Education in Africa and allowed FAWE to build on already existing research programs on women's participation and experiences in higher education in 14 universities in nine countries. The specific goals of the research program were to promote gender equality in higher education institutions; understand experiences of women in higher education; formulate, implement, monitor, and evaluate gender-responsive university policies on sexual harassment and equal employment opportunities; communicate strategies for combating sexual harassment to enhance performance and career development; and create safe, gender-sensitive environments in higher education institutions.

FAWE worked with eight African universities: Busitema University, Uganda; Kenyatta University, Kenya; the National University of Comoros; University of Yaoundé I, Cameroon; Copperbelt University, Zambia; the University of Swaziland; Cheikh Anta Diop University, Senegal; and the University of Ghana. The study confirmed that women were still a minority—less than 30 percent—in university management. Seven of the universities had established Gender Equality Advocacy Teams (GEATs) by 2011, staffed by university personnel and FAWE representatives. FAWE continues to work toward this project's goals to enable access, professional development, and promotion of women in higher education through gender-responsive research, innovative advocacy strategies, and leadership training. Reflecting the Rockefeller Foundation's basic principles, the project is built on collaborations—with, for example, the Association for Strengthening Higher Education for Women in Africa (ASHEWA), the Association of African Universities (AAU), and the Southern and Eastern Africa Consortium for Monitoring Educational Quality (SACMEQ)—as well as on building strategic alliances within universities. A key element of the project is to establish the African Women in Academia Tracking System (AWATS) to track patterns and trends of gender-responsive transformation in employment and promotion within the participating universities.

Progress and Lessons Learned

More than two decades after it was first conceptualized in Manchester and formulated at Bellagio, FAWE represents one part of an enormous social shift gradually taking place in Africa. Although women and girls still struggle with gender bias in many legal systems as well as unequal access to economic resources, they are gaining access to the ladder

of opportunity. In Rwanda, for example, where women accounted for only one in five university graduates in 2000,
they received half of all degrees awarded in 2006. Women
are increasingly moving into positions of political power.
When she was inaugurated in Liberia in 2006, Ellen
Johnson Sirleaf became the first woman elected president
of an African nation. In Rwanda that year, women filled
49 percent of the seats in parliament, the highest percent-
age of women in a national legislature in the world.
In addition, women were serving as vice presidents in
Mozambique and Zimbabwe, and five members of Sudan's
postwar cabinet were women. Women are also increasingly becoming entrepreneurs and driving economic growth,
especially in the small-business sector. Remembering the
moment in Manchester in 1991, FAWE's founders can take
great pride in their accomplishments.

FAWE's achievements and its long-standing relationship with the Rockefeller Foundation highlight the
success of the Foundation's strategy to build human capacity in collaboration

In September 2012, twenty years
after the Forum for African Women
Educationalists was created, founders
and leaders gathered at the Rockefeller
Foundation's Bellagio Center to discuss
the progress of their movement and
plan for the future. Oley Dibba-Wadda,
Nacera Mogul, Hendrina Doroba, Amany
Asfour, Yumiko Yokozeki, Chikezie
Anyanwu, Kim Ki-Seok Korbil, Katherine
Namuddu, Stella Smith, Nora Fyles,
Daphne Chimuka, Anna Obura, Cheryl
Faye, Irene Mkondo, Marie Louise
Baricako, Christine Dranzoa, Marie Toto
Raharimalala, Marjan Kroon, Sail Ebrima,
Kadiatou Baby, Simone De Comarmond,
Ahlin Byll-Cataria, Nyokabi Kamau, and
Ann-Therese N'Don-Jatta posed for this
group photo. (Rockefeller Foundation.)

with networks and institutions on the ground and to work in partnerships with other donors. These donor partnerships can be complicated, but the mission remains simple. "Female education correlates highly with income growth and lower fertility rates," Peter Goldmark had written in his 1992 President's Review. The education of young women belonged at the heart of the Foundation's program, he asserted. The education of women fit together with improved health services and agriculture to form the foundation of social and economic development. Development (and the demographic transition) would have been impossible without the empowerment of women. It had been a conceptual breakthrough of enormous significance.

The successful partnership with FAWE had been anchored by decades of experience in the field of human reproduction. It also reflects the Foundation's increasingly important role as convener and catalyst in partnerships where timing is critical. The Foundation has steadily embraced a strategy of working through partnerships to accomplish goals that required big investments over long periods of time that were beyond the scope of a single institution.

But FAWE also reinforced an important insight about the nature of these partnerships. Collaboration means that, over time, projects could be profoundly affected by shifting government priorities, pressure on international multilateral agencies, the stability of the global economy where the portfolios of philanthropies were invested, and even the fundraising potential of small NGOs. Nevertheless, this role as convener and catalyst offers great potential. As FAWE showed, when this strategy was combined with the experiences of working with women in Africa, it could provide enormous benefits, especially for African women.

The work done over the past three decades on women's issues in Africa would have a profound effect on the Foundation's projects, opening the door to questions about local expressions of global problems and about the role of communities and families in addressing the impact of poverty and disease. Although the Rockefeller Foundation had always worked with local and state institutions, these decades of addressing women's needs alongside women from a wide range of African countries shifted relationships that had been based on giving into partnerships. The Foundation's work with women, especially through organizations like FAWE, acknowledged the extent to which the problems that the Foundation was trying to solve were already being addressed directly by local individuals, organizations, and governments. All of these insights and the experiences of working with women and local communities would prove critically important as the Foundation sought to help Africans confront the onslaught of AIDS.

AIDS AND THE RETURN
TO PUBLIC HEALTH

I
n a small clinic in the town of Eldoret in western Kenya, David Mushiri
and his wife Cecilia Onjero explain to a group of anxious parents-to-be
how they can minimize the risk of transferring HIV to their unborn
children. David and Cecilia, both HIV-positive, have a young daughter
born HIV-free. They are also both healthy, with access to antiretroviral
drugs through the clinic and other programs designed to keep them that
way. Having benefited from the clinic, they now work as volunteer peer
counselors helping other families to stay healthy. The clinic in Eldoret was
funded by the Rockefeller Foundation's Mother-to-Child Transmission Plus
Initiative (MTCT-Plus), which did what now seems obvious for HIV/AIDS
programs: it moved beyond treatment strategies for preventing transmission
at birth to focus on whole families, including fathers, to help everyone
maintain their health.

This focus on the whole person in the context of family and community,
which has characterized the Foundation's HIV/AIDS programs in Africa
since the 1990s, builds on a century of public health work in Africa. It also
underscores the way in which HIV/AIDS programs in Africa have relied on
the strong scaffolding erected by the Foundation's work on human capital,
agriculture, family planning, and women's education.

The Foundation's work on HIV/AIDS began in August 1987, when its AIDS Task Force met to study the reasons for the relatively equal distribution of HIV infection between the sexes in Africa. The following year, the Foundation funded a task force on child health and donor coordination to help the Ugandan Ministry of Health develop an AIDS prevention education program. Given its long experience with population stabilization, the Foundation could understand how the epidemic affected and was shaped by family life, migrant labor, food security, and women's education.

The Foundation's joint programs in Health and Population began to support a variety of initiatives that enabled scientists from developed and developing countries to work together on aspects of the AIDS problem that were not receiving sufficient attention. These grants concentrated on the relationship between AIDS and other reproductive health issues, such as sexually transmitted diseases, contraceptive effectiveness and use, and maternal-infant transmission of HIV. The grants also funded studies of factors that contributed to heterosexual transmission of HIV, measures that could be effective in preventing HIV transmission, and ways to communicate project results to policymakers and program managers.

In these early days of African AIDS funding, the Foundation worked with a wide range of possible collaborators. They included the Kenya Medical Research Institute in Nairobi for a training program in laboratory techniques applicable to the study of HIV; the African Fertility Society in Nairobi to compile information on AIDS research projects in Africa; the anthropologist Brooke Schoepf for research on the control of AIDS in Zaire at the Centre de Recherche en Sciences Humaines in Kinshasa; the Task Force for Child Survival in Atlanta, Georgia, to provide the Ugandan Ministry of Health with technical assistance in reestablishing the country's primary health care system;

The Mother-to-Child Transmission Plus Initiative (MTCT-Plus) works with families to maintain the health of HIV-infected members, and to prevent the transmission of the virus to the next generation. As part of the program participants are provided with antiretroviral drugs, as well as access to education and counseling. (Rockefeller Archive Center.)

the University of California, San Francisco for a collaborative study with Makerere University of heterosexual transmission of AIDS; and the International Women's Health Coalition in New York to extend its reproductive health program to selected countries of sub-Saharan Africa.

As the epidemic grew, however, some staff looked for ways for the Rockefeller Foundation to do more. In April 1989 Jane Hughes, an expert on adolescent health, wrote to President Peter Goldmark and Vice President Kenneth Prewitt with a detailed analysis of the challenges of HIV/AIDS in developing countries as well as the possible solutions on which the Foundation might work. Hughes highlighted the need for public-private collaboration, suggesting that governments and large public organizations like the World Health Organization (WHO) needed foundations and nongovernmental organizations (NGOs) to "tell it like it is" in order to confront the epidemic head on. Organizations working at the front lines of community health, she pointed out, were more attuned to the challenges of prevention and education. Hughes wrote that AIDS would be one of the defining issues of the age, especially for the United States, not least because "AIDS in the developing world is to some degree a by-product of the urban, mobile lifestyles of western patterns of development, and because, more than many other major diseases in the developing world, it is rooted in behaviors people have some degree of choice about. These factors mean that how well we address AIDS in Africa, Latin America and Asia will have a greater political and social legacy than how we address malaria, or the next drought."

Hughes also recognized that Americans shared this crisis with people in the developing world, where many of its aspects were the same as in the United States: "the research issues, the orphans, the dilemmas about how to reshape sexual behaviors, the civil liberties issues." She understood that Africa would be one of the most important regions for the fight.

Hughes proposed a program of aggressive education and prevention efforts that would target adolescents, especially those still too young to be sexually active. She suggested that the Foundation encourage international and indigenous private volunteer organizations with a respected track record in developing countries to incorporate AIDS education into their activities. Private philanthropy could sponsor politically risky interventions that governments might shrink from, aimed particularly at the highest-risk subpopulations. She proposed that the Foundation help convene a panel for an independent, nongovernmental examination of AIDS in the developing world. This panel would then frame an agenda for the United States—or developed countries generally—that would encompass NGO and government actions needed to address the crisis.

Hughes's recommendations led the Rockefeller Foundation to incubate and launch an international effort to raise and channel donor funds to developing countries for HIV/AIDS initiatives. These efforts came to fruition in December 1993 when the Foundation brought together nine major donor agencies in Paris to form the International HIV/AIDS Alliance, with the goal of providing money and technical assistance to developing-country NGOs engaged in HIV/AIDS prevention and care. The donor groups—which included the European Union, the Organisation for Economic Co-operation and Development (OECD), and WHO—pledged more than $5 million for the project's first three years. These funds helped national coalitions in developing countries act as linking organizations, channeling small grants and technical assistance to grassroots NGOs working on AIDS prevention and care.

As the Foundation's AIDS initiatives in Africa developed through the 1990s, this focus on prevention and care would continue along with a separate set of projects designed to accelerate research on the disease with the hope of developing a vaccine.

Coalition Building

As the AIDS epidemic progressed and the number of organizations and institutions working to address the crisis increased, the Rockefeller Foundation's comparative advantage continued to lie in coalition building and the development of institutional networks for research. Confronting agricultural issues through the Green Revolution, the Foundation had come to understand the importance of building research capacity within developing countries where the need for solutions was most urgent and where feedback between the field and the laboratory was more direct. These lessons, embedded in the Foundation's culture by the 1990s, shaped the development of research coalitions related to HIV.

In 1988, for example, the Foundation joined with the International Development Research Centre, the John Merck Fund, and the Ford Foundation to create the AIDS and Reproductive Health Network as a mechanism for strengthening developing-country HIV research. In the absence of a vaccine, the network supported research on intervention and funded efforts by a network of scientists to find cheaper and less invasive tests. The Foundation also convened a meeting in August 1991 that included representatives of WHO, OECD, and seven bilateral aid agencies to consider how private voluntary groups, unions, churches, business groups, and academic institutions in the developing world could best be encouraged and funded to take roles in combating the HIV/AIDS epidemic.

Coalition building in other areas of public health also provided a platform for AIDS initiatives. The campaign for universal childhood immunization, originated at a Rockefeller Foundation-sponsored conference on child health in the 1970s, had brought together several governments, four international agencies—UNICEF, WHO, the United Nations Development Programme, and the World Bank—and other, smaller service organizations like Rotary International, to work towards the goal of universal childhood immunization. By 1990 the campaign had been able to raise childhood vaccination rates from 5 to 80 percent. Based on the success of this coalition, the Rockefeller Foundation and its partners launched a research project to develop a magic-bullet vaccine to protect children around the world against 18 viral and bacterial childhood diseases. To attack HIV, the Foundation focused on a similar convening and coalition strategy.

Seth Berkley had come to the Foundation from Uganda, on the front lines of the epidemic. At the Foundation, as associate director of Health Sciences, he became a champion for vaccine research. Berkley believed that only a vaccine could beat AIDS, but no one in government or private industry was actively pursuing that solution.

A collaborative effort between the private and public sectors, the Development of Antiretroviral Therapy in Africa (DART) brought together national governments, foundations, and pharmaceutical companies to develop cheap and effective drug therapies for Sub-Saharan Africans. (Jonas Bendiksen. Rockefeller Foundation.)

Chapter Thirteen: AIDS and the Return to Public Health

Foundation President Peter Goldmark supported the idea of investing in vaccine research. Reflecting on the world's experiences with smallpox, yellow fever, polio, and measles, Goldmark would later write in the 1996 annual report: "Never in history has a serious viral public health threat been eliminated without the use of a vaccine." But Goldmark was concerned about the overwhelming expense—no single nonprofit foundation could manage the costs of developing a vaccine—as well as the long timeframe for research and the ways in which an initiative would be organized. Seth Berkley and others suspected the effort might take 20 years.

With the trustees' support, Berkley convened a series of meetings with experts and representatives of political entities and international agencies to talk about a vaccine for AIDS. The experts came together in 1994 at the Foundation's retreat center in Bellagio, Italy. *Science* magazine described the meeting as the most important and diverse that had ever been held on AIDS vaccines. Soon after the conference, the Rockefeller Foundation organized an Ad Hoc Scientific Committee on "Accelerating the Development of Preventive HIV Vaccines for the World."

Berkley also brought together leaders from developing countries, some of whom were uneasy with the idea of a new initiative. They asked if the effort would divert resources needed for treatment. To address this situation, the Rockefeller Foundation began to work on developing an innovative public-private partnership to support vaccine research and clinical trials in the developing world. In September 1995, at a meeting of leading scientists gathered in Chiang Mai in northern Thailand, the Foundation announced that it would help create the first nonprofit, nongovernmental organization dedicated to the development of a vaccine.

The International AIDS Vaccine Initiative (IAVI) built on the Foundation's long and rich history in global health. In a new context and a different era, it continued the tradition of vaccine research in Africa initiated with yellow fever research in Nigeria in the 1920s. But it also incorporated lessons learned in completely different arenas. In agriculture, for example, during the Green Revolution of the 1960s, the Foundation had sparked the development of research institutions focused on particular crops. These unique international institutions were collaborative efforts among governments, private enterprise, and university scientists. The success of these institutions, many of which thrived long after the Foundation ended its initial support, created a belief within the culture of the Foundation that reputational capital could allow it to play a key role in bringing others together to launch new institutions targeting emerging problems around the world.

Berkley and his colleagues at the Foundation suggested that IAVI would follow the "social venture capital" model, in which the Foundation would fund scientific research in collaboration with pharmaceutical companies as long as the drug companies pledged to distribute vaccines widely to poor nations at a reasonable cost. The Foundation's initial grants to IAVI, which totaled $8 million in the first decade, provided critical funding. Other foundations, nonprofits, and agencies soon joined the initiative, including the Bill and Melinda Gates Foundation, the Starr and Alfred P. Sloan foundations, Foundation Mérieux, Until There's a Cure Foundation, the Elton John AIDS Foundation, the U.K.'s National AIDS Trust, and the World Bank. IAVI had a war chest of $239 million by February 2001, with a goal of raising $550 million to support research and clinical trials.

The Foundation also invested in other drug development initiatives. It played a catalytic role in the Development of AntiRetroviral Therapy in Africa (DART) trial, which was sponsored and funded by the UK Medical

Public Health Schools Without Walls (PHSWOW) was established in 1995 by the Rockefeller Foundation as a way to train a new cadre of public health workers to work on the frontlines of African health care. Operating in Zimbabwe, Uganda and Ghana, PHSWOW offered students like Nelson Musoba (pictured) of Makerere University in Uganda to obtain a Masters in Public Health by combining academic study with practical fieldwork. (Steve McCurry. Rockefeller Foundation.)

Research Council with additional funding from the UK Department for International Development and the Rockefeller Foundation. The Foundation granted $1,645,310 in 2005 and 2006 to the University of Zimbabwe in Harare and the Joint Clinical Research Centre in Kampala, Uganda, for participation in a multicenter clinical trial to assess the safety and effectiveness of two strategies for the use of antiretroviral drugs against HIV/AIDS in sub-Saharan Africa.

Like the International AIDS Vaccine Initiative, DART included a key role for pharmaceutical companies and the private sector. Antiretroviral drugs given to trial participants were donated by GlaxoSmithKline, Gilead Sciences, Abbott Laboratories, and Boehringer Ingelheim. These companies also provided funding for some of the studies that were part of the DART trial. The results presented at the International AIDS Society Conference 2009 in Cape Town showed that, irrespective of group, the survival rate in the DART trial was among the highest reported from any trial, study, or antiretroviral therapy program in Africa. Historical comparisons—based on data from follow-ups with similar patients in Uganda who did not have access to antiretroviral therapy—made it clear that few of the DART trial participants would have been alive after five years without the drugs. In fact, the success of antiretroviral therapy played a key role in the larger campaign, funded by the Rockefeller Foundation, to revolutionize primary care and HIV/AIDS treatment in Africa's poorest communities.

INCLEN and Public Health School Without Walls

Even as the effort to find a vaccine was getting underway in the mid-1990s, the Foundation was continuing to look for innovative ways to integrate the battle against HIV with primary health care in developing countries in Africa. In the late 1970s, the Foundation had recognized that the field of public health, which it had worked so hard to define and build over the course of the twentieth century, had in some instances lost touch with the needs of communities in the developing world. To promote the development of a new "population-based" medicine that relied on the increasingly powerful tools of epidemiology, the Foundation created the International Clinical Epidemiology Network (INCLEN) in 1980.

INCLEN provided fellowships to physicians from developing countries to spend a year studying population-based medicine and epidemiology at one of the Foundation-supported centers established at a handful of leading medical schools. These fellows were then encouraged to return home to train other health care professionals in epidemiological methods and to conduct research that would guide national health policy.

The Foundation hoped that with additional grants these fellows would help establish clinical and epidemiological units within local medical schools in their own countries. In this way, the international network would grow organically with researchers sharing information related to patterns of infectious and chronic disease.

Within three years of its establishment, INCLEN had created 16 of these clinical and epidemiological units in developing nations, including one in Ibadan, Nigeria and another in Addis Ababa, Ethiopia. Teams of clinicians and researchers conducted population studies to guide the efficient and equitable allocation of health resources to serve whole communities, including the poor and disadvantaged.

With INCLEN's success, other international donors joined the initiative in the mid-1980s including USAID and the World Bank. The network expanded. New sites were added in Africa in Cameroon, Egypt, Kenya, Uganda, and Zimbabwe. In 1988 INCLEN incorporated and began to move toward full independence. Long-term viability was enhanced in 2000 with the creation of the INCLEN Trust. By 2013 the network included nearly 90 clinical units in developing countries around the world, including eight in Africa. Most importantly, INCLEN had helped to pioneer new methods of disease surveillance and epidemiology that played a fundamental role in shaping health policy in Africa and other developing nations.

The Foundation's support for INCLEN also sparked other innovative efforts to address community public health in Africa. By 1995 the Foundation had established its Public Health School Without Walls (PHSWOW) in Zimbabwe, Uganda, and Ghana. Although not specifically focused on HIV/AIDS, this project sought to meet the desperate need for properly trained health workers in regions hardest hit by the pandemic.

Established in 1992, PHSWOW offered a new training model for in-country Master of Public Health degrees. The project allowed students to learn by doing. It concentrated on practical problem-solving skills, and emphasized a process of lifelong learning. It also sought to address the continuing shortage of skilled public health practitioners, an important factor that limited the overall development of health services and the implementation of specific health programs such as the control of HIV/AIDS and malaria or the prevention of maternal mortality.

Despite some hiccups involved with providing computers, getting local administrators on board, and keeping up with transportation needs, by 1999 three universities in Africa—Makerere in Uganda, the University of Zimbabwe, and the University of Ghana—were key participants in the PHSWOW program. The program also provided limited support to the

University of Kinshasa in the Republic of the Congo and, in South Africa, the Transvaal School of Public Health and the University of Western Cape. In all, PHSWOW had produced a total of 108 graduates at the M.P.H. level—29 from Uganda, 26 from Zimbabwe, 29 from Ghana, and 24 from Vietnam.

As a 2001 evaluation of the PHSWOW programs in Africa noted, the AIDS crisis was leading to a transformation in the management of public health. PHSWOW reflected the change. It was sensitive to local contexts and worked to enhance access to and participation in public health services for the poor and excluded. PHSWOW had had a substantial impact on health systems, especially at the district level, in reducing the barriers between the academic programs and the ministries of health. Its graduates were at the forefront in responding to major public health crises, such as the Ebola outbreak in Uganda and the plague outbreaks in the Matabele region in Zimbabwe, as well as to HIV/AIDS. In Zimbabwe, leadership provided by PHSWOW program graduates in the Ministry of Health's disease surveillance had a tremendous impact on disease control programs.

Highly flexible, the PHSWOW model encouraged collaboration between a country's national university (or equivalent national training institution) and the Ministry of Health. The guiding principle of PHSWOW is that public health training is best provided through a combination of rigorous academics and extensive supervised practical experience emphasizing the capacity to pursue rather than memorize knowledge. The Rockefeller Foundation has emphasized faculty development over the years, making possible overseas academic training as well as teaching apprenticeships for local public health practitioners. PHSWOW was also sustained by frequent North-to-South networking and through the Rockefeller- and WHO-supported Network of African Public Health Institutions.

STEPPING BACK

At the end of the 1990s, after more than a decade of involvement with HIV/AIDS in Africa, the Rockefeller Foundation established a Working Group for AIDS Exploration to determine whether the Foundation was appropriately addressing the still-mounting crisis of AIDS, especially in Africa. This self-reflection stemmed partly from the realization that the impact of AIDS went far beyond health, that it was a multidimensional problem for economic and social development.

This review led to a pivotal international meeting in Kampala in 2001, which emphasized AIDS care in the fight against the epidemic in Africa. Organized by the Foundation in cooperation with the Joint Clinical Research

Centre in Kampala, Uganda, the conference on "AIDS Care in Africa: The Way Forward" was attended by nearly 200 African as well as international scientists and citizens from academia, multinational agencies, and governmental research councils and institutes, including bilateral donors, private foundations, and NGOs. Some of the world's leading AIDS scientists also attended, including two of the most distinguished—Anthony Fauci and Luc Montagnier.

Attendees came because the fight against the AIDS epidemic in Africa had reached a crucial moment. The revolution in antiretroviral drug treatment for HIV/AIDS had previously bypassed the more than 25 million Africans infected with the virus, but falling drug prices meant that many Africans would now have access to effective treatment for the first time.

A convening of key players at a critical moment once again helped foster coalition building and an innovative strategy. At the Rockefeller Foundation, the conference led to a new focus on AIDS work in Africa under the rubric of a program called Nenda Mbele (Go Forward with Care). Distinguished from "treatment," which emphasized medical approaches to disease, the concept of "care" included not only medical therapy but also the core dimension of humanistic relationships. Its essence had been captured at the 2001 confer-ence by Reverend Gideon Byamugisha, a Ugandan Anglican priest who co-founded the African Network of Religious Leaders Living with or Person-ally Affected by HIV and AIDS. "AIDS care is a judgment," Byamugisha explained, "on how we relate to, educate, train, value, care and support each other in our global village."

The conference raised important issues about the ethics of and strate-gies for AIDS work in Africa, and especially about the consequences of improved antiretroviral drugs. The attendees had to discuss uncomfortable questions about who in Africa would benefit. Would the beneficiaries be only the rich and powerful? What about the poor and excluded? In bridg-ing the North-South gap, how could we avoid opening and widening new divides within Africa?

The conference helped to establish the African Dialogue on AIDS Care (ADAC) with the goal of enhancing clinical research capacity and ensuring coordination, standard setting, ethical review, resource mobilization, and the policy relevance of research. ADAC sought to foster dialogue within Africa and to create links with other regions. In essence, ADAC hoped to become a broker for the continent's interests related to AIDS care. The creation of ADAC also had an important influence on the development of a critical project that had been launched in the mid-1990s to address the issue of mother-to-child transmission.

For a number of years in the mid-1990s, the Foundation had supported efforts to address mother-to-child transmission of HIV. The Foundation sponsored a workshop on the topic in November 1994, hosted by the Network of AIDS Researchers of Eastern and Southern Africa. Twenty-four researchers and program implementers attended, addressing questions about vertical transmission as well as counseling and community- and home-based care. The workshop helped to develop collaborative linkages among researchers in the region and to trigger new research, training, and intervention-related activities. Insights gained from this conference, from other HIV/AIDS initiatives, and from the Foundation's efforts to empower women in Africa fed a growing interest in mother-to-child transmission.

In the United States, Wafaa El-Sadr, a Columbia University physician and medical researcher focused on AIDS in Harlem, was developing an approach that combined treatment and prevention by working with whole families, not just infected individuals. Her goal was to lower mother-to-child transmission, and this meant ensuring the continued health of the mother as well as of her partner(s). Tim Evans and Ariel Pablos-Méndez of the Foundation's Health Equity program were interested in El-Sadr's work. They believed that the Foundation needed to do more to address the terrible impact of HIV/AIDS on poor communities around the world.

Conversations and meetings with El-Sadr and her team at Columbia University led to new insights. Based on her experience and research, El-Sadr believed strongly that treatment and prevention had to go hand in hand, which meant that HIV/AIDS programs needed to address the whole family and not just the individuals known to be infected. Her approach fit well with the Foundation's long-term work on family planning, women's education, and public health, especially in Africa. As a result of this dialogue, the Foundation committed to exploring the possibilities of a treatment and prevention program that could be applied throughout the developing world.

Many doubts were raised regarding the proposed approach. Some people feared it would be impossible to distribute antiretroviral drugs at the community level, that the stigma surrounding AIDS would prevent families from coming into the program with their infected relations. Some suggested that giving pregnant women medication to reduce transmission would encourage HIV-positive women to become pregnant. The concerns only made El-Sadr and her team more determined to show that people in resource-poor environments could be successfully treated for HIV/AIDS and that this treatment would have an effect on prevention as well.

Although there were substantial risks of failure, the Foundation backed the project. New grantmaking guidelines established at the beginning of the new millennium pushed the Foundation to deepen its commitment to fighting AIDS. It also recognized, echoing insights that reached all the way back to Wickliffe Rose, that AIDS interventions could lead to efforts to address broader shortfalls in health and social systems.

With Foundation funding for Columbia University's Mailman School of Public Health, El-Sadr's team developed the framework for the Mother-to-Child Transmission project (MTCT-Plus) and sent out requests for proposals for implementing the concept at the community level. They deliberately kept the program flexible. There were no rigid guidelines, but rather a set of principles for treating the whole family and whole person affected by HIV/AIDS. These principles were to be adapted to meet the needs of specific communities.

Obtaining and distributing drugs was a key part of the program and it presented major challenges, requiring complex negotiations with pharmaceutical companies and state health services as well as local pharmacists and physicians. Along with the life-saving drugs, women and especially pregnant women were provided with general and maternal health care. They were also offered education on prevention and staying healthy. Most important, they were encouraged to bring in their partners and families, however those were defined, in order to learn about maintaining health and reducing the chances of infecting anybody else. Despite all the skepticism, clinics, hospitals, and NGOS around the world sent in applications. These institutions understood the value of addressing HIV/AIDS on a community level.

Eight sites were awarded Rockefeller Foundation funds to partner with Columbia in the MTCT-Plus program, adapting its basic principles and the developed scaffolding for their local resources and environment. Doctors, nurses, and other clinic or hospital staff in many of these programs began to work together on AIDS treatment as a team. And for the first time they took comprehensive medical records of their patients, treating the family and not just the virus.

The Rockefeller Foundation committed money, time, and resources to the project. President Gordon Conway, who had traveled extensively in Africa in 1998 and visited the many sites of Foundation-funded projects, campaigned tirelessly to recruit support and collaboration from other foundations as well as the private sector. MTCT-Plus was a new kind of medical program and thus a hard sell, but it offered a model for HIV care in resource-limited settings that could be replicated and scaled up.

Effective implementation of MTCT-Plus required current, integrated, and accurate information on participants that could be easily accessible to caregivers. In order to facilitate this access, the Rockefeller Foundation funded the Electronic Medical Records program at Moi University and the Mosoriot MTCT-Plus Health Centre in Kenya. The Medical Records System was aimed at developing a simple stand-alone information system that could be used on individual computers as part of an integrated, paperless web-based network that would enable more effective monitoring and management of larger numbers of patients through a centralized data repository. These technological innovations provided real-time capture of data critical to the care of HIV/AIDS patients and the management of HIV/AIDS care programs.

By 2006 MTCT-Plus had established care and treatment programs at 14 sites in sub-Saharan Africa. It had enrolled approximately 12,560 individuals, including 4,985 children receiving HIV/AIDS care along with 3,045 adults and 423 infants or children. The project's work was groundbreaking on a number of levels. It made a strong case for early diagnosis, demonstrating why virologic tests of HIV-exposed infants were important during the first months of life. The project also initiated peer-based programs for supporting adherence in antiretroviral treatment clinics, and it illustrated the essential role that a team approach could play in HIV/AIDS prevention and treatment by emphasizing the importance of an entire care team—from the receptionist to the lab technician.

Deo Wabwire, a physician who worked with the Makerere University-Johns Hopkins University Research Collaboration site in Kampala, Uganda, since the start of the MTCT-Plus Initiative, asserted that providing antiretroviral treatment made a difference in the way clinicians cared for patients, many of whom were bedridden upon arrival. Margaret, for example, the clinic's first patient, "had lost all the hope and we had nothing to offer her. But when she started antiretroviral drugs courtesy of [MTCT-Plus] she did quite well. . . . We've actually now employed her as a peer educator. She was formerly a teacher but she has now crossed over to share her experience with the other people starting ARV treatment. And she's been very, very good."

Margaret spoke in December 2009 about what the program meant to her and her family, and what it meant for the treatment of families and children throughout Uganda: "On the first day he [Deo] gave me [antiretrovirals] he knew that I was going to die because the ARVs are very strong, and me at that time I had no energy. And when he saw me coming back after one week to collect the ARVs, he said, 'Oh! Are you Margaret?' I said I'm the one. He said, 'You really have life!' Then I think from that day he knew I was going to progress on very well."

The success of MTCT-Plus changed the mindset of many funders and other organizations working on HIV/AIDS by demonstrating that it is possible to provide treatment and prevention together in poor communities. In fact, the visible effects of treatment, evident to families and community members, provided hope and reinforced the message of prevention. As El-Sadr posits, no prevention campaign could make a dent if people felt that they were already doomed.

IMPROVING HEALTH SYSTEMS

The MTCT-Plus Initiative, in combination with the Foundation's other work on health issues in Africa and the developing world, underscored the importance of health systems. After Judith Rodin became president in 2005, the Foundation focused more tightly on "Transforming Health Systems" and aimed at "repairing weak, outmoded health systems" to make modern health systems stronger, more affordable, and more accessible in poor and vulnerable communities.

Within this modified framework, the Foundation continued to forge partnerships with long-term goals and big ambitions. In 2008 it hosted a conference at the Bellagio Center called "Making the eHealth Connection: Global Partnerships and Local Solutions." More than 200 health, financial, and technology leaders

In an effort to strengthen global health systems, the Rockefeller Foundation is harnessing technology to both modernize health care and to make it more accessible. Accessibility remains a challenge in many African communities where many people rely on traditional healers, like James Musigo (pictured), to treat a variety of illnesses including HIV/AIDS. (Steve McCurry. Rockefeller Foundation.)

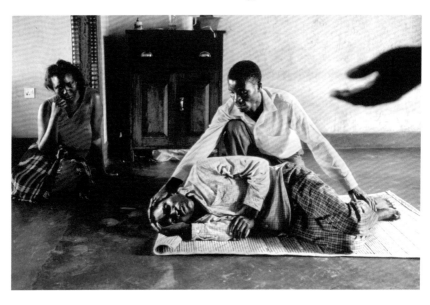

became signatories to the Bellagio eHealth Call to Action, which advocated for enhanced capacity; better—and better-coordinated—funding; new collaborative networks and public-private partnerships; and sharper focus on interoperability. The Foundation also promoted the development of disease surveillance networks in Africa and the developing world, including the Southern African Centre for Infectious Disease Surveillance and the East African Integrated Disease Surveillance Network. Operating across multiple countries, these networks were designed to conduct surveillance within their own borders and to share with their neighbors a focused regional response to infectious disease outbreaks. Many of these initiatives had roots in lessons learned from the spread of HIV/AIDS.

Indeed, it is hard to ignore the important lessons learned from the HIV/AIDS epidemic and its impact on health systems in Africa. In a recent visit to one of the first Zambian clinics to be awarded Rockefeller Foundation funds for MTCT-Plus, Wafaa El-Sadr was overjoyed by the welcome she received and the testimonials from nurses, still working at the clinic, who initially implemented her principles in caring for communities and families affected by HIV/AIDS. The clinic staff showed her a room full of patient files collected during early implementation of the MTCT-Plus treatment and education plan. The files offered testimony to the success of the original design and the resourcefulness of health care workers who—even in the most economically deprived circumstances—were able to take advantage of resources offered by an institution like the Rockefeller Foundation to develop sustainable and effective community health care programs.

The Foundation's subsequent and continuing work in health systems in Africa reveals the value of lessons learned from MTCT-Plus, which built on the Foundation's long history in public health and mobilized its core principles in the areas of women's education and the combination of science with community. The work also demonstrated the power of collaboration, not only across agencies, organizations, and communities, but also across Foundation programs. Such collaboration on the development of health programs required that education, work, transportation, gender equity, and agricultural development would all have to be at least considered. Finally, through its investments in health systems, disease surveillance, and the treatment of patients with HIV/AIDS, the Rockefeller Foundation contributed to a revolution in philanthropy in Africa, one based on cross-agency partnerships and conversations.

In Africa, cities are growing more quickly than on any other continent in the world. By 2025 more than half of Africa's population will be living in urban environments. Like cities around the world, however, these burgeoning urban communities will face serious shocks and stresses brought on by climate change and globalization.

In 2013, as part of a series of centennial initiatives, the Rockefeller Foundation launched the 100 Resilient Cities Challenge and committed $100 million to create a new, independent nonprofit to serve as a hub for thinking and action on issues related to urban resilience.

In Africa, Durban (pictured here) and Dakar were among the first 33 cities to be chosen. Resources from the 100 Resilient Cities network allowed them to hire or fund a chief resilience officer, to develop a resilience plan, and to benefit from new tools and resources developed by the network to foster innovative finance, new technology, and improved approaches to infrastructure and land use. All of these efforts aim to foster greater community and social resilience and ensure that urban areas are places of increased opportunity for future generations.

Physician, activist and anthropologist
Mamphela Ramphele joined the
Rockefeller Foundation board of trustees
in December 1999, becoming the first
African to serve on the board. (Rodger

CONCLUSION

At the beginning of the twenty-first century South African physician and anthropologist Mamphela Ramphele became the first African to serve on the Rockefeller Foundation's board of trustees. More than anyone else, she symbolized a new era that permeated all of the Foundation's work, and her life story connected with key moments in the Foundation's history. Ramphele was the child of school teachers who lived in the northern Transvaal. She fought her way into medical school at the University of Natal, the very program that Sidney Kark and George Gale had built with Foundation support. At Natal she met her life partner Steve Biko, who founded the black consciousness movement. As a physician, Ramphele organized a community clinic for poor Africans in Zanempilo. Banned by the apartheid government in 1977, she went into exile in the Transvaal, where she opened a second community clinic at Ithuseng. When her exile was lifted, Ramphele returned to the University of Cape Town, where she earned her Ph.D. in anthropology.

Ramphele had many connections to the Rockefeller Foundation's work. She was an early participant in the Forum for African Women Educationalists (FAWE), attending the first FAWE meeting at the Bellagio Center in 1992. She helped form the interim steering committee for FAWE's South African chapter. In 1996 she became the first black vice chancellor of the University of Cape Town. When she joined the Foundation's board of trustees, she was managing director of human development for the World Bank.

Ramphele reflected both the results of a century of human-capital building and the realization of what the Rockefeller

Foundation's elders had originally anticipated, the creation of world-class African leaders united by the bonds of science, education, and humanism. She also epitomized the continent's energy and growing optimism. On the board of trustees, she contributed to the evolving process of adapting global philanthropy to the needs of Africa.

PHILANTHROPY'S PROGRESS

In 2013, with so much of Africa experiencing unprecedented economic growth and progress, the role of philanthropy is very different than it was when the Rockefeller Foundation was established a century ago. An unprecedented number of large private foundations have committed generous sums of money to health, education, and agriculture programs in Africa. The most successful projects are driven by local communities and adapted to local needs, but they are supported by global networks that incorporate multiple stakeholders. More than ever before, foundations are collaborating with one another and with local agencies to improve the well-being of the people of Africa. As a result, Africa is making substantial progress in addressing health care, poverty alleviation, and education.

The Rockefeller Foundation's century of work in Africa and its own institutional evolution have been instrumental in instigating and furthering this new model of global philanthropy. The Foundation's commitment to taking the best scientific and technological resources from around the world, both human and structural, and applying them in local contexts provided the basis for many of these large-scale collaborations. The Green Revolution has been credited with saving as many as a billion lives in developing countries, but fewer people are aware of the ways in which its collaborative models, developed for research and implementation in the field, helped to shape the Foundation's institutional strategies in other arenas, including education and health care in later decades.

Just as importantly, the Foundation's sustained commitment to education and training has played a key role in the development of new institutions. In the mid-1980s, Foundation President Richard Lyman identified the need to increase the research capacity of African institutions as well as the number of African fellows in the sciences. The aim, he wrote, was "to produce a future generation of African social scientists versed in multidisciplinary research and sensitive to the human and social complexities inherent in the agricultural transformation process." This revitalization of human-capital development programs helped Africa meet challenges well into the new millennium.

This investment in human capital has helped to strengthen institutions. In 1995, faced with a changing global context, President Peter Goldmark asked David Court in Nairobi for advice about the future of the Foundation's activities in Africa. Court suggested that "all RF programs face the dilemma of weak institutions on the one hand and the need to foster indigenous initiatives, develop problem-solving capacity and nurture an ethic of accountability, on the other. Bridging this divide in program implementation requires on-the-ground intelligence, flexible responsiveness, and monitoring capacity here, accompanied by effective bridges to the New York office." Over a hundred years, these have been critical components of the Rockefeller Foundation's strategy and its institutional culture in Africa and around the world.

Work in Africa has also been aided by a global strategy
that was inherent in the Foundation's mission from the very
beginning. After Judith Rodin became president in 2005, the
Foundation reaffirmed the importance of this international
approach: "Globalization is the product of world-wide revolutions
in the technology of transportation, finance and especially
information. It is in our time what industrialization was at the
time of our founding: neither an intrinsically good or bad thing,
but a pervasive and irreversible trend, with implications both
beneficial and challenging."

Though it has not always used the terms, increasing equitable
access to opportunities and to society's resources has always been
an important component of the Foundation's work. The reality
of growing inequality in the twenty-first century, alongside
the expansion of technological innovation, interconnections,
and interdependence, have led the Foundation to deepen its
commitments to solutions that meet the needs of the poor and
marginalized in Africa. Digital Jobs Africa, for example, a $100
million initiative launched by the Rockefeller Foundation in 2013,
aims to benefit a million people in Africa by training low-income,
high-potential African youth and developing job opportunities
for them to enter the digital economy. By improving coordination
and communication between businesses, training providers,
governments, and nonprofits, the initiative works to create and
expand opportunities for young adults in Egypt, Kenya, Nigeria,
Morocco, South Africa, and Ghana. The project seeks to help
Africans benefit from the global expansion of the information,
communications, and technology sector.

Despite many setbacks, the Foundation has never been
defeated by political and social changes in Africa, in part because
it created new ways of practicing philanthropy. Its experience and

reputation, combined with its funding, aimed at strengthening international institutional architecture and made the Foundation a catalyst for partnerships that could link weak domestic systems with rapidly improving global standards in health care, education, and agricultural development.

Over the past century, Africa has often been the place that made the Rockefeller Foundation rethink its global efforts and the way it designed its programs. For nearly half a century the Foundation struggled to find a way to work in Africa, but success was limited by the institutions of colonialism, the Foundation's still-developing understanding of Africa, and larger historical forces. Nonetheless, it remained resolute in its commitment to the continent. A new strategy, developed as the nations of Africa were becoming independent, has been anchored in the idea of investing in people.

Innovators and leaders empowered by education and training have created and developed new institutions to address Africa's challenges. The Rockefeller Foundation's support helped bring these innovators and leaders together in networks to collaborate and then disseminate good ideas and basic knowledge. In turn, this information and these ideas helped improve systems in education, agriculture, and public health that affected the lives of millions of individuals throughout the continent. At the heart of all of these efforts was a faith in human capacity—a faith in the ability of young girls to learn and grow to take control of their destiny and shape their communities; in the ability of young scientists struggling to learn and discover new knowledge far from the world's elite universities; and in the ability of Africans everywhere to unleash the creative potential of the continent to improve the well-being of all of its citizens.

Shared Journey is part of the Rockefeller Foundation's Centennial initiative. While much of the Foundation's work in agriculture and health has been explored by historians over the years, the Foundation's grants and operations in Africa over the last century have been less well documented. This book, therefore, demanded more original research in the Foundation's records and presented unique challenges. It truly depended on the collaboration of many people.

As the vision for this book developed, various members of the Rockefeller Foundation's staff were deeply involved in helping to understand and interpret the story. Given the Foundation's current work in Africa, Dr. Judith Rodin saw the need for a book that would put this work in historical context. Michael Myers was persistent and thoughtful in pushing everyone involved to uncover the lessons learned along the way. In the Foundation's Africa office, Wairimu Kagondu and Mwihaki Kimura Muraguri, working closely with Carolyn Bancroft in New York, reviewed multiple drafts, provided excellent insight, and were extraordinarily patient with the process. Others at the Foundation read the manuscript and provided helpful comments, including Mamadou Biteye, Neill Coleman, Gary Toenniessen, and Charlanne Burke. Robert Bykofsky, Elizabeth Pena, and the staff in Records Management were always willing to find historical documents, often with short notice, and provided a home away from home when our team was in New York City. Kathy Gomez collected spectacular photographs highlighting the Foundation's recent work, and Juanita Frazier-Martin found important key images from the Bellagio Center. In the General Counsel's office, Shari Patrick read the manuscript and she and Erica Guyer provided legal guidance and feedback.

At the Rockefeller Archive Center (RAC) in Tarrytown, New York, President Jack Meyers and Vice President James Allen Smith welcomed our team. Senior Fellow Patricia Rosenfield offered insights from her work with the Foundation's Africa staff. Michele Hiltzik went out of her way time and again to help us find and digitize important photographs and documents from the Foundation's archives. James Washington handled much of the scanning. Archivists Nancy Adgent, Monica Blank, Beth Jaffe, Tom Rosenbaum, and the others on staff provided key documents and files. Members of the RAC's centennial project team, especially Barb Shubinski and Teresa Iacobelli, shared their research, and Teresa graciously agreed to help write captions as the project went into production.

Members of the team from Teneo Strategy, the Foundation's strategic partner for the Centennial, helped guide this book to completion. Thanks especially to Andy Maas, Max Dworin, and Michael Coakley.

Researching and writing this book was a team effort. Sam Hurst did much of the initial research and provided a rough first draft manuscript to work with. Developmental editor, Madeleine Adams, and series editor Eric John Abrahamson helped shape and reshape chapters to sharpen the narrative. Lois Facer tracked down over a hundred photographs to help enrich the book and compiled the list of illustrations. Ernie Grafe copyedited the entire work. Amanda Waterhouse proofed the galleys. Craig Chapman and Vivian Jenkins compiled the index. Mindy Johnston and Leigh Armstrong researched photographers and copyright holders to make sure we recognized the creators of works that have been buried in the archives for many years.

At Pentagram, Michael Gericke, Matt McInerney, and Janet Kim brought the words and illustrations together in a gorgeous book. Tim Hamilton and the folks at Blanchette Press beautifully printed and bound the final product.

Kathryn Mathers

	Description	Creator. Source.
57 & 59	Josephine Mary Namboze fellowship application and photo (1961).	RAC.
58-61	Josephine Namboze, Kasangati Health Clinic, Uganda.	RAC.
62-63	Malawi women with baby (2006).	Jonas Bendiksen. RF.
65	Mt. Kenya, late evening on road from Nyeri (1936).	Matson Photograph Collection, Library of Congress.
67	Bronislaw Malinowski (c. 1930).	Library of the London School of Economics & Political Science.
68	London School of Economics, main entrance (c. 1933-1938).	RAC.
70	Lucy Mair fellowship card (1931).	RAC.
73	London School of Economics, interior (c. 1920).	Library of the London School of Economics & Political Science.
75	Jomo Kenyatta, May Day, Nairobi (1969).	Marc & Evelyne Bernheim. RAC.
76-77	Dakar roofs (2011).	Jeff Attaway. Flickr Creative Commons.
79 & 81	Ali Al'Amin Mazrui application and photo (1960).	RAC.
80-83	Great Mosque Djenné (2003).	Andy Gilham. WikiMedia Commons
85	The Atlantic Charter (1941).	National Archives and Records Administration.
86	East African soldiers, Garden of Gethsemane (bet. 1940-1946).	Library of Congress..
87	Ralph Bunche, senior year, University of California, Southern Branch (1927).	Los Angeles Public Library Photo Collection.
88	Crown Mine, Johannesburg, South Africa (c. 1935).	Library of Congress.
90	Brookings Institution (1939).	Leet Brothers. RAC.
91	W.E.B. Du Bois in the office of The Crisis.	Photographs and Prints Division, Schomburg Center for Research in Black Culture, The New York Public Library, Astor, Lenox and Tilden Foundations.
94-95	Title page and map from *Africa Advancing* (1945).	RAC.

	Description	Creator. Source.
132-133	City street, Nairobi (2009).	Antony Njuguna. RF.
135	Program for Anansegoro (Spider Plays) by Efua Sutherland (c. 1958).	RAC.
136	Robert July.	RAC.
138	Wole Soyinka (1969).	Keystone. Hulton Archive/Getty Images.
140	Kenneth O. Dike with John Weir (1963).	RAC.
143	Students in class, Siriba Training College (1961).	RAC.
144	Women students, Siriba Training College (1961).	RAC.
147	Teacher Matthew Kayuza and student, Cuttington College, Liberia (c. 1961).	RAC.
149 & 151	Bethwell Allan Ogot fellowship application and photo (1959).	RAC.
150 - 153	Entrance to the Royal College, Nairobi (c. 1962).	RAC.
154-155	Felicia Akejiuba, assistant to Dr. Dike, University College, Ibadan (c. 1960).	RAC.
157	Ralph Bunche, leaving Elizabethville Katanga Province (1960).	Dennis Rayle/Associated Press. RAC.
158	Tower Court and Administration buildings, University College, Ibadan (c. 1963).	RAC.
159	Dedication of the International Institute of Tropical Agriculture with J. George Harrar, Will M. Myers, and Major-General Yakubu Gowan (1970).	RAC.
162	Sketch of Kitchener Memorial Medical School, Khartoum.	RAC.
163	Undergraduate students in chemistry lab, Faculty of Agriculture, University of Khartoum (1961).	RAC.
164	University of Khartoum veterinary scientists and students (1962).	RAC.
165	Students at University of Khartoum (c. 1966).	Marc & Evelyne Bernheim. RAC.

	Description	Creator. Source.
217	Rural health station (1961).	RAC.
218	Lango schoolchildren and parents (1966).	RAC.
221	Katwanyaa mother and child (1988).	Wendy Stone. RAC.
222	Dr. Mati at Norplant clinic.	RAC.
224	Nairobi office staff (c. 1990's)	RF.
225	Children on slide, Tanzania (2006).	Jonas Bendiksen. RF.
227 & 229	Albert Chinua Achebe fellowship application and photo (1960).	RAC.
228-231	Chinua Achebe, Buffalo (2008).	Stuart C. Shapiro. Wikimedia Commons.
232-233	Students, Kalangala Island, Uganda (c. 2001).	Steve McCurry. RF.
235	Maimouna Kane (Senegal), UN Conference (2008).	Per Jacobsen. United Nations, photo #66206.
236	Provincial Girls' School, Kano, Nigeria (c. 1965).	Educational Services Inc. RAC.
237	Ayele Ajavon, graduate in chemistry (c. 1960).	RAC.
239	Fay Chung.	RAC.
242	FAWE leaders, Bellagio (2012).	RF.
244-245	Agape Children's Village, Tanzania (2006).	Jonas Bendiksen. RF.
247	Institute of Virus Research, Entebbe, Uganda (1989).	RAC.
250	District dispensary, Rufiji, Tanzania (2006).	Jonas Bendiksen. RF.
252	Nelson Musoba, Uganda (c. 2001).	Steve McCurry. RF.
260	James Musigo, traditional healer, Uganda (c. 2001).	Steve McCurry. RF.
262-263	Durban (2008).	Vince Smith. Flickr creative commons.
264	Mamphela Ramphele (1993).	Rodger Bosch. RAC.